EARLY PRAISE FOR *UNMANAGED*

"Skeels's extensive experience in building and teaching how to create successful teams and organizations is shared through models, examples and illustrative stories. You may ask, 'Do I need another business book?' If you're looking for new and better approaches, then you'll definitely want *Unmanaged*."

—MARLA KAPLOWITZ, CEO, The American Association of Advertising Agencies (4As)

"*Unmanaged* is an indispensable guide for leaders in today's rapidly evolving world. Jack brilliantly dissects traditional management styles and offers a field-tested roadmap to successfully steer organizations through change. This book is a wealth of wisdom and a must-read for any leader committed to thriving in the face of change."

—JOHN LARGE, Dir., Strategy and Operations, Janssen, Inc.

"*Unmanaged* is one of those rare books that helps you see that the answers to your most pressing organizational problems are the opposite of what you thought they were."

—BLAIR ENNS, Author, *The Win Without Pitching Manifesto*

"Unmanaged" deconstructs the discipline of management and makes the compelling case that knowledge workers perform much more effectively for "Humble Gardeners" than "Angry Ranchers." With decades of experience working with hundreds of professional service firms, Jack Skeels presents a convincing case for how the chronically misunderstood agile framework can produce transformational results."

—TIM WILLIAMS, Partner, Ignition Consulting,

D1096114

"Whether you've been through Jack's trainings or not, *Unmanaged* is must-read for anyone who leads teams or projects at an agency. Every reader will recognize (and commiserate) with the situations [described in the] amusing and relevant examples. *Unmanaged* provides a clear guide on how to navigate through them, and preferably avoid them, in the future. Once you're done, you'll be ready to make some deep-rooted process and cultural changes that will also yield significant results."

—LAURIE RICHARDS, Founder, ClearRiver, LLC

"In *Unmanaged*, Jack Skeels takes lessons from the hundreds of chaotic digital agencies he helped transform and combines those lessons with his command of human dynamics, process models, and continuous improvement. Leaders looking for different way to make their project organization more successful would be wise to consider *Unmanaged* as part of their playbook. This book is a must-read if you want to learn how to deliver projects brilliantly. The only thing that would have made it better is if it also included our story: The very first project that we brought Jack in on was the biggest project we had ever undertaken. We were halfway through and thought we were cruising. When we applied *Unmanaged* methodology, we realized that we were going to come in 300% over budget and almost certainly were headed to financial ruin. Jack helped us not only realize that but showed us how to communicate it in a way where the client ultimately was able to join us in reframing the scope of work and budget, leading to a mutually beneficial outcome. On that project alone, we literally owe our company to Jack."

—JUSTIN KABBANI, Co-founder, Hardhat Digital

WHAT PEOPLE SAY ABOUT THEIR SUCCESS
WITH *UNMANAGED* METHODS

"By the time we had finished the five-day workshop—I sometimes forget that we were actually doing it for the first time and it was really "training"—we had accomplished a lot. Our client told us so, telling us that she saw more progress in this week than she would normally expect from months of meetings and PowerPoints."

—MIKE SOMMERS, SVP Group Account Director,
Global Team Blue

"AgencyAgile's team-based training has the potential to be transformational. Those teams that have experienced the training are excited about the process, and there is now real demand for their approach to scoping across the agency. Arguably one of the smartest training investments we've made."

—SARAH HOFSTETTER, CEO, 360i

"Our marketing services organization is incredibly complex, with dozens of stakeholders, streams of work, and hundreds of projects with priorities shifting on a daily basis. AgencyAgile's training and coaching took us to a whole new level of capability. . . . It seems a bit unbelievable, but . . . the quality of the work we're producing is much better. We also attract, engage and retain employees in a way that we could not before. Work for our teams has become much more fun.

—LARRY SHAFFER, SVP Marketing and
Business Development, Insperity

"We knew enough about consulting to know we needed a Tenzing Norgay. We weren't going to bet our agency on a few business books and a half-baked internal change management strategy. We wanted nothing less than total transformation; and we knew we needed a fresh, outside perspective to guide us. One call with Jack Skeels was all it took to know the AgencyAgile methods would be our guide, our Norgay."

—BRET STARR, CEO, The Starr Conspiracy

"AgencyAgile has intimate knowledge of best practices in team structure and management. They help identify processes that empower high-performing teams to continuously improve. They work seamlessly across agency organizations and helped us appreciate and achieve the promise of Agile."

—PETER DENUNZIO, CEO, HelloWorld (now Merkle)

UNMANAGED

MASTER THE MAGIC OF CREATING EMPOWERED AND HAPPY ORGANIZATIONS

FIRST EDITION

JACK SKEELS

AgencyAgile, Inc.
www.agencyagile.com

Published January 2024

Cover and interior design by Wolf Design and Marketing

27 26 25 24 23   10 9 8 7 6 5 4 3 2 1

To my father, Jack William Skeels.
Love you, dad.

CONTENTS

Introduction

PROJECTS THAT STRUGGLE AND FAIL are everybody's problem. And most projects struggle more than you probably realize. At first blush, that sounds like a project management problem—but it is not. At the heart of the challenges that projects face are lessons about how we can better manage and be managed. Over twelve years ago, projects became my learning laboratory because they are self-contained stage plays in which one can see a blindness in how most leaders think about managers and their impact on organizational success.

This book is not written for project managers, but for the broader group of leaders and managers in what are called *project-driven organizations*. They are the organizations of the future. As automation becomes more dominant in the repetitive work of both factories and service organizations, human-driven organizations will increasingly do things never done before: work that requires adaptation, customization, innovation, or creativity.

Project-driven organizations, like projects themselves, often struggle. It is a difficult business, the doing of new things. Our prevailing management models, mostly based on a factory mindset, are counterproductive to project and organizational success. The truths that we'll uncover tend to be universal for managers in most situations, even factories.

This book invites you on a journey into a new way of thinking about managing, which I've termed *unmanaging* because, at its core, it is about doing less of managing and, of what remains, doing it differently and much better. Unmanaging is different, and it is much more fun.

These techniques are proven to boost your customer's happiness and also that of your teams and workers. Their happiness goes up not because of free lunches or skateboards in the office, but because they are delivering projects and working together better than ever. Most leaders realize that happy organizations outperform unhappy ones, but get it backward: delivering well and working together well makes everyone happy.

That includes managers: managing well, and having things go well, is a wonderful pleasure in itself. And you will prosper in other ways that include making more money.

I've always been intrigued by the idea that we could all work better together—and then someone gave me a push, suggesting that I might be part of the problem. That began my quest into whether there was a way of managing that could make everyone work better together.

The answer is yes. The story is in here.

Origins

HOW WOULD YOU DESCRIBE THE PATH OF YOUR CAREER? Like many, I've been a pinball, bouncing off the bumpers of companies, roles, and even different professions. I've founded three companies that have endured the tests of time, and I've even won awards for my work as a manager and leader. Yet, like most business entrepreneurs, I have had many failures as well. At one time, I strived to be a master plumber, but my boss promptly fired and admonished me, "You belong back in college." One less smart-mouthed plumber in the world is probably a good thing.

Another bounce happened when I was laid off from my leadership role at Sapient, a global consulting and marketing agency, during the global economic downturn in 2009. As head of their Los Angeles office, I'd already seen several amazing people go, but exiting among good company hardly makes these things easier. This pinball bumper had a little extra bounce to it thanks to a parting shot from my boss, who said I had "never been that good of a manager anyway."

That set me on my current course as I spent my considerable severance money on research to write the book that would prove that I did, in fact, know how to manage.[1] A few bounces prior, I had been a senior management sciences analyst at RAND, a prestigious research organization, so my bar for proof was pretty high. I spent weeks poring over a hundred popular and scholarly business research articles and books, then developed an outline of thirty-seven key concepts for managing a great workplace. With all the evidence that I had sought in hand, I reached the unfortunate conclusion that pretty much everything I had been doing as a manager was, well, wrong.

Okay, maybe there was another bumper to come.

THE PROJECT ON FIRE

In 2010, having hit pause on the book, I clung gratefully to a VP sales job at a midsized digital agency in Santa Monica, California, named Blitz. It was a fun place, with some wicked talent and a really nice roster of clients. We were supporting the upcoming release of a new chapter in one of the world's most popular video games. Our client, the video game manufacturer, wanted a website, mobile app, social media elements, and all the trimmings that come along with that. It was a great project, and also a horrible one.

As often happens, the sales team pitched it as a murky dream involving too little money and even less actual understanding of what the client truly wanted or needed. A very talented client services director that reported to me had been managing it, but it had turned into an out-of-control freight train, picking up speed, flames and sparks coming from the wheels, heading toward a deadly turn.

There were plenty of people trying to fix it. Four managers, not including myself, worked mostly full time overseeing a team of twelve designers, developers, testers, and others. The team depended on multiple departments as well, so all the department managers were "contributing" to the firefighting of the disaster.

After the video game's global launch, millions of people would flood to the website we were still building. Last I had heard, with ten weeks to go, we had twenty-two weeks of work. We were in some serious trouble. Time to close the gap.

That was two weeks ago. Now the director was sharing the type of news that strikes fear into every project manager's heart: the latest projections showed we now had twenty-four weeks remaining.

Seasoned project managers—yes, I had been one once upon a time— know that when the time needed to complete a project is increasing, despite work being done, it means just one thing: nobody really knows how much work remains; the project is still uncovering its scope. This was going to be a disaster.

But this was a moment I had been waiting for. I asked the client services director whether they would mind me taking the project over. I'm pretty sure they cried tears of joy upon hearing that.

What I knew then, and hoped I could prove, was that bad ways of doing things only get worse when times get tough. I believed that we had the wrong people in charge, and I was going to fix that.

One of the project managers was a guy named Brian. He and I had worked together previously at Sapient, and I trusted him completely. He had been hired at this agency on my recommendation. I walked over to the room where the team was working and asked him to come back to my office.

"I want you to move the other two project managers off the project," I told him. He was aghast. Before he could say another word, I added,

"And go out there now and send everyone home for the day. They need some rest." This was true. They had been working eighty hours a week for months, and they looked like the walking dead.

Brian started to object, pointing out that we didn't have time for such things, but I cut him off. "I need them fresh for tomorrow. Have them here at 9:00 a.m. in the big conference room. Plan on us working together all day." I'm pretty sure Brian thought I was nuts, but at least now they could blame me—not him—when they dug through the wreckage of this failed project.

The next morning, everyone was there on time, sitting at a U-shaped table, looking at me, wondering what the heck was going on. I was at the front of the room, sitting on a stool. My opening words were, "I think you all know that this project is in trouble." Everyone nodded. "So, we need to fix it." There wasn't much reaction to that, but I'm pretty sure they were girding themselves for a verbal flogging ("How could you possibly let this project fail?") or some form of managerial rah-rah, including the obligatory Mike Tyson or George Patton quotes.

Instead, I asked, "So, what do we need to get this done?" Blank looks on their faces. Dead silence.

I waited.

I'm pretty sure they figured this was some devious or torturous form of managerial rhetoric to command them to do work they'd already planned to attempt. But I had no idea at all what they should do. I had no idea of how to fix the project, save for what I had already done so far. So, I waited. I repeated my question and fiddled with the dry-erase marker in my hand.

We waited. It felt like twenty minutes, but it was probably closer to five. That's still a long time to sit in fear-tinged silence. I repeated the question and added, "I ask because I have no idea what needs to be done. It is your project and has been for months now."

Although I did not know how to fix the project, I did know that the best way to start was to let the group do what groups of people have successfully done for thousands of years. They, as a group, would decide what to do.

So, we waited.

Finally, someone broke the silence. "We need a separate server for the client to use so they don't mess up our work." I looked around the room.

"Does that make sense to everyone? Is that needed?" Most people nodded, so I wrote it on the whiteboard: "Sandbox server for client access."

Then I sat down again. "What else?" The responses started coming. I quickly became quite busy, writing their ideas down, looking for confirmation, and trying to write down the points they made as the discussion roiled through the room. I had to get them to slow down, make them take turns. Three hours later, the large whiteboards that covered three of the walls were filled with tasks that needed to be done. We were all exhausted. It was just barely noon. But we were on our way.

We all walked to lunch and talked about other things, all not project related. On the way, Brian, who had been furiously transcribing my whiteboard scribbles into his laptop said, "We didn't have half of those things in our project plan." Ugh, that meant we were even further behind than anyone knew. After lunch, and a much-needed stop at Starbucks, we went back to the room and sat down again.

"Cool list, eh?" I said, smiling. "Okay, so what needs to happen first?" Brian started to speak, but I shook my head. As good as humans are at problem-solving, we are also really badass at planning. I waited with dry-erase markers in hand.

It was a shorter wait this time. Then, all of a sudden, we were deep in a complex discussion. I color-coded their comments into logical waves—groupings of actions that could and should be done together. The team's creativity automatically paired with their instinctive self-organization abilities as they started to check that each wave fit the work. They were simultaneously planning and optimizing. I, as the VP in the room, was earning my pay, arguably better than any of the project managers or my director had been doing for months, by playing scribe to the team and simply asking an occasional question.

I had unleashed the power of the team by unmanaging them: removing many of the common managerial behaviors and enabling twelve wonderful minds to take on solving the very difficult problem of how to finish the project. It was still not clear that they could get it done in time, but probably for the first time in that project, they clearly knew what needed to be done.

And, to the amazement of all, including themselves and the client, they killed it. They completed 97% of the project's scope in time for the launch. The client was so amazed they gave us even more money to add to the work, including paying us a second time for work the team hadn't finished. And they gave us three more large projects that year, all of which I ran using this same underlying philosophy and a growing body of techniques I was piloting. Those projects were the most on-time and in-budget projects the agency had that year.

The success of that project was a bittersweet confirmation that my boss at Sapient was more correct than either of us knew—I had been a horrible manager. And I wasn't alone. I'd learned how to manage from years of observation and mimicking how everyone else managed. Somewhere in those last few pinball bounces, I seemed to have, like Neo in *The Matrix*, made the "red pill" choice, and saw the whole world of managing from a completely different perspective: the way we as managers and leaders (and society) think about managing is tragically flawed.

THE COSTLY EPIDEMIC OF OVERMANAGEMENT

Only years later did it sink in that how (poorly) we manage projects is but a symptom of a larger and costly management chaos, an organizational challenge and opportunity at a massive scale. It was an indictment that struck at the very heart of how we manage today's work, workers, and teams.

Managing is ridiculously costly. The direct costs of a manager—which may be formidable—are often dwarfed by their many indirect costs. These include the impacts of overmanaging and its evil cousin, bad managing, which in combination represent one of the largest expenses in any organization. But the idea that management can be very costly remains largely unexamined because managers are deemed to be a good thing (by managers), so in some strange way, more managers must be better. But is that true?

Once you start asking questions in this direction, the answers you find only get worse and somewhat unbelievable. Some leaders I have worked with had at least nagging doubts about whether those managerial dollars were well spent. Over a decade ago, a VP of operations asked me, "Why do I have so many project managers?" She had twenty project managers for an organization that only had about one hundred people.

The counterintuitive shift that I invite you to make is to explore what I call the *manager tax*, the cumulative set of costs that managers and their managerial activities place upon the organization. This tax is in many ways hard to see until you train your eyes to it. Managers always seem to have the gift of being able to describe how what they are doing is valuable.

If you care about productivity or profits, then this is worthy of your attention. Let's look at the Project on Fire example to see why:

The direct managerial cost was probably four full-time managers if we count project managers and the several other managers providing fractions of their day to the project. Since this was a six-month project, we can assume their cost to be half of their annual cost, or $300,000.

Had the project really failed as it seemed to be destined, the rescue and recovery costs would have been hard to calculate, but we can take a crack at it. If the project had truly been a disaster, then the client would have canceled its multimillion-dollar book of business (there were other projects) and probably stopped payment on the existing project. If lawyers had gotten involved, then it would have been way more, including returning whatever had been already paid to Blitz. This is, of course, the worst scenario, and ridiculously costly. Frankly, having been around projects like this, my heart is racing as I write this. Maybe you've seen one or two.

Had the project struggled and underperformed without failing (and assuming that the client was a bit kinder in their response to the project's problems), then the teams would undertake a massive effort to recover the project. Several hundreds of thousands of dollars would be spent, with the potential for future (and ongoing) business with that client being diminished or eliminated.

The difference between the existing managerial model for that project and what I did was a five-to-six-figure impact. At least.

And you might be saying, "Yeah, but hey, it didn't fail. You rescued it and you are a manager." And I would reply in this way: "Yes, but I am an unmanager, and the team rescued it, not me, because I removed most of the managers who—because they did not understand the costs of their actions—were causing it to fail."

Let me try again without being so manager-centric: What *enabled* *the team* to successfully deliver the project was a massive reduction in the number of managers and the general activity of managing, plus some simple changes in the way the project was managed. My actual time spent managing the project after the first three days was minimal. I didn't want to be a tax.

The way you manage matters. A lot.

THE SYMPTOMS OF THE OVERMANAGED ORGANIZATION

We've done a wealth of survey work with our new clients—it is part of our kickoff process—seeking to quantify what impedes them from being more productive. The project-driven organizations we work with almost uniformly respond with three challenges:

Workers often do not understand what they are being tasked to do. Often the leaders and managers overseeing the work are not aligned on the work either.

Worker coordination and focus are often difficult to attain because of competing demands from multiple managers and projects.

Productive time (Flow) is scarce. People resort to working off-hours or extra hours to just keep up. Some things just don't get done. Often, things are late.

Additionally, organizations that are not project-centric also report the same challenges. Our unmanagement techniques work well for them too.

The three symptoms are related to each other, of course, and produce a ripple effect—one begets another, and they tend to occur together.

For leaders, this means that the *ethos of management* in your organization will have a profound effect on managers' choices. Do your managers assume, like ours did at Blitz, that their intentions matter more? How could they be doing wrong when they are trying to help? This is an example of managerial exceptionalism: nobody was asking, even for a moment, if more managers and managing was helping the situation. Nobody.

For managers, these symptoms highlight the need to really understand how and when to manage. How hard could that be?

DO WE REALLY MANAGE WELL?

The answer is complex.

Most tend to think that business schools teach people how to manage. They don't. When I was laid off from Sapient, I had already earned my MBA from a top-ranked business program, with honors no less, and some accolades from the faculty, which included a rare postgraduate teaching role. Still, I was rightly labeled a bad manager. Part of the challenge is that getting an MBA will not help you very much—or at all—at being a great manager.

Noted researcher Henry Mintzberg wrote an underrated book on the subject.[2] He argues that managers need to be incredibly aware of themselves and the context in which they are managing, which is not easy at all. We hardly discuss these issues in business school, if at all. At the highly-ranked West Coast graduate school I attended, the only classes that even came close were targeted at entrepreneurs to help them understand themselves better. In Western society, encouraging emotional intelligence often seems too touchy-feely to feel appropriate in business cultures. Our current notions of managing are shaped by its military-industrial origins, where workers were likened to soldiers who needed to be prodded into conformance.

I've noticed that people think they understand what managing is, but when pressed, they struggle to define it beyond some familiar tasks or a circular definition.

CAN YOU REALLY MAKE RICE?

"Managing is what managers do." Having devoted the last twenty-plus years to focusing on managing, I can assure you that managing is much more complex than that. I often equate it to the question, "Are you a rice maker?" Managers tend to respond to the question, "Are you a manager?" in the same way:

"Yes, I have made rice."

"I do know how to make rice."

When I press, and ask, "What do you need to do to make really good rice, to be a superb rice maker?" Most people don't have more of an answer than what they gave at first.

And the problem is how to measure what good rice is. Arguably, one of the best types of rice is sushi rice. So let's ask, "Do you know how to make really good sushi rice?" Pretty much everyone, except those who have been trained, will just blink.

Your favorite sushi restaurant takes its rice seriously. It is not unusual for a novice, aspiring sushi chef to spend about a year learning how to make great rice. Doing something well is never simple. Sushi rice is to ordinary rice as correct managing is to what most managers do.

WHY IT IS CHALLENGING TO MANAGE WELL

Managing with a clear method and consistent application is not easy. To do so, you must overcome prevailing managing "wisdom" and your own often flawed "intuition" to address the following challenges:

The actions required to manage well are contextual. What a manager needs to do at any given moment depends on the moment itself. To manage well, you need to be fairly brilliant (and humble) at assessing the situation and choosing a path forward. There are patterns, which we'll explain, but they are not obvious to most. Because of the manager tax, your choosing wrong may be quite costly. In any given moment (context), you need to choose *only* the actions that will have a positive impact. And in turn, avoid others and instead choose inaction (doing nothing), which can be ridiculously difficult to do.

Work type and organizational complexity further create a fog of war. The type of work your organization does has a profound effect on what you and other managers should and (more importantly) should not focus on. Also, as the organization gets more complex thanks to additional managers, multi-allocated teams and workers, and a growing mix of clients and stakeholders, the best managerial actions become even less obvious and less effective because you, as the manager, are not the only one impacting productivity. Other managers' actions may make your actions worse.

The needed techniques are neither obvious nor familiar. Unmanaging requires a skill set that is nearly the opposite of what society and business cultures expect. At moments you may feel like you are swimming against the tide of popular opinion. And that will probably be true. Worse yet, if you are a manager who came up through the ranks as a specialist, then most of what you mastered will point you away from great managing. You'll need to toss out that old compass.

HOW COSTLY CAN A BAD MANAGERIAL CHOICE BE?

When I read the paragraphs above, I think, "C'mon, Jack, lighten up! How hard could this really be? I mean, I do fine enough already, and now you're just making this all complex and my job harder." To which I say, "Harder, yes, but only if you want to do it well. That's why they call it work."

Most managers that I have met—and I have met many—coast along in their decision-making by mimicking other managers or just using their intuition. How bad could that be? I mean, how much impact could a small, but incorrect, intuitive decision have?

In the year that followed the Project on Fire, I started a consultancy, AgencyAgile, which today has worked with well over two hundred client organizations, helping shape and refine their managerial mindset using the principles now in this book.[3] That's saying it backward though. This book is the product of what we learned. Our two-hundred-plus clients have been a learning laboratory. Theory is great, and even useful, but practice is how we can verify our actions as managers. Here's an example of how subtle it can be:

Our training program includes a daily coordination meeting that, on the surface, resembles the stand-up meeting you are probably familiar with.

Daily stand-up meetings, of course, are useful for both coordinating what people will do that day and also a good time to introduce new information, such as a decision made late the previous day that will impact the team. Our version of this meeting, however, has been supercharged to deal with the managerial context, one aspect of which is the transfer of new information to the team.

Let's see how much difference a small, intuitive, but incorrect decision might make. Consider this: How, as a manager, should you introduce new information during a stand-up coordination meeting? What is the best way and moment to do that? Should you tell everyone right away, before they start, before they talk about and coordinate their plans for the day, or should you wait until after, when they are mostly finished coordinating?

And would it make a difference which choice you made?

Pretty much every manager I have ever met would say the former and tell everyone right away. When I ask why (and I have, many times), they explain what probably seems (intuitively) obvious to you as well: "Why let them go through all of that mistaken planning and tell them at the end, which would mean the previous discussion was a waste of time?"

To which I would reply, "Why are you so sure it is a waste of time?" While some will respond by explaining their arithmetic, nobody provides a cogent answer. Nobody is thinking of the most important question deeply and skeptically: When is the best time for a manager to introduce new information to the team?

Because I saw this situation frequently in our trainings, I started wondering. I'd been wrong enough times to loathe the crutch of untested assumptions. It was time for a test. I and a few of our coaches tried out both approaches on our current clients, having the managers provide new information before and after.

The experiment didn't last long, just a few weeks, and we laughed about it on our weekly internal call. Adding new information at the start of the meeting extends the meeting longer than adding it at the end. And it wasn't even close. Adding the new information later or at the end has a lower time cost for the attendees, and our subjective assessment was that people felt far more confident in the daily plan than when the information was provided early.

Counterintuitive? Yes, for sure. There's really not much research I was able to find on groups' effectiveness of replanning (in this case, new info at the start) versus plan repair (new info at the end or at least later on). Repair works better in this situation, we believe, because at the start of that meeting, most people already had a solid idea about their day (plan), so it was far better to let them finish nailing that down and then add the new information, allowing for a quick repair of only the pieces that need change.

How much impact did the choice have? Now it's my turn to do some arithmetic:

- The meetings had (on average) twenty-five attendees.
- The time difference was about ten minutes, at a minimum.
- That's 250 minutes, which is four-plus hours of productivity.
- There is also the intangible of the (lack of) energy from confusion, versus the positive energy from resolution and alignment.

I would guess that there is at least a day or two of productivity gain or loss in that group of twenty-five people because of this one shift in managerial action. That's about 4%, maybe more, potential productivity loss or gain from just one (intuitive) managerial action.

If you've been front-loading your meetings, don't be too hard on yourself. How would you have known? And different meeting styles probably have different dynamics. Our AgencyAgile team, despite our deep theoretic knowledge of better managing and having worked with well over one hundred client teams at that point, really didn't know what the right choice was. We were able to do some A/B testing, but that would be a lot harder for an individual to do, even within one company.

But the fact is, most managers—including the younger me—have killed some serious productivity with a well-intentioned interjection. One little managerial choice—one managerial moment—can have a tremendous impact on a team. Doing the right thing as a manager is often not easy or obvious. Effective measurement, as was the case here, is a critically important compass.

As a leader, the least-costly thing about your managers is probably their salary.

MANAGING A MILLION MANAGERIAL MOMENTS

That stand-up meeting was just the first fifteen to thirty minutes of that day. How many more moments throughout the day will managers need to correctly choose how and whether to act? I'm guessing there are hundreds of these moments—maybe thousands on some days. Multiply that by how many managers you have. How could anyone handle that? Fortunately, unmanaging is a mindset that, though somewhat complex, follows patterns that you can learn and apply to new situations as they come up. And you don't need to get them all right either—just the big ones.

The big moments matter far more than others, and there are four types of them we'll cover, which I call the *key managerial moments*. Managers tell us that other moments become easier to navigate as they gain mastery of those key managerial moments.

Growing awareness often makes a manager more tentative in their actions. That sounds like a bad thing, right? "The manager was tentative." But if we assume that thoughtless action is one of the sources of overmanaging and also bad managing, then being tentative means that the manager tax may be reduced in that moment.

For many of us, when we don't know better, we just react. A key move, for anyone who is adopting this mindset, is learning to prioritize less-reactive behaviors and mastering a reflective posture. Yes, a bit more Zen. Like Buddha.

THE POSTURE OF UNMANAGEMENT

I can think, I can fast, I can wait.
—*Siddhartha* by Herman Hesse

In Herman Hesse's *Siddhartha*, there's a scene where the young Buddha is seeking a job. His prospective employer astutely asks what skills he could provide, and the young Buddha replies, "I can think, I can fast, I can wait." Young Buddha would make a great manager.

In Western business culture, we often see doing and being as intertwined: the busy manager must be a good manager. But young Buddha offers a different perspective. His overall posture is that of someone who will act only when they see it is time to act. Doing, for him, is but one style of being. Another style is stopping and waiting. I invite you to think of being (and unmanaging) as an essential skill that includes *not* doing. Let's break down the three components of young Buddha's stellar resume that should be on every manager's mind:

- **Thinking.** You will need to understand the nuances of how good managing works. This includes being able to see through a flawed idea of managing, workers, and teams birthed over one hundred years ago in the Industrial Age. That's the purpose of the first two sections of this book.
- **Fasting.** This practice refers to patiently sacrificing your own needs for a greater purpose. In Hesse's book, young Buddha learned to fast from the ascetics, who believed that enlightenment came from rejecting one's desires. The ability to resist the many impulses around taking action, being in charge, being managerial, and many other desires is what helps leaders and managers choose the correct action (or inaction) in a managerial moment. Sometimes the most effective choice is less satisfying, and you'll need to hang with that.

You'll see this laid out in the many techniques I illustrate in this book.

- **Waiting.** Speed is a problem in many ways. One is how speed differences in cognitive and learning processes among workers and teams impact their understanding of the work. Another speed challenge is within our managerial selves: the impulse to quickly solve or direct the solution to problems or situations, often compounded by our limited and biased skills of perception and assessment, makes for poor decisions and even sometimes worse actions. Slowing down your decision-making and switching to question-making will increase your presence in the managerial moment and aid your thinking. You'll find many lessons on these topics in this book, especially the last section.

Often, managers just *do* because it is easier than *being*. The best way I know to teach this is to show you how it works in practice. That's what we do when we work with an organization—we train everyone in how it should work, how it feels, when to talk, when to not, and so on. If you've ever trained in martial arts, you might recognize this approach. It is about mastering patterns that create better outcomes.

When we train our clients, we train with real, live projects; everyone experiences hands-on learning. In this book, I'll focus on telling you stories about some important key moments. The opening vignettes and discussion in the chapters to come will attune you to what is probably a familiar situation, and then I'll show you unmanaging techniques for those situations that you can apply and try yourself.

THE FOUR KEY MANAGERIAL MOMENTS

Taiichi Ohno, one of the great management thinkers of the last hundred years, famously stated that when you lower the water level in the river, you expose the rocks. When things are going well (plenty of water), it is hard to see what needs fixing. But when things get difficult (not enough water), the hard parts become more apparent. Ohno was a practitioner of lowering the water, which spurred the growth of the "Lean" school of process management.

Your organization's rocks are likely not easy to see while hidden in the muddy water below, yet the river still runs slower because of them. Lucky for us, my team and I have seen plenty of rocks. In our work with high-performance organizations, where time is so scarce that every misstep can create another crisis, many rocks become glaringly obvious. These key moments, the rocks, are when incorrect managerial choices become especially costly. Said another way, because most organizations fail in these moments, they have a tremendous opportunity to improve and save money by fixing those moments—doing them better.

There are four that stand out. They can be your organization's greatest strength or greatest weakness:

I. **The Why Moment.** This is probably the most important and also the most poorly managed (or rarely occurring) moment in our modern, Western-culture workplaces. Here the manager or leader must ensure everyone, individually and as a group, understands the reasons for the work.[4] The natural human reaction after being told to do something is to ask, and even need to know, why it's needed. It is a necessary precursor for an effective What Moment.

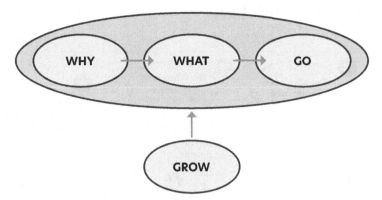

Figure 1: The Four Key Managerial Moments

2. **The What Moment.** This is the moment in which the manager enables everyone to know, both individually and as a group, what the work entails. In a project, one form of What is often called scope: what is needed for a successful delivery. Another key detail is how to do the work and who should do what. If the What Moment is not managed correctly, then the Go Moment often falters.

3. **The Go Moment.** The Go Moment is when productivity happens. The Go Moment includes the moments of active coordination and the doing of the work, and managers must ensure that they do not impede this moment directly. If the Why or What Moments have been poorly managed, then the Go Moment will struggle.

4. **The Grow Moment.** The Grow Moment is when managers' actions are directed toward making things better in broader and more holistic ways. This includes moments of opportunity and inclusion, learning, measurement, reflection, and mentoring. Too often managers today, laser focused on (over)managing the Go Moment, underserve these opportunities.

A FOUR MOMENTS FAILURE MODEL

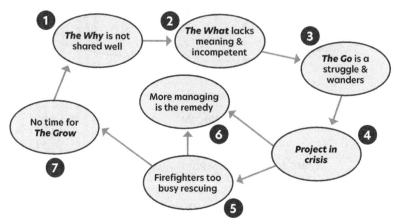

Figure 2: The Four Moments Failure Model

Using this framework, let's look at an example of how inefficiencies are introduced to the organization during the inevitable times when things get challenging. What results is a self-reinforcing loop of dysfunction.

- The Why is neglected or shared narrowly. Workers and teams are blind to it. They know they will need to do something but don't understand how it came about, why it is necessary, or where it fits among the rest of the organization's work.
- Everyone's understanding of the What suffers, especially when the What involves newness, complexity, uncertainty, the need for innovation, and so on. You've experienced this—it is the moment when you might pause the person telling you the What and say, "Hold, on, I need to understand the bigger picture" (the Why).
- Lacking a Why connected to the What, workers in the Go Moment struggle. The more unknowns in the What of the work, the greater this effect.

- Things go wrong. Sometimes the schedule or plan for the work is overly optimistic in one or many ways, or people just struggle because they don't understand enough about what they are being asked to do. Fires start.
- Someone has to put out the fire, so senior talent—the go-to firefighters, often managers who were promoted—take on major project responsibilities to save the day. This is not managing but becoming a worker.
- Simultaneously, additional managers are brought into the mix. These additional managers do not improve the understanding of the team's Why or What but instead add more complexity to the project.
- Firefighters and managers can't help less-skilled people develop their skills while the project burns. Skills development, mentoring, and general growth in capabilities and people are neglected. Workers and teams become more prone to failure because they lack proper development.

For some of you, this cycle will be hauntingly familiar. Worse, as a result of this, managers may view the workers as incapable because they could not make the project succeed, so why should they overinvest in explaining the Why and the What next time?

LARGE, COMPLEX PROJECTS DRAIN THE MANAGEMENT RIVER

As I mentioned in the introduction, AgencyAgile has learned from projects because they were both a problem that cried out for a solution, and also because they have boundaries that allowed us to isolate actions and impacts. The bigger and worse the project, the more there is to see and learn; the rocks become vividly clear.

We've seen profound patterns when managers face tough situations; their intuitions and instincts betray them. All too often, even the most well-intentioned managers slip and use one or more of these success-reducing behaviors:

- **Hoarding understanding, alignment, and wisdom.** Managers typically overmanage information in a multitude of ways, which decreases (or delays) the flow of it to workers and teams, impacting their ability to do quality work productively. Ironically, this hoarding also makes their jobs as managers more difficult. We'll address this when discussing ways to better manage the Why and What.

- **Stealing volition, control, and ownership from workers and teams.** Managers typically demand too much control over their workers' focus and the work itself. The overcontrol of focus decreases productivity in many direct ways but is also amplified when the manager's ownership of the work enables a dynamic of "dis-ownership" within workers and teams. The team's resultant detachment from the work ("I'm just doing what you told me to do") squanders the natural skills of workers and teams in terms of problem-solving, adapting to changing needs, and optimizing processes. We'll discuss this alongside our methods for better managing the What and Go Moments.

- **Ignoring managers' bias in the assessment of workers and teams.** Managers assess workers and teams poorly because of biased and somewhat invisible behaviors in their decision-making around participation in the work. This bias then pervades managerial assessments of capability and merit. These incorrect assessments of workers result in lower inclusion and participation, which then squanders their potential contribution to the organization. This lost capability makes the organization more fragile. I address this when discussing methods for better managing in all four key managerial moments, but especially when discussing the Grow Moment.

One would hope that you could just explain the above behaviors and trust that managers would do better. But for reasons we'll explore further, that doesn't generally happen. And so, the Four Moments matter. When managers act correctly in those moments, then the model changes its nature.

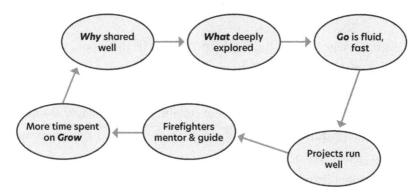

Figure 3: A Four Moments Success Model

In our opening story, The Project on Fire, which I will refer to many times throughout this book, the organization needed three-plus managers when it was running poorly. But with its moments correctly managed, it needed less than one full-time manager. In a very real sense, the project had become unmanaged; the impact of the challenging managerial behaviors discussed above was almost completely eliminated by remedying the failures in the first two key moments (Why and What) and some more-subtle adjustments to the Go Moment.

THE UNMANAGEMENT MINDSET

Unmanaging does not mean no managing or imply unruliness, as in *uncontrolled*. Nor does it mean no managers. Instead, the *un* of *unmanaging* emphasizes that managing less is often a key component in managing better.

Unmanaging is a mindset that seeks to understand whether action is needed and, if so, guide the manager to act only in ways that create better results for the organization, its workers, and teams.

> Unmanaging is a mindset that seeks to understand whether action is needed, and if so, acting only in ways that create better results for the organization, its workers, and teams.

As a manager, if you follow the principles in this book, you will be doing less, often much less, of what passes for managing today, rejecting the prevalent attitude of managerial exceptionalism: if something or someone needs fixing, solving, or any sort of oversight, then a manager should do it. Much can go quite well without a manager's help, and almost always it turns out just as well or better.

But leadership matters even more. As we'll explore later, the managerial ethos of the organization plays a significant role in shaping managers' behaviors, and in our experience, no enduring shift can happen without the direct support of an organization's leadership.

UNMANAGING AND TODAY'S "LEADERSHIP IMPERATIVES"

Leaders face a relentless barrage from the "management advice" industry, a juggernaut that includes consultancies, publications like the *Harvard Business Review* and *Entrepreneur*, and of course, my fellow authors who churn out thousands of business and management books every year, most of which contain the urgent imperative that managers and leaders shape their people and organizations to:

- Deepen collaboration
- Work better cross-departmentally
- Increase innovation
- Take on more complex projects
- Enable agility
- Be more equitable and inclusive

- Increase the diversity of thought
- Think outside the box
- Reinvent their ways of working
- Empower their people to take greater ownership

It is the slow Gregorian chant of the world of management today: "*Innovatus agilitus*, empowering *diversitas*, and so on."

I believe that all of the above "imperatives" will be tangibly impacted by unmanaging. Why? Because they are also core aspects of the companies in our client base: highly innovative, creative, and collaborative advertising, marketing, and digital agencies.[5] They are incredibly productive, schedule-driven organizations that eat, sleep, and breathe the imperatives listed above. And they tell us that they become more of that when they adopt this new approach to managing.

And yet I also claim—and have case studies to support it—that regardless of your industry, the unmanaging mindset will enable you to manage better and unleash the potential of your workers and workplace. Whether your business is about assembly lines, health care operations, or research, unmanaging will transform your workplace.

SPEAKING OF TRENDY LEADERSHIP IMPERATIVES: SOFTWARE AGILE

A few years back, Harvard Business Review had *Agile* on its cover. That was the peak of the hype around Software Agile, a set of techniques packaged in 2001 that today are misunderstood. For the unwashed in this matter, Agile is well-proven set of techniques for running a very specific type of project (very large software development) very well. The term *Agile* owes its popularity to some amazing successes in that narrow space, but more so to an amazing amount of marketing. More on this in my many articles, which you can find on online.[6]

Why do I bring up Agile? The first reason is that my company has *Agile* in its name. I confess we decided on the name AgencyAgile as a marketing device, knowing full well that we could do something much better than Agile (i.e., it would actually work in broader business contexts, and it does) and that people were more likely to buy Agile than, say, "My name is Jack and I'm here to help." Ironically, because we never really gave our technique a name (until now, with unmanaging) our clients started calling our version AgencyAgile, or just Agile, so we ended up in a conundrum: hang on to the Agile moniker or let it go. So far, we've kept the name.

A second reason for bringing up Agile is that the techniques you'll read here may feel Agile-like. Naturally, many of the ideas and methods used in Agile existed long before anyone used that term. Agile is an agglomeration of best practices for large projects, and AgencyAgile's unmanaging techniques draw from that same well. As with Agile, we've assembled some great ways for people to work better together, including a few that Agile used. Plus, we created a few new ones as well.

The last twenty-plus years have not been kind to Agile. Millions of people and probably hundreds of thousands of organizations have tried to adopt its very specific methods to a wide range of business activities. In my opinion, the whole thing has been a messy failure. A good number of you reading these words will be nodding in confirmation. You can go look at popular forums, such as the Agile subreddit from https://reddit.com/, to hear this conversation in more detail.

Having used dozens of team-based methods over the decades, including many precursors to Agile, I think that those failures come from people hewing too strictly to a set of Agile rules, instead of understanding why the rules worked for that situation (context) and how, if at all, they should be used in this new context.

If you as a leader or manager have been tasked with "being more Agile," then a good bit of what I'll share in this book will help you navigate that challenge. On occasion, we even hire out our coaches to run other people's Agile teams and projects. We do this even though we know bad managing happens when you use the wrong techniques in a given situation, and that's what most Agile looks like these days: people doing what they think is right without really thinking.

I like to think of unmanaging as being the smarter and more-useful second cousin of Agile. There are some genetic similarities, but we're talking about different branches of a family tree. Think chimpanzees versus humans. We're not as good at swinging from branches, but we're amazing at almost everything else.

WHAT YOU CAN GET FROM THIS BOOK

Depending on your managerial role, what you gain from this book may vary. I'll take a crack at setting your expectations here:

- **Leaders of organizations**, this book will help you shift to seeing managing for what it is, including its benefits and costs. If I have done my job, you may be inspired to join our clients in unlocking the unmanaged potential within your organization. There is also much actionable guidance for you as well. Your forthcoming mastery of Why Moments, which sit at the core of some of the best leadership practices known, will make you a better, more-inspiring leader. I believe you will also grasp the essence of what good managerial action looks like, and your awareness will help shape the behavior of your managers as well.
- **Managers**, especially those in project-driven and knowledge-based workplaces, this book should be your handbook. The exercises were designed for you. Prepare to be delighted by an almost annoyingly comprehensive collection of information about what we do wrong as managers. Your understanding that we can do better is the first step toward change. We'll also arm you with multiple variations on managing in the key moments so you'll be prepared for the road ahead.
- **Workers and team members**, I hope you'll enjoy this. In some ways, it will probably validate experiences that you've had with

managers, some of which might become more comprehensible as a result. When we train client organizations, we always train the workers as well so that the managers know that the workers know better. Hopefully, the knowledge here brings you some power in that way.

- **AgencyAgile clients and alumni**, here are the underlying big ideas: a handbook to accompany our trainings. A reminder, and hopefully, a few laughs for you from the stories, vignettes, and models that we have shared with you over the years. Although our high-intensity, hands-on training format spurs the adoption of new, better behaviors, the words spoken can easily fade from memory. This book should remind you of the why behind many of our techniques and methods.

- **Those in "Agile" workplaces**, this book will help you decode some of the ideas in the original Software Agile.

YOUR JOURNEY OF CHANGE

A very wise client of ours named Dave, having mastered many of the techniques listed in this book, once remarked, "I think my real success secret now is to remember what I used to do in each situation and try to do the opposite of that."

The golf legend Jack Nicklaus wrote in *Golf My Way* that despite his verified greatness, it may be that none of what worked for him will work for his reader; every golfer is different, even at the pro level. In that way, there is no one way to lead or manage. I am regularly amazed by how our clients have maintained the spirit of unmanaging while adapting its techniques to their own needs and style.

You have your own better way, and it will probably depend on the type of work you do and the organization you are in. On your journey, I hope you gain the eyes, ears, and mind to become a great manager or leader of managers. So much goodness springs from the kind of shift you're going to make. Prepare to make lives better: your team's, your client's, and your own.

Find reader resouces at
https://unmanagedbook.com/resources

Managers, Organizations, and Metrics

This section is a boot camp to teach you the core ideas of unmanaging and discusses the origins of managing and managers. From there, we'll go on to define the project-driven organization and how its structure and successes often pose challenges. For fun, we'll also look at what happens when we take unmanaging to its extreme and have no managers at all. We'll wrap up by talking about how we measure managers and the effects of managing.

CHAPTER I

The Eternally Costly Manager

The ad agency executive took the stage and regaled the crowd with a story about an experiment one of their teams conducted. For two weeks, they had sequestered twenty workers in two New York City brownstones during the day. The workers were told to disconnect from all email and ignore all other communications except between their fellow workers in the brownstones. They had been given an assignment—work that needed to be done for a client, a large beverage company.

The executive proudly exclaimed that the work the team produced amazed everyone in two ways. First, its quality: they had delivered some really solid work. Second, it's quantity: in the executive's words, they had done a year's worth of work in those two weeks.

The executive was very proud. Everyone clapped. But all I could feel was embarrassment for him . . .

WHY EMBARRASSMENT? A year's worth of work in two weeks seems astounding, but what he was actually saying with that boast was, "The way we manage our workers and teams is so costly to quality and productivity that we only get one twenty-sixth of what we could." That's less than 4%. In other words, if the team was able to do a year's worth of work in two weeks, what was stopping it from doing the same all year? The answers can all be found in the manager tax.

....

The paradox is that, despite managers wanting to create productivity, they become its nemesis. This is the manager tax.

....

THE ORIGINAL MANAGER TAX

Management can be costly to productivity. This idea is not new, but it may be new to you. It came to prominence in 1937, in the later parts of the industrial age, and was heralded by Ronald Coase, a young PhD student at the Oxford School of Economics. In that time between the two great wars, industrial economics followed the maxim, "the bigger you get, the bigger you can become." The concept of economies of scale had become popular, especially following the development of mass manufacturing as embodied by companies like Ford and DuPont.

As these companies grew larger and standardized their resources, processes, and products, they found they became even more efficient, competitive, and profitable.

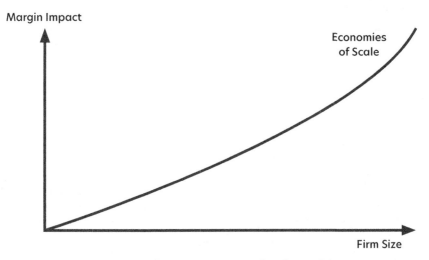

Figure 4: Classic Economies of Scale Model

Coase's analysis, however, produced an interesting point: If the concept, "the bigger you get, the bigger you can become," is true, then why are there still so many smaller firms around?[7] In fact, he pointed out something that was probably being ignored: that in virtually every industry, alongside the one, two, or even three extremely large firms, there were far more companies that were smaller by comparison, and often hundreds if not thousands of even smaller companies that competed with them. How could they possibly compete with the scale (and price) advantages of the big firms?

The only reasonable explanation was that although production economies of scale do occur, making them more competitive, it amplified another set of costs: the costs of coordination—that is, the activity of keeping people and teams moving in the right direction. Increasing size increases coordination costs.

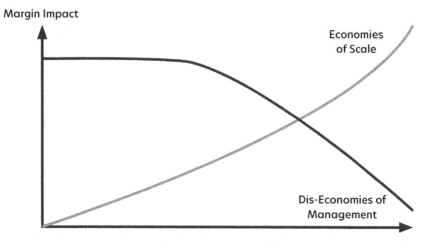

Figure 5: Coase's Dis-economies of Management

Coordination is another way of describing the primary job of managers, and here Coase went further. He found that managers and managing become more costly as the firm grows and as more managers are added. That managers are often the most expensive type of worker, amplifies this effect.

Ultimately, Coase surmised that a firm's competitiveness was bounded by the increasing cost of managing the business, meaning that tradeoffs between size, profitability, and many other factors would ultimately shape the organization, both in terms of its limits and also its configuration.

For example, General Motors, once the largest manufacturer of automobiles in the world, with a staff of three hundred thousand, was also the largest single purchaser of tires and batteries. It manufactured neither of these products, finding it more cost effective to allow smaller (yet still large) firms to make them rather than start a whole new division. At that time, only half of every finished GM car hit the market because of GM activities. Suppliers, who were smaller and more efficient, produced the rest.

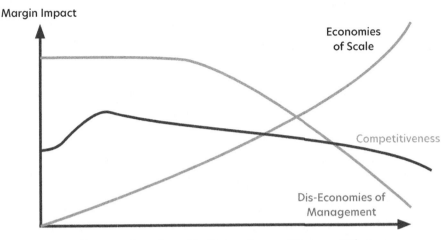

Figure 6: Resultant Declining Competitiveness Effect

The idea that managers were a drag on an organization's growth and ability to scale was revolutionary and somewhat controversial in 1937, but in the decades that followed, researchers identified other transaction costs that might influence a company's decision to scale. For instance, consider the choice over in-house versus external legal counsel. One of the transaction costs might be the difference between an in-house lawyer's salary versus the external lawyer's hourly rate. Another could be the value of having a broad-capability law firm available versus one internal lawyer, who would likely have a less-broad set of skills. We often call these pros and cons in decision-making, yet as you'll see, this same sort of tradeoff discussion is somewhat rare when choosing whether to hire an additional manager.

THE MULTITUDE OF MANAGER TAXES

In today's organizations, the costliest feature of managers is usually not their salary or the basic coordination cost that Coase identified, but the way they interact with the people who actually produce the work. More precisely, managers tend to interact in ways that reduce the productivity of workers and teams.

Over the years, Coase's research has spurred important discussion about the many costs involved in having and hiring managers. What follows is a list of what we refer to as the manager taxes:

1. **Managers tax profits.** Since managers are not directly part of the production function in the organization—that is, adding a manager does not add a worker—their cost reduces overall profits.

2. **Managers tax productivity.** In general, the more managing that occurs, especially as it relates to interactions with workers and teams, the lower their productivity.

3. **Managers tax managers.** Every new manager taxes existing managers. If a firm has only one manager, that manager operates at 100% managerial efficiency. But as the organization adds managers, the existing manager gets less efficient because of the cost of coordination between managers. This coordination cost can grow quickly, even geometrically, because as the per-unit cost of managing goes up,[8] the firm gets less managing per managerial dollar spent.

4. **New managers provide diminishing returns.** New managers themselves are less efficient than existing ones because they too experience the manager-to-manager coordination tax.

5. **Bad managers increase taxes.** Managers may perform suboptimally. The above taxes exist even when managers are perfectly efficient and effective. But managers are human and, like all of us, may perform suboptimally due to a range of factors, including lack of skill, a wide range of misbehaviors, and plain old bad decision-making.

This last point, which Coase, as an economist, shrugged off as an inevitable aspect of humanity, is often the single greatest tax of all the manager taxes. Incorrect managing, especially in a project setting, multiplies the impact of all of the other manager taxes. Productivity loss can easily reach 30% or more![9]

A final note on Dr. Coase: if his insights (and their implications) strike you as a bit ingenious and ahead of their time, you're in good company. In 1991, Coase won the Nobel Prize in Economics for this pioneering work and a few other amazing ideas he hatched later in his career.[10]

MANAGING VERSUS PRODUCTIVITY

I've always found it ironic that the act of managing is, in general, a negative force on productivity. A wide body of anecdotal evidence (which is far more common and useful in the business world than quantitative data) supports this idea. As Peter Drucker famously noted, "Most of what we call management consists of making it difficult for people to get their jobs done."

An organization's productivity is inversely proportional to the number of managers it has and how vigorously they manage—and that assumes that they are all managing well. It only gets worse if managers, as Coase noted, perform suboptimally, producing so-called bad managers and the bad managing tax.

It is a difficult paradox to get one's head around: managers can be useful, but less actual managing and fewer managers overall can be a good thing. Often, when workers are asked to identify the most productive hours in their day, they answer "very early" or "very late," which really means, "when the managers and their managing activities are not present."

I can tell you with great confidence that no manager goes to work asking themselves, "Hmm, how can I mess up productivity today?" I believe most managers want to make their organizations better. But I'm also pretty sure most of them are unaware of the productive cost of many of their managerial actions. I wasn't.

THE ABSENT MANAGER: WHOM SHOULD WE SEND HOME?

How taxing are managers (and their activity) to knowledge worker productivity? We present this question in our leadership workshops in a very simple way, using an organizational pyramid. We call it the "Away for a Day" exercise. I must give credit to Dave Laughran, a senior economist who I used to go for runs with when I worked at RAND, for the idea that maybe we, any of us, don't contribute to success as much as we think we do.

Imagine your organization is a pyramid with three layers. The executive layer, at the top, steers the organization but does not touch the production function. The middle layer consists of the managers who directly or indirectly touch the production function. The bottom layer is, of course, workers and teams that *are* the production function. For the purposes of this example, we're going to ignore the fact that these layers can be a bit blurred, as in the case of a manager also doing production work.

Figure 7: The Sources of Productivity Pyramid

Let's look at the impact of sending people home and telling them to do no more work for the day. If we send the people at the bottom layer of the pyramid, the workers, home for the day, what gets done? A fairly accurate answer would be "not much" or "way less." Yes, some things might get done because managers are still there, some of whom can perform the worker function. On the whole, however, sending workers home would pretty much decimate the organization's productivity that day.

Now get ready for this.

What if we send all the managers home for the day? Would workers be more productive? When I suggest this during our two-day leadership workshops (we often ask our clients to have most or all their managers in attendance as well), there is always a sort of embarrassed laughter as managers realize what I am suggesting.

That's what happened at a recent leadership workshop for a client in Brooklyn; the managers also laughed when I first explained the idea.

Coincidentally, after we were done for the day, the company had scheduled a happy hour at a nearby gastropub (arranged prior to the scheduling of our workshop) for the whole company. When the managers arrived (our workshop ended a few minutes late), they asked their worker colleagues how their day had been. The workers answered, "Really productive!"

Happens all the time.

During a run with Dave at RAND, he remarked that government policymakers made multibillion-dollar policy decisions based on his research papers. Dave was quite self-effacing, adding, "But as with all research, I could be wrong! Or I might only have discovered part of the problem, and spending money in that way could be a complete waste, or worse!"

I laughed and said, "So what you're saying is that maybe they should sometimes just pay you to stay home and save billions of dollars?" We both laughed at that, but at the core of it is a truth managers should consider: despite your best intentions, your actions may generate more problems than solutions. Choose wisely.

....

Take a holiday from the manager tax: productivity often
increases for workers when the managers are away.

....

AGILE CALLED AND SAID, "YES, AND LET'S LOSE THE MANAGERS AS WELL"

Codified in 2001, *The Manifesto for Agile Software Development* proved to
be a modern-day, digital equivalent of Martin Luther's act of nailing his
theses to a church door in Germany five centuries earlier. At the core of
Software Agile are key ideas about breaking away from a monotonous and
procedural approach to software design and testing and replacing it with
something nimbler and more bespoke or, in their terms, Agile.[11]

But Software Agile and its repercussions extend beyond software development because of key principles that reframe management:

- **Worker productivity and quality of work are two primary
  measures of success.** The Agile founders were ruthless about
  measurement. Large projects are notoriously hard to measure or
  complete, often remaining "90% finished" for more than half of the
  project! The Agile founders measured how much good code was
  produced per worker hour. If the number went up, then whatever
  you were doing to manage the team and project was good; if it went
  down, then the opposite. It was all about the team.
- **Protecting the team matters.** There is a basic rule in well-practiced
  Agile about how managers should interact with their teams. Here's
  the rule: "Stay the fuck away from the team."
- Using the metrics above, the Agile founders found that an increase
  in managerial interactions tended to lower team productivity. In
  fact, it turned out to be more effective to let the team make mistakes
  and fix them afterward than to allow managers to intervene (or
  fiddle) during their work. While true Software Agile teams are a bit

rare, this rule is embedded in some of the key managerial moments discussed later, especially the Go Moment.[12]

- **The team is a team, not just a group of workers, and the work belongs to all of them.** All work is an assignment in common. That means everyone gets to know everything. Everyone works together, hears everything, can ask questions, learn, interact, and relate. Humans work better this way than they do in silos. We've also embedded this throughout the four key moments that you'll learn.

As if this were not radical enough, Software Agile's founders state their strong team-centric bias, preferring:[13]

- Individuals and interactions over *processes and tools*
- Working software [taking action] over *comprehensive documentation*
- Customer collaboration over *contract negotiation*
- Responding to change over *following a plan*

If you think about who "owns" the items italicized at the end of those bullets, you'll recognize three managerial roles: project manager, requirements manager, and client manager. One of the biggest problems the Agile founders uncovered was that all these managers and their managing created more confusion and distance between the team and the customers in an already very challenging type of project.

How much better did things get? According to research on the topic, the productivity of Agile teams increased by as much as 500%;[14] teams would become up to five times more productive using the Software Agile approach to managing.

If you're salivating at the idea of enabling your workers and teams to go five times faster, know that the projects that Software Agile fixed were burdened with massive delays and sky-high failure rates driven by their sheer complexity and size. Bad managing can be a massive multiplier in bad situations, and have the opposite effect when alleviated.

THE JOURNEY TO BETTER MANAGING

So, yes, managers can be costly, perhaps costly no matter what we do. The least-costly manager is the one who overcomes their intrinsic managerial taxes on profits, productivity, and their fellow managers by having a positive effect on the production function of the organization. The most important thing is to avoid the three main ways that the bad manager tax happens:

- **Managing without method.** Many people manage without a cohesive theory about how to do it and why. Many ascend into managerial roles, especially in knowledge work organizations, with little or no formal training in the principles of management (and truthfully, there is very little good management training available). More often, they just do what they have seen those above them do. Other times, they may just do what feels good to them, which usually turns out badly for others.
- **Managing without regard for context.** Even if managers have a method, a sturdy set of managerial behaviors, or knowledge of management theory, many use the wrong ideas or approach. There is no one way of managing, and good managing happens when one chooses the techniques that create the best outcomes given the context in which they operate: the type of business, the type of work, and their managerial role.
- **Warring with other managers.** Managers sometimes act against other managers, and not necessarily by ignoring their boss or acting contrary to their wishes or demands. In certain types of work, managing doesn't look like a pyramid, meaning multiple managers may have an opinion about what the correct course of action is for any given worker or team. When these managers lack

alignment, they may compete with each other to enforce their desired actions. In such environments, managers may not recognize the boundaries of their authority, so they attempt to assert control over work that other managers are responsible for.

Does this sound familiar at all to you? Have you seen it in other managers or even in yourself? But also, it all sounds kind of crazy, doesn't it? How did things get this way? Where did we get lost?

CHAPTER 2

Origins of Bad Managing

Andreas the master saddle maker is standing in the workshop watching the apprentice test how the rear jockey, the part of the saddle behind the cantle, lies on the saddle skirt. This is a critical part of the fitting process, and the apprentice is focused.

The apprentice keeps on testing it, seeing if he can get it to lie so only the right pieces are showing while it is lying flat. Andreas notices something amiss despite the apprentice's efforts.

Andreas, being a master, can see quite clearly what the problem is; with his steady hand, it could be fixed in just a few minutes. But the master's job is different from that—the master is a teacher, and all of his actions are directed toward helping the apprentice become a master someday.

He walks over and asks, "So what do you see?" The apprentice replies that he can feel that it isn't fitting but is not sure what the problem is.

During the next several minutes, the master continues to ask questions, asking the apprentice to think about what the solution might be. The master knows that the apprentice might spend all day or even two trying to figure this out, and the saddle may end up being late for the promised delivery.

THE WORK, meaning the good or service being delivered, is a product of the worker, their skill set, and their experiences. In the story above, we see a patient, thoughtful teacher painstakingly guiding his apprentice, using a Socratic questioning method.

Some may say it is an overly romanticized story set in a time when classrooms were rare, literacy was uncommon, and YouTube videos didn't exist, so the only way to teach was through guided hands-on experience. Nonetheless, despite the fact we all have access to online resources, guided hands-on experience remains one of the best ways to teach and learn. This has a fancy name today, actionable learning, and it is probably the best way to train knowledge workers so that lessons stick.

But why does this master-apprentice-Socratic approach seem quaint and ancient even though it is verifiably effective? The answer is that we took a detour from this approach when we entered the era of factories and automation. Around the turn of the twentieth century, the nature of work changed dramatically. We traded a model that made masters for one that made money. And we can't seem to let it go.

THEN WE STARTED CALLING IT MANAGING

In centuries past, managing people was not called *managing*. In fact, the use of the word *manage* spiked to its current level in the 1920s (see diagram below).[15] The word *manage* comes from French, Italian, and Spanish words, all pertaining to holding the reins of a horse and derived from the roots *manus* (hand) and *agere* (to act). Therefore, actual management was a literal hands-on activity intended to guide livestock of various types.

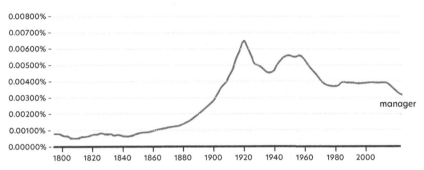

Figure 8: Historical Usage Frequency of the Word "Manager"

In the thousands of years of human activity before that, the act of managing people came in two forms. One form, symbolized by the Andreas mentorship story above, involved creative, productive, but often artisanal endeavors to train and mentor individual craftspeople. The other form was the command-and-control approach, led by charismatic or terrifying authoritative personalities driven to meet often-impossible military, industrial, and economic objectives. Think wars, the pyramids, and humanity's horrific history of slavery.

At some point around two hundred years ago, a new epoch of industrialization began. Machines powered by nonhuman energy (water, steam, and electricity) and the standardization of production became the norm. When industrialists sought the best management method for this new era, they made the military command-and-control approach their starting point.

This choice of styles—and its perceived effectiveness—is now woven into our social fabric and has formed modern notions of what a manager should be and do. But it is almost entirely wrong for today's worker and workplace.

THE BIRTH OF BAD MANAGING

In the 1800s, the focused artisanship of earlier centuries gave way to increasingly complex automated and powered machines that could replicate actions previously performed by people but much more consistently and at much lower cost.

Consider the sewing needle. A thousand years ago, the needle-making process involved eighteen artisans, each specialized in their step of the process.[16] Centuries later, around 1500, in England, the process involved twenty-five artisans in sequence, and in all of England, there was only one person, a Spaniard, with the skills to actually make the wire for needles. English needle-makers, therefore, imported the bulk of the wire they needed from Germany or other countries where people could more readily produce it.

As automation expanded, machines and networks of companies replaced artisans. Factories still required some human assistance, but no one with the skill of an artisan. In a sewing needle factory, workers handled and moved metal pieces from machine to machine, possibly even pulling a handle or turning a crank. We see the same thing today in modern car assembly lines and Amazon fulfillment centers; robots and conveyors do most of the work, but a few humans are always there to tidy up the messy loose ends.

There is nothing artisanal about the factory process. Its philosophy has always been to enable standardization through automation. Every single sewing needle must be indistinguishable from the next. In that same way, the economic power of the era of industrialization brought in a new way of managing, where distinctions between the qualities of people become secondary or ignorable, replaced by the question of whether they could keep the machines producing. This new world of work needed a new way of managing.

THE WORST-EVER WAY TO MANAGE PEOPLE

With the lower costs and higher productivity of industrialization came more competition. Commercial items of all kinds went from being artisanal works, where the maker mattered a lot, to commodity products, where the maker didn't matter at all. The race to create mass-market, competitively priced goods meant the cost of production was everything.

Machines and factories cost a lot, but people's labor did not. Cities filled up with immigrants and farm workers seeking the better (yet still scant) wages that factories offered. Most were illiterate or barely schooled. Machines were simple and fairly reliable at this point, and the biggest variable was how fast the workers could feed the machines. The faster the factory ran, the greater the profits, and ideally, the lower the costs.

What industrialists needed was a new way to manage workers to make them work as quickly as possible, hopefully as fast as the machines. In this moment, many of our current notions of managing were born.

A mechanical engineer named Frederick Taylor developed a way of managing workers in these repetitive, automated processes, and called it Scientific Management. Taylor asserted that managers should measure how quickly workers were doing their work and compare them to *time standards*. For example, someone operating a punch press to punch holes in metal would be expected to be able to punch, say, 250 pieces per hour. The measure of the worker, then, was their ability to meet the time standard for that job.

It wasn't as if productivity didn't matter for artisans like Andreas and his apprentices—it did—but the introduction of machines and assembly lines made it a necessity. Quality, learning, and speed usually involved a tradeoff in the artisanal process, but in the Industrial Age, quality was the responsibility of machines, and speed became the primary standard by which to judge people.

WORKERS BECAME THE PROBLEM

Because the primary constraint on the profitability of a factory had become the workers, an industrialist who wanted more profits would see workers as *the* problem to solve.

Taylor applied the military idea of command and control to create what were essentially production platoons in a production line, called departments. Each leader of each department was called a manager and was responsible for making sure the department produced at the maximum speed. Ironically, this brings the word "manage" back to its origin: a literal hands-on activity intended to guide livestock—in this case, dehumanized workers. Taylor's managers were ranchers of a sort, and his Scientific Management model enabled workers, departments, and managers to be measured and molded to ensure a smoothly run operation.

The worker's jobs were not wonderful, and this era is renowned for its mind-numbing working conditions and mindless, repetitive tasks.

Some industrial historians (yes, that's a thing) note the shift when the predominant pay model went from piecework to hourly. Piecework rates would tend to align the worker with the capitalist—"the more product you make, the more we all make." The shift to an hourly rate changed this to "the more product you make, the more the boss makes." This is likely the origin of the phrase "greedy capitalist." Although the shift to hourly wage meant that that workers could be assured of a certain daily wage, it also meant that the owners and managers needed to focus on how to get every last bit of productivity out of the wage paid to the workers. Whereas Taylorism's initial focus had been on whether the machines were running at capacity, this shift in pay model meant that the employers could claim they were paying for the worker's time as well as their productivity.

This was a new lens—a quite chilling one—as owners started making claims that workers were "stealing" from them by taking breaks or not trying to work hard enough, knowing they would get paid anyway.[17] Drawing on the military management analogy, Taylor called this inherent laziness "soldiering" as if war-weary soldiers would only march and fight when commanded to or when threatened with punishment.

At one point, Taylor also noted that some workers needed to be "treated as if they are oxen." And those ideas, that workers are intrinsically lazy, became woven into the fabric of the manager-worker relationship and the very definition of what managing means. It was so terribly wrong, yet is still with us.

The manager was to be the hammer to the anvil of time standards. Said Taylor, "the duty of enforcing the adoption of time standards and enforcing this cooperation rests with management alone." With Taylor's management framework, the model of the patient, thoughtful Andreas was sidelined in favor of a much harsher profit-driven notion of what a manager should do and be: an enforcer of cooperation.

Taylor eventually realized that Scientific Management might not be the best approach. By the 1930s, he admitted that the whole framework was "dehumanizing" and that there were probably better ways to manage. But we seem to have never shaken his ideas out of our heads or out of corporate culture.

Today, his ideas are more commonly referred to as Taylorism. He is also widely recognized as the first management consultant.

The Taylorism term managing now meant
enforcing the need for workers to go faster and
work harder than they would otherwise.

TAYLORISM LIVES ON

It was 2016, and we had just finished the first training for a new client, a sixty-person marketing services group within a large finance company in New Jersey. Our first day is always for the managers and leaders, helping them understand what is possible if they master the techniques to empower teams, and to begin the process establishing the sense of rigor required of leaders in such an organization. Ideally, those leaders go home feeling a different path is possible, even probable.

We were packing up our training materials when the two top leaders in the group gave me one of those head motions that signals, "Hey, can we go chat in the hallway?" I nodded, smiled, and followed them.

"Jack, I want you to know this is great stuff," said Kathy, who had been instrumental in bringing us in.

I looked down, suspecting they were ramping up for some sort of "but" statement. I composed myself, looked up, and smiled at the two of them. "Well, I'm glad you liked the material. I'm pretty sure the trainings will have an impact for you."

"We just have one problem . . . or maybe a concern." There it was. "It's around timing. You see, we are in a tough location. It's hard to find good marketing people. Despite New York City being only two hours away, the market for this talent is so tight that we really can't afford most people, and when we do get someone good, they often move on."

I nodded in acknowledgment, trying to hide my real feelings.

She explained. "About half of our people are not the right people. We hired them because we needed people, but they aren't who we think we need." She looked at me intently to see if I understood how important this point was.

Now frankly, I'm not that good at hearing these excuses because my ears are listening for the why of the excuse. What I instead heard her say is, "We don't really know how to inspire people to be great at what they do, and possibly we don't even know how to mentor them into that greatness. Rather than admit those failures, though, we're going to fire or lay half of them off, then hire some new people with whom we will eventually have the same problems." I nodded and waited.

She continued, "So, we're not sure if we should train all of these people and then let half of them go, only to have to train the new people as well. We're thinking we should wait until we have the new people on board?" She left it open, seeking an answer to the unspoken question at the end: What should they do?

The implication caused my brain to short-circuit. All I could hear was, "Despite spending the whole day today learning about how most of our challenges are managerial, we still think that our people are the problem. We're not bad managers. Firing people who are not a fit is certainly an important managerial function and will prove that we're on the job."

Okay, that's harsh. But it was a long day already, and I was dismayed that I had not gotten my point across. I think part of the problem was that they thought we were going to train their teams.

To be fair, we do train teams. But teams are easy, and managers are
the challenge. I felt like I had already said that several times during
the day, yet we were still speaking different languages. I replied in
my best manager-ese: "I think you can go ahead with the training.
Afterward, you will be able to do a better job of choosing who to let
go." It was actually the truth, though I meant something very differ-
ent from how I think they interpreted it. I wasn't thinking of team
members being let go, but rather the managers.

Workers, especially knowledge workers, are misperceived through the lens of the factory management model and, even in knowledge work today, highly underestimated in terms of their capability and potential. Multiple forms of subtle bias and misunderstanding plague managerial decision-making to the detriment of worker and team development.

DO YOU HAVE THE RIGHT PEOPLE?

A persistent narrative among managers and leaders focuses on this question. In fact, General Electric used to have a policy of "up or out," also known as forced ranking, in which workers are judged by where they are in the performance ranking (this is a very subjective list made by a manager or managers), and then the weakest performers get "moved out." This system fits perfectly within a Tayloristic lens where work standards apply (e.g., a capable machine operator ought to produce x number of products), but in less-repetitive or ad hoc work, this ranking often becomes very subjective and fraught with bias.

Do today's managers judge workers well? Not really. One of the best studies on the topic showed that performance reviews were extremely biased, with the manager's personal idiosyncrasies being far more influential (63%) than actual results or quality of the work (21%).[18]

WHERE THE OTHER THREE FINGERS POINT

Bill, a business partner of mine a few decades ago, often told a story about how, in a previous role, he needed well beyond one hundred people to staff his technology program at a large aerospace company. After a few months, he had only hired about twenty people, and his boss called him in to ask what the problem was. Bill quickly pointed out, "There just aren't enough good people out there." Bill's boss asked to see the resumes, and Bill brought a big stack of them in as proof that he was looking at a lot of candidates. Bill's boss peeled the top one hundred resumes off that stack, handed them to Bill, and said, "Hire 'em, give 'em a chance, and fire the ones who don't work out."

Bill's boss knew on some level that most people can work out if given a chance and that having the chance is the first and most important move to developing people and a strong team.

Bill said most of them worked out just fine.

What most managers don't realize is that complaining about the talent in one's organization and providing justifications for it, as Kathy did, is basically the same as saying, "I don't know how to develop the potential of my people or enable them to productively learn." The index finger points at the worker, but the other three fingers point back to the manager.

The middle finger refers to the most-important job of any manager, especially first-level department managers: developing the potential of their people. When this doesn't happen, many managers blame their own failure on the worker. Do these managers think their job is merely to wrangle perfectly formed talent and then, like some sort of angry rancher, cull them when their workers have any significant shortcomings or just need some help? If there are seven people in the manager's department, and five of them are underdeveloped by 30% relative to their experience (which is quite common), that's one and a half people's capacity going undeveloped and unutilized. And that is just the beginning of the tragedy.

The ring finger points back to the manager, as in Bill's case, for ignoring the person's potential, a potential that lies within virtually all of us. A person's failure to learn is almost always a teaching problem, not a student problem. A manager may encounter one exception to this; but if more than that, then the manager is probably delusional. The biggest problem those workers have in common is the manager.

BEWARE THE DISMISSIVE MANAGER

Take Jeff Fisher, former coach of the Los Angeles Rams. In the 2016 season, Fisher shrugged off two quarterbacks, Jared Goff and Case Keenum, deeming them not worthy of being starting quarterbacks in the NFL. But in 2017, no longer working for Fisher, both were having impressive seasons, leading their teams into the playoffs with winning records of 9–4 and 10–3, respectively.

Dig a little deeper, and you'll see that the Rams had losing seasons for all five years that Fisher coached them. He blamed the losses on a lack of quarterback talent. In all, six of the quarterbacks that played under him (including Goff and Keenum) were part of winning teams in 2017.[19]

In 2018, under a new coach, Sean McVay, Goff took the Rams to the Super Bowl.

If you say you have thirty out of sixty people that need replacing, we know at least one more person we should add to the list—maybe at the top of the list.

The pinky finger points to the manager's ignorance of how profoundly biased they are and how difficult it is to be truly "objective" in any assessment. And yet, it *is* that manager's job to be objective or to discover one or more unbiased metrics that can shed light on the real skills and skill gaps of the worker.

THE FALLACY OF MANAGERIAL SUPERIORITY

Let's assume a sixth finger on each hand, one that indicates the fallacy of managerial superiority. This belief echoes Taylor's idea that the manager understands process and product much better than anyone else. The fallacy is not about the fact of this superiority—often the manager is more skilled in some ways. Instead, the fallacy is believing that any difference in skill or knowledge matters very much. The reality, contrary to Taylor's idea of workers being like oxen, is that people are actually quite amazing and far more similar than we typically admit or perceive.

Workers are generally free from guilt or sin because they are blessed by a desire to learn, which is their birthright, and it is proper for them to expect to receive that opportunity and the support that comes with it.

THE WORKERS WHO WERE NOT SO GOOD

My business partner Greg heard from Kathy about one year after we finished the team and managerial trainings for her sixty-plus-person organization. He relayed what she said:

"Hi Greg—I am so excited. We just left a meeting with the internal client who had been (for years) our strongest critic. The team presented the plan they had developed, and this amazing conversation

ensued where the client got so excited that we learned things we had never known about their business and their needs. I stood back and watched as this happened . . . the team led it all. We have the most amazing team!"

There was more, but that was all I needed to read. I quickly replied to Greg and Kathy, asking one question: "Hey, just wanted to check and see how many people you ended up letting go?"

She replied, "We only lost one, but she left on her own because her husband's job moved, and they left the state."

Kathy's thirty-plus people who weren't good enough became thirty-plus people who were awesome. What changed? The way they looked at their people and, as a result, the way they developed their potential.

So much can change when we look at knowledge workers as the solution, not the problem. We'll come back to factory workers later, but first we need to clean up some other distinctions that will help us make managerial choices and better understand the various contexts in which managers operate.

CHAPTER 3

The Work and Organizational Context

IF YOU STOP AND THINK ABOUT IT, Taylor's ideas enable a very simple work model—people will perform repetitive tasks to keep a string of machines working. In essence, this is a product-driven model: make the same product as fast and well as you can. But the world of work has always been much more varied than that, and that is even more true today. The implication here is obvious: while the simplicity of Taylor's hierarchies and time standards may be attractive, there is no reason to assume that they work well in other situations. They weren't even the best way to manage the work they were intended for—factory work. In practice, what we see matches what some researchers have noted: the type of work shapes the organization, which in turn shapes the correct managerial practices.

BEYOND COMPANIES AND DEPARTMENTS: DEFINING ORGANIZATION

As researcher Henry Mintzberg illustrated almost fifty years ago, form (the structure of the organization) follows function (the work that is being performed).[20] These are the key elements of the organizational context, the nature and shape of the organization within which we manage. But the word *organization* can be a muddy one, as are many business terms. For instance, it can refer to one's company, team, department, or project, to name a few.

In our usage here, the term *organization* means a group of managers and workers who work together to deliver a style of work, the inputs and outputs of which tend to be similar. Most companies, as I'll explain, have many organizations within them, such as a law firm with a litigation organization and a finance organization within it.

Organizations can span department boundaries (for example, the electric company's residential customer service organization might depend on people from many departments) or even company boundaries (for example, a project implementation organization may include external vendors and people from several internal departments).

An organization is a collection of people who get things done.

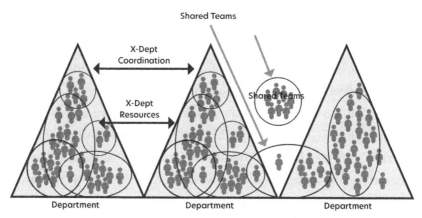

Figure 9: Organizations Take Many Forms

With the increasing complexity of work these days, organizations exist as a varying combination of people, departments, roles, and even parts of other companies.

Departments and hierarchy matter less these days, and managers will need to manage effectively in an organization comprised of a diverse set of people. They may even be managing more than one of these organizations! Success as a manager will depend on their grasp of the work being done, not the source of the people doing the work.

Part of good training for managers includes understanding the organizational context. Every organization has DNA from at least one of three basic organizational work types. Identifying which type matches your organization will have a major impact on your success as a manager.

THE PRODUCT-DRIVEN ORGANIZATION

We'll start with Taylor. The challenge he sought to address was a product-driven problem: How can an organization make a consistently high-quality product as efficiently as possible? This is a very specific work production style where uniformity is cherished, both in terms of work outputs and also in worker and manager behavior. It is about repetition.

> The product-driven organization was the target
> of Taylor's management techniques.

Now here is the important part: you could say that Ford Motor Company is a product-driven organization: the primary organizational function of the company is to reliably produce vehicles. But Ford, the company, has other organizational functions within.

For example, Ford needs to design new cars, and each design needs to be new, different, and unique in some (or many) ways. This function enables Ford to produce new products, but it is not strictly necessary, as they could choose to produce the same car model over and over. In fact, Ford's first car, the Model T, was first produced in 1908, and it was only nineteen years later that production ended in favor of other models. Ford owned about half of the US car market at the time, in part because of how they optimized production to make the Model T highly affordable to the growing middle class. Ford is a product-driven organization.

But what of the other parts, the other organizations within Ford?

THE PROCESS-DRIVEN ORGANIZATION

It is safe to assume that Ford has a finance and accounting organization within the company. What do they produce? Are they product driven? No, this is an example of our second of three forms, the process-driven organization, an organization that is responsible for the optimal execution of a process, which usually takes the form of a set of rules or policies. In the case of our example, the rules and policies include tax and accounting regulations, internal process controls, and reporting, to name a few. The process-driven organization at its heart is a service-based organization that operates to ensure that the rules are followed.

Figure 10: The Two Most Common Organizational Styles

Often, the process-driven organization is filled with managers, as much of what goes on is simply managing a process to ensure the organization conforms with the rules. This means that actual workers may be called managers, as in a "client success manager" who speaks to you when you call a support phone line.

While some process-driven organizations operate under a very formal and strict rule set, others, like a customer service organization, may use the rules as a framework for how things are done.

While the process-driven organization may measure itself by its throughput (how many policy actions were done by a given worker), it is primarily measured (and managed) in a bureaucratic way: Did we follow the rules, and how well? Doing it right can often be valued more than doing it fast. Bureaucracies are not necessarily efficient, but they are very effective, even if you don't like what the DirecTV customer support person told you.

Another example of a process-driven organization is the CPA firm that does my and my company's taxes—I and they measure their work quality primarily by whether they followed the rules.

Figure 11: Management Styles Are Influenced By Organizational Style

As you can see in the diagram above, these two types of organizations rely on two different ideas of management, Taylorism for the product-driven organization and bureaucratic management for the process-driven organization. A manager in one of those organizations would have a different managerial focus than a manager in the other type.

THE PROJECT-DRIVEN ORGANIZATION

But what about the types of work where repetition and rules aren't as helpful? In the messy real world, a growing number of organizations perform work that is varied, new, and nonrepeatable.

The project-driven organization is anything but repetitive or rules-based. It excels at doing things in new ways. Because of this high level of work uniqueness, workers and managers are in a constant state of figuring things out, being creative, innovative, etc. The project-driven organization is a knowledge-work organization where its product comes from people's minds, not policies, rules, or assembly lines. These people are often referred to as *knowledge workers*.

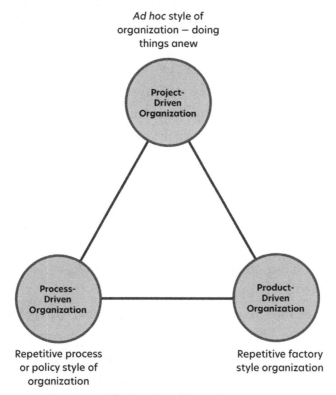

Figure 13: The Project-driven Organization

Before we go further, let's clean up some terminology: *project* is an overloaded and potentially confusing word. Cleaning my house can be called a project, as can building a massive bridge or designing a new car for Ford. It is the right word for where we're going in this book, but because of the overuse of the word, you may have to bend your brain around it, ignoring more common uses, like I had to. This will (later) include letting go of the idea that project management has anything to do with managing product-driven organizations.

In general, project-driven work has many, but not necessarily all, of these challenging attributes:

- **Time-bounded activity.** Projects have a start and end that can be measured: did we accomplish what we set out to do? Often the end is a deadline, a time or date by which the project should be completed. This is different from product production, which, if we gave a project-like name to it, might be called a production run—a number of units that we produce in a batch. This, likewise, is different from a process-driven activity, which we might call a *case*.
- **Unique context and output.** A project typically involves creating something that has not been done before. If Ford designers set out to design the Model Z, they will not do another Model Z project. They likely will do other projects like it but with different results. Each project has its own unique result.
- **Uncertainty.** During projects, workers are figuring out things, solving a problem, or building something anew. A project might be to find out what consumers think of our new product, for example. Projects end when we have the answer—unless we just give up.
- **Innovation.** Projects involve making something that is better or different from what has been made before. This can also take the form of creating a new way of doing things, such as a new survey technique or a more efficient way of running an organization.
- **Creativity.** This is often treated as synonymous with innovation, but our clients tend to see creativity as more inspiration driven, focusing on ideas, insights, or designs that do not seem incremental but seem, well, a bit inspired. Innovation would be more incremental or obvious in comparison.
- **Collaboration.** Almost everything we do, unless we are completely alone, involves collaboration. In a project, however, workers are uniquely interdependent: the work result is a team-based result, or the work is done together rather than sequentially as in a product- or process-driven organization. Adding to this is the uncertainty of *how* the team will work together and how their pieces of the

puzzle will be solved together to create a cohesive or integrated end product.

- **Complexity.** Often related to the size of the project, complexity makes the whole picture above unclear. At the start of a project, a team may need to answer questions such as, what innovation and other team members do we need? This is, by the way, what Software Agile was created to solve: massive 200-plus-staff projects that were highly complex and whose details were often incomprehensible.

Mintzberg initially called this the *ad hoc organization*: it responds to ad hoc project requests (from clients or stakeholders) and does so adaptively, assigning workers or, more often, teams to execute the project. After the project, the team often dissolves, its members reappearing in other teams. The classic form of the ad hoc organization is a matrix organization, where workers (specialists) reside in departments for "housekeeping purposes" but functionally work in cross-departmental teams, delivering projects.

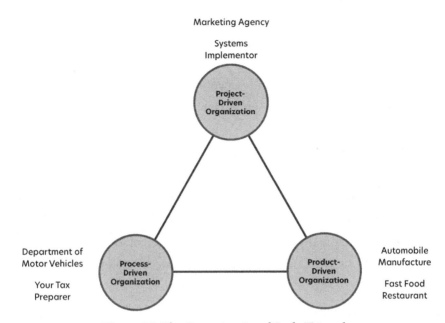

Figure 14: The Organizational Style Triangle

The project-driven organization is less similar to the other two types—it does not live in the world of repeatability like the other two. For managers, the managing that needs to be done, the processes needed, the staffing, the schedule, the outputs—pretty much everything—can vary with every single project.

Project-driven organizations will underperform when overmanaged. No surprise there, as Coase already taught us that *any* type of organization will perform worse when overmanaged. But project-driven organizations generally have more managers because of their matrix structure and their ad hoc work style. In this organizational context, the impact of suboptimal managing by individual managers—which is a problem for any type of work—gets multiplied by the prevalence of other managers. Mintzberg noted that these project-driven organizations often:

- Do not function well with traditional Tayloristic principles of management
- Grant quasi-managerial authority to a wide range of personnel (which challenges the Tayloristic idea of control through hierarchy)
- Lack a rigor called "unity of command," meaning that it may not be clear whom, or if anyone, is in charge

THE MESSY MIDDLES

We've covered work that involves repetitive activities, whether producing things or following policies and rules, as well as the chaotic, new work of the project-driven organization. But the real world is not as simple as I state, and many organizations are a mix or blend of these types. For example, many styles can exist between the process- and product-driven organizations:

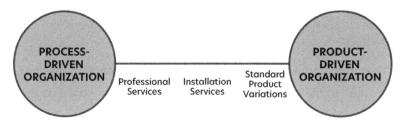

Figure 15: Organizations Along the Continuum

- **Professional services.** One of the key factors in a successful professional services organization (process-driven organization) is creating service options that can be bought and delivered as products.
- **Installation services.** Many product-driven organizations also have an installation organization that follows specific rules for how to install the product.
- **Standard product variations.** A product-driven organization may have a product that can be customized through a process or service (e.g., a new car).

Since we learn best from extreme examples, I focus on project-driven organizations throughout this book. They are, I believe, the hardest organizations to manage well, and the methods we'll explore for solving their managerial challenges are also useful in the other types of organizations.

This last point surprised me when we first discovered it, and I am grateful for knowing clients who, despite not being like our typical clients, said, "I think we need to learn that. I think it could help us." But it makes perfect sense: in general, every company looks a bit like Ford, with a mix of all three types of organization within.

OUR PROJECT-DRIVEN FUTURE

I also believe that all organizations are becoming more project driven in nature, as evidenced by the list of common business imperatives noted in the "Origins" section of this book. Part of that shift, I believe, is also being driven by the very same forces of technological automation of work that started in the Industrial Era and also continue today, including recent advances in artificial intelligence.

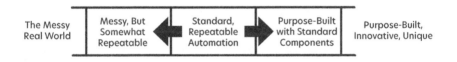

Figure 16: Automation and AI Will Drive Humans To The Edges

The diagram above shows a continuum of sorts, where automation continues to claw its way to the edges. Toward the left edge is work that deals with the messy real world, problems that require human touch, insight, adaptation, or presence. This, in its own way, is also project-driven work. Toward the right edge is work more like what we defined as project driven, creative, innovative, unique, and so on. The middle is where much of the product-driven and process-driven work happens.

Work that requires humans will increasingly shift to the edges, or said differently, machines will become increasingly better at the middle, working their way outward. At some point, what will remain human oriented is just the project-driven work, whether messy or unique. By learning to manage complex projects, you prepare yourself for the inevitably project-driven future.

CHAPTER 4

The Managerial Context

In 2002, I took a job as a CTO/COO of a dot-com that had been funded only a week before the bubble popped. Still flush with cash, we had about forty-five of the original hundred-plus people still on board. I inherited thirty or so of them and set to meet them and learn what they were doing.

One of the people, whom I'll just name Sam, was "Senior Manager of X." Sam was the only person in his department, and after a quick inquiry to our HR person, I discovered that had always been the case.

I asked Sam about it, "So . . . what is it that you manage?" He replied, "I manage the work that I do."

LIKE MANY TERMS USED IN BUSINESS, the term *manager* is broadly used, often in ways that have nothing to do with managing. Sam probably got the title of senior manager because it was a condition of his being hired from somewhere else or maybe because it costs nothing to give away titles. But, in my view, Sam was not a manager.

Managers fill many different niches and roles, but in this book, managers are the people who play a *coordination role with the production function*. They interact with workers, play a role in how the work is handled and defined, or directly support the worker's execution of the work or process. (Be careful with this last piece, as many forms of direct support are actually counterproductive.)

Those in leadership are not managers unless they otherwise qualify as described above. For instance, the CEO of a small fifteen-person firm may still spend part of their time as a worker or, more likely, have some direct managerial role around the work. Roles (and actions) are more important and distinguishing than titles.

We can also exclude managers from what I would term corporate or administrative functions, like human resources or finance. These are managers, for sure, and as vital as they are, their interaction with the production function is peripheral. If they manage poorly, the organization will take a hit, but the production function generally will be unaffected.

One last distinction. Managers fall into two basic categories of purpose: the vertical manager and the coordination manager. The vertical managers are typically what we would call a department manager, someone who became a manager due to their expertise and experience in that department's focus; their position is often depicted in a vertical hierarchy for that department:

- **Department manager (DM).** These managers oversee a group or team that is primarily in a production or worker role—those who produce deliverables or services. Most departments have a specialty: a craft or skillset or an area of focus. In a pharmaceutical company, there might be a medical affairs department, a group of medical policy and research experts. A consulting company might have a Microsoft Dynamics 365 product configuration department to set up software for specific clients. In a marketing agency, this could be the strategy department or the creative department. In general, these managers bear responsibility for onboarding, training, developing, and mentoring everyone in the department.

The other main category of managers is the coordination managers, who exist because of the coordination needs within the life cycle of the work. As organizations grow in size, the need for coordination grows. Coordination managers tend to fit into one of three roles:

- **Project manager (PM).** This refers to managers who primarily coordinate and manage schedules and other resource aspects of a project. That said, PMs often cover every aspect of managing a project, including those of the other roles listed here. Still, they rarely do the work. Perhaps ironically, some of the greatest forms of overmanaging in project-driven organizations come from this role, whose name includes the word *project*. In popular business literature, the scope of project management is so wide reaching that it could claim ownership over at least three (Why, What, and Go) if not all four of the key managerial moments mentioned at the beginning of the book.
- **Client manager (CM).** These managers coordinate between those for whom the work is being performed (customers, stakeholders, etc.) and the teams and workers. Client managers typically "live" in their own department of other client managers.
- **Requirements manager (RM).** These managers help define or collect requirements for the work or service being performed. They know *about* the work and may even do some work to define the work, but they are actually managers when you look at the impact and style of their role. Needed most when requirements

are complex, RMs coordinate and manage the existence of that information.

One other important difference between the DM and the other coordination-style managers is that the coordination managers tend to be managers throughout their career. For example, if someone is hired as a PM, they begin managing a project immediately. You can see this in in their titles: the entry level might be a project associate, then project coordinator, PM, senior PM, and so on. They all start with their specialty being a managerial role.

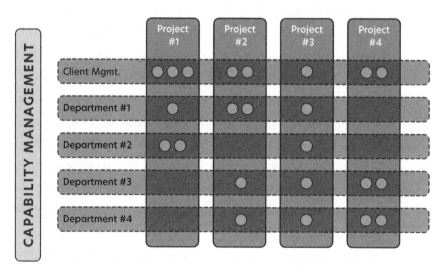

Figure 17: Matrix Structures Enable Multi-Managing

As shown in the diagram above, this multiplicity of managerial roles often exists because project-driven organizations have a *matrix structure*, where (horizontal) department specialists are "enrolled" into (vertical) projects that are then populated by some selection of the other three types of coordination managers.

THE MANAGERIAL SWARM IN PROJECT-DRIVEN ORGANIZATIONS

While product-driven and process-driven organizations may gradually gain managerial complexity as they grow, project-driven organizations more rapidly proliferate managerial roles, mostly due to the ad hoc nature of the work, but also in response to the decreasing effectiveness of any given manager as the complexity within the work-mix and overall population of managers grows.

Let's look at some numbers. The top parts of the pyramids below are manager full-time equivalents (only equivalents because some managers may be fractional, retaining worker responsibilities as well). The bottom of the pyramids are workers. The size of each pyramid corresponds to the size of the organization.

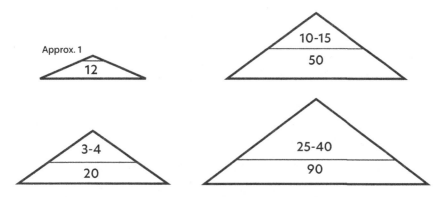

*Figure 18 : Project-driven Organizations Often
See Rapid Increases in Managing*

It is somewhat shocking that a hundred-person project-driven organization routinely has upward of thirty-five managers, meaning that there is one manager for every two or three workers. This accelerating growth of managers (as a percentage of the overall organizational population) is a breeding ground of sorts for all forms of the manager tax. One of our clients (a COO) noted that this stems from bias toward using managers as a "creeping workaround" for almost anything that seems to be not working.

What do all those managers do, and how do they work with workers to ensure optimal and prioritized productivity? How should they work with each other? Those questions will be answered, but first we'll start with the worker's direct department manager, the DM.

THE BIRTH OF THE DEPARTMENT MANAGER

Where do department managers come from? While they can be hired, most DMs in project-driven organizations begin as specialists who are promoted within their departments to become managers.

The promotion moment is both the beginning of the new journey into management and, more significantly, the culmination of a competitive race to the top that confirms which specialist was best. While "best" often includes subjective elements, there is usually some real truth to the promotion of the best specialist (hereafter the "deep specialist"). This person has done great work or been instrumental in a large number of wins (or rescues) for the organization.

Many challenges arise out of this style of promotion, but before we explore those, it is worth noting the positives. Such a promotion ensures the retention of that specialist, which is incredibly valuable since a good percentage of the organization's capability may ride on this person's presence. Their departure would create a major capability gap. The promotion also solidifies the ethos and career progression of the organization: become an expert and get a higher title, more recognition, higher pay, and so on by being promoted to the top role in the department.

Many leaders do not realize that this actual success moment for the deep specialist is not quite what we imagine; nor is it a necessarily positive event for the organization overall.

THE MERITOCRATIC MANAGER AND THE HORRIBLE CHASM OF PROMOTION

A company's tendency to promote based on merit creates a hierarchy known as a meritocracy. Being promoted into management on the basis of merit or seniority does not ensure the person is skilled at managing. A person can be an excellent nurse, graphic designer, or accountant, but a terrible manager. And this is often the case.

Promoting specialists on merit creates a failure point for the new manager: a large portion of the job of managing is new to them, often something that they don't know how to do or likely never had the inclination or opportunity to try. When we do leadership coaching for new managers, they almost uniformly agree that at the top of the mountain lies a chasm looking both before and behind them.

In a meritocracy, once one has climbed the mountain, one cannot go back down without, at a minimum, a loss of reputation. The promotion closes the door behind the specialist—beware of what you have sought! But looking forward, one will see that the skills needed to be an effective manager are mostly the opposite of what the specialist developed during their ascent. Instead, a different chasm, the managerial skills chasm, exists because of their lack of competence.

In our leadership coaching practice, we see new managers struggle with how to be managerial. Lacking true manager skills, the new manager will instead revert to behavioral models that were useful for them during the ascent. The two most common forms seem to be:

- **Being dismissive of others' skills.** While this can be a very effective way to aid one's own ascent, when delivered to a worker from the position of managerial authority, it can be quite toxic.
- **Replaying the internal narrative of the specialist.** This narrative is the story they told themselves to drive their work styles and habits, which often includes ample amounts of harsh self-criticism. When the manager leans on that critical voice when managing their

team, even with the best intentions, morale and productivity will likely suffer. It is one thing to be critical of yourself but an entirely different thing to be critical of others.

More generally, the new manager's reaction to the unfathomable mystery of managing is to control harder. It is what they know: it was their assertion of (personal) control that helped them rise. It becomes very difficult for this type of person to suddenly relinquish control. Instead, they become experts in micromanaging and, consequently, terrible bosses.

Again, most cases of these behaviors are very well intentioned—they enabled the specialist to ascend, and they wish to share them to benefit the team. However, the specialist has little awareness of, nor training as to, how things might be done differently.

THE FIREFIGHTER MANAGER

Andrew walks out of his office and looks over toward the new designer. He feels concerned that this person—like so many others—will turn out to be a waste of time. It's so hard to find good talent out there, and the fact that so many of his hires already had to be let go (with more to follow) is starting to worry him.

The new hire looks busy, Andrew muses, but you never know. He moves closer. "Hey, what are you working on?" he asks. The new hire appears shocked, unprepared for the question.

"Um, just looking back at the work we've done on this campaign in the past," comes the reply.

Andrew feels a wave of irritation rise within him. "This employee is wasting time," he thinks to himself. "Time is being wasted here when work needs to be done." He had given clear instructions and can't fathom why they are not being followed.

"What inspired you to do this?" he asks. "Was I not clear when I briefed you?"

The new hire reacts defensively, pulling back, and frowning slightly. But that's neither here nor there, Andrew thinks. This person needs to understand how his department works.

The new hire replies, "I was telling Rena what I was working on, and she said that there had been some great ideas in years past and that I should take a look. I think she's right. Look at this one from three years ago."

"Hey, I didn't ask you to recreate the past!" Andrew exclaims. "We're building the future here. We need to do things better."

Andrew glances at the screen and sees the old campaign the new hire is reviewing came from before he took control of the department. People did say good things about that work, he had to admit. But copying work done under his predecessor's watch, no matter how good it was, would not help Andrew prove himself as the better manager.

He takes a deep breath and contemplates what to say to get this person working the way he should.

"Look," he says, "I can understand that you're new and have a lot of questions, but I need you to be productive, and that means following directions."

The new hire nods, "Okay . . ."

"I see you have your notes from our conversation," Andrew continues, "so just follow those, and then we can look at what you've done."

Andrew shakes his head. He can't think of a way to make it clearer. He's struck by the feeling that everyone he hires is just so, well, stupid. Does he need to do their job for them? But that's what he has to work with. It's my job, Andrew reflects, to whip them into shape.

Let's compare Andrew to Andreas, the saddle maker we met at the start of the book.

While Andrew's story is one of the few fictitious ones in this book, the persona that he presents is extremely common in project-driven organizations. You have likely experienced one or both sides of this exchange.

Andrew's words and attitude completely destroy the new hire's natural desires to understand, learn, and take control of their growth journey. This kind of Tayloristic management makes me cringe whenever I see it, mostly because it reminds me of how I was. "Where did that come from?" I wonder. It wasn't like I was working in a factory.

This behavior contrasts sharply with the almost magical wisdom and practices of Andreas the saddle maker, who patiently allowed his apprentice to explore and learn and who actually took pleasure in observing the development—even the mistakes.

VERBAL DOMINANCE AND FACTUAL AUTHORITY

With time and growth, the meritocracy's management ranks fill up with promoted deep specialists, creating a culture of management colored by the better-than-you ethos of those who claimed their managerial crowns. Abraham Maslow, in his only book on management, referred to the manager as a "superior being": put simply, the smarter, stronger, faster person.[21] We can think of them as a plus—great to have on our side. But they are, in a very real sense, a two-edged sword because of the very behaviors that gave them prominence.[22]

At some moment in our evolutionary selection, dominance (and the group response to it) must have been a major factor in natural selection. I would hate to admit it came from the human-on-human warring that we have done over the millennia, and so I tell myself a different story, a decidedly hominid one, where the emphatic expression and communication of a fact to a group was needed to cause beneficial action:

Imagine two parallel hominid tribes, one of which had learned that the threat of lions coming over the ridgeline was best handled by a dominant person saying, "Everybody grab a stick and get into the cave!"

The other tribe was more sanguine toward these "Chicken Little outbursts" and eventually became dinner for the lions.

This is a simplification, for sure, but it illustrates the relationship between factual superiority (a person knows more about something, such as the threat of lions, than others) and verbal dominance (the effect of the intensity and quality of presentation of the speaker).

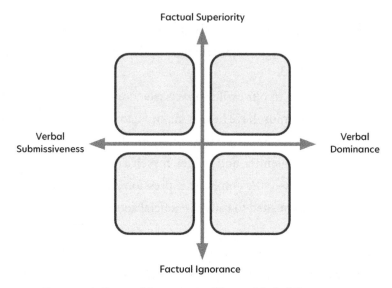

Figure 19: Factual Superiority Versus Verbal Dominance

Research has shown that, left to our natural styles, those in a group discussion will be biased toward those who seem to know more about whatever topic is being discussed. Those who demonstrate a dominant affect appear more knowledgeable than others, who in general become submissive *regardless of whether* the verbally dominant person possesses a higher level of factual superiority or not.[23] As in the lion-over-the-ridgeline example, when it works, it works really well.

But human behavior is driven by many things, and it is not a great stretch to imagine that a newly minted manager uses verbal dominance as a "prop" of sorts to hide gaps in what they know. Research from RAND, examining the effects of dominance and factual knowledge in group decision-making, produced some interesting findings that question the effectiveness of this behavior in specialist managers:[24]

- People who know less, when confronted by dominance, speak disproportionately less than the difference in knowledge; they exhibit *excess submissiveness*.

- That means people with knowledge not possessed by the dominant speaker(s) often will not bring it up.
- Therefore, even when everyone in a group has roughly the same level of knowledge (this is what RAND studied), and the goal is to explore options or solutions, the dominant speaker(s) suppress the size of the solution set and options discussed.
- If the group is seeking to be innovative, inclusive or explorational, as in say, a brainstorming session, then results will be suboptimal.
- When this group is pressed to come to a decision, social pressures, such as a desire for harmony or compliance, will shape behavior and result in a suboptimal exploration of solutions or even a suboptimal solution. This is called groupthink.
- It is common for people who express verbal dominance in one or more topics to be unaware of their knowledge boundaries, so they may speak with dominance on topics for which they have no factual superiority. This is known as "false authority." These statements are often accepted as fact by the rest of the group.

Maslow mused that perhaps we should remove loud voices from the room if we really want teams to work well together. In some ways it sounds like a sad invective for our deep specialist turned manager: congratulations on your promotion, now stay away from the team!

THE STEEP CLIFF OF MANAGERIAL IGNORANCE

We've all experienced the steep cliffs of factual knowledge, and I am no exception.

I have been a wine lover (okay, snob) for years now. Even knowing this, I can feel myself slipping off the cliff of factual knowledge when I am intoxicated (yes, maybe in more ways than one) with the thrill of demonstrating my knowledge to a group.

After I share some illuminating quasi-facts ("Oregon's pinot noir vineyards are at the same latitude as those of Burgundy in France, which is one of the reasons why this Oregon wine tastes . . ."), I notice that my comments about flavor elements ("I get a smoky, cherry scent . . ."), despite being decidedly nonfactual, carry an outsize weight in the group discussion.

Over the years, I have learned that I am not that good at tasting, even if my verbal style suggests otherwise. People will spend ten minutes chasing my comment, "Some scent of rose petals," rather than just use their own (often better) nose and sense of taste.

We can use this verbal dominance framework to illustrate the ascent of the deep specialist through knowledge and verbal affect:

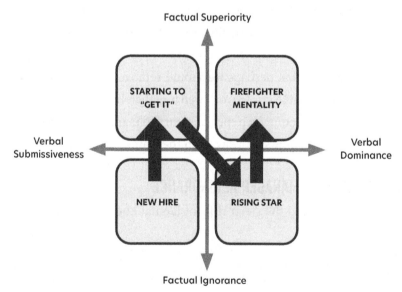

Figure 20: Example of Firefighter Career Progression

- New hires will tend toward submissiveness in the face of their situational ignorance ("not sure what to do it this situation").
- As someone starts to "get it," they put their factual knowledge to good use and may even advise other new hires.
- This rising star becomes verbally dominant about their ignorance, which foreshadows their potential as a deep specialist. Those who ask for more help and ask more questions grow their skill sets faster.
- Eventually, the confident expert emerges.

We, as a culture, often revere this person, the expert. We idolize them as a sort of superhero with the self-reinforcing powers of knowledge and force of personality. As the name "Firefighter" implies, they often are known for rescuing projects as well.

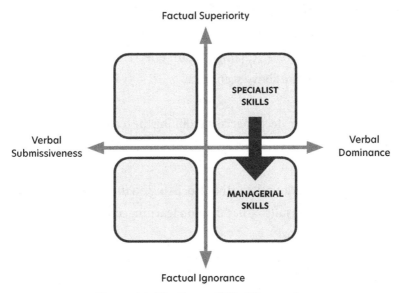

Figure 21: The Steep Cliff of Promotion

Yet the sudden shift to a managerial role means that the deep specialist is now swimming in unfamiliar factual waters, being relatively ignorant of optimal managerial behaviors. Yet sometimes we do not know what we do not know, and the new manager does not understand their own ignorance regarding correct behavior. Meanwhile, verbal dominance remains.

It is within this dichotomy that the television show *The Office* lives. Virtually every episode relies on the plot device of Michael, the factually ignorant manager who was previously a salesperson, trying and failing epically to invoke some form of managerial action.

As you can imagine, the experience of this ignorance can also cause discomfort in a new manager. Rather than begin the learning process anew, however, they likely revert to what they know well—how to be a specialist—and wield that knowledge over and through their people. Their critical internal voices get externalized, leading to verbally dominant attempts to overcontrol the rest of the department.

FIREFIGHTER MANAGERS MAKE FOR WORSE TEAMS

Research on managerial style and team performance point to three key attributes of managers that hamper team effectiveness, all of which are typically present in the above scenarios:

- Promoted as a deep specialist, robbing the team of their best worker
- A tendency to overmanage, micromanage, and intervene in others' work
- An overly serious demeanor (focusing on the work rather than the people, on results rather than on learning, etc.)

This invites a comparison. How comfortable do you feel about this manager?

Patrice walks into the office midmorning with a box of bagels in hand. Walking past the team, he holds up the box and smiles. "It looks like they're off to a good start," he thinks to himself. He sets the bagels out in the break area, grabs one for himself, along with an espresso, and walks back to his desk. He scans emails quickly to see whether anyone needs anything from him. He and his team agreed they would reach out to him immediately if they needed anything, which means he need not interrupt them several times a day. Not that Patrice is the best person to answer a specialist question—he was not the most skilled on the team—but he is good at being there for everyone and making sure people get the tools, time, and support they need to meet their project due dates.

Patrice might not be a good fit in a firefighter meritocracy, yet there is much to suggest that his style could be an effective one. He might actually be a very good manager.

CHAPTER 5

The Good Manager Compass

HOW DO WE AS MANAGERS find our way back from the influences of Taylorism and the meritocratic organization? Here we'll explore ideas about the other directions you can take to unleash your teams. Along the way, we'll plot a few compass points on a map you're building in your mind.

Rensis Likert conducted some of the best research on managers and workers.[25] Most people know about Likert indirectly from his Likert Scale, a survey method in which people record their passion toward a topic by selecting from a range of answers: strongly agree, somewhat agree, neutral, somewhat disagree, or strongly disagree. Likert developed this very scale in the 1950s to survey workers in factories on subjective topics, such as how much the workers felt their managers valued their opinions. He wanted literally to understand workers' opinions on how valued and included they felt.

By comparing the attitudinal answers of workers to the organization's business performance data, Likert opened the door to understanding what good managing and bad managing might look like and how much it mattered.

In the Tayloristic view of managing, when a department was not running well, it was assumed—maybe because it was the easiest, most expedient thing to do—that the problem was lazy, shirking workers. How could it be the manager? So like any good researcher, Likert set out to test whether that was true.

In one experiment, Likert chose two geographically separate factory workplaces that were owned by the same company but that had vastly different manufacturing performance. Presumably, this difference had been ascribed to differences in the quality of the workers and their output. But Likert's initial survey revealed that the differing managerial styles of the two workplaces might be to blame.

In the well-performing factory, workers scored managers highly and took part in workplace decision-making. In the poorly performing factory, the scores were the opposite: workers felt managers did not inclusively engage with them.

This finding was revelatory and provided early proof of what became known as the Theory Y management style, which assumed the fundamental goodness of workers. Theory X was Taylorism and its enforcer-manager. Theory Y workplaces ideally replace the enforcer-manager with an inclusive and mentoring manager. It is now widely accepted that factories (and virtually ANY other type of organization) will run better using Theory Y management styles.

Likert's initial research, however, spoke only of one situation involving two factories. He lacked the data to say the management-worker relationship *caused* the differences in the two workplaces. So Likert searched for more evidence, swapping the managers of the two factories. The results were positive: the so-called bad workers that received the good managers started to perform better; better managing causes better results. Being "oxen" was an outcome of how you were managed, not a result of being a worker!

Interestingly, the team that received the bad managers did not get worse. This, Likert surmised, was because they had already experienced good management and were able to retain its principles. Strong managing had made them resilient to weaker managing. These findings have been supported by countless studies since the fifties.

A few years back, we at AgencyAgile fielded a modified version of Likert's survey with several clients and were able to see the positive effects of these principles in the scores given by the workers and managers, pre- and post-training.

REPUDIATING THE FIREFIGHTER CULTURE OF CONTROL

Likert's findings support the idea that firefighter, deep-specialist managers who believe they are the best source of information and decision-making are worse managers than those who are, frankly, humbler on that matter.

There is a great irony in how many Theory X behaviors we see in project-driven organizations, given how directly counterproductive they can be. The minds of the workers are the productive machines, so any demotivation of workers strikes directly at the production function.

At the center of this is the paradox of control. Taylorism taught that managers should be in control. Most project-driven organizations seem to have an underlying Tayloristic managerial mantra: "As long as we have control of this, things will be fine." In many ways, the judging of a manager is done on this basis rather than how they affect the production function.

THE MEASURE OF THE MANAGER

I didn't believe it when Ben, the CEO, described his organization. I assumed he was lying. Many of the organizations we work with have 30–40 managers for 120 people: a 1:3 or 1:4 ratio. Ben had just told me he had 8 managers overseeing 120 people. That is a 1:15 managerial span of control, which is pretty rare and pretty cool.

You're probably expecting me to talk about the transformation that we did for them. But this was my first meeting with Ben. He had unmanaged his organization on his own. It was one of those wonderful moments when I got to be the student rather than the teacher. I dug in.

"So, how did you end up with so few managers?" I asked.

Ben looked around the beautifully renovated SOHO office space—it was nicely modernized while retaining the original midcentury charm—and with a dramatic gesture he said, "I never wanted ours to be like other companies, and so I vowed I would make my decisions differently. Every time I had to make a business decision, I would say to myself, 'What would they do?' and then I would do the opposite or something different."

I smiled and nodded. Amazing. He was a contrarian, and that's useful if you want to manage well.

"I noticed how often they would have chosen to hire a manager, and I just didn't do that. Sometimes I had to, of course, but most of the time we could just find another way to do it or let people self-manage—do it themselves."

Ben had called me there because, while he did know how he got to this point, he was not sure how to sustain it. His biggest fear was that as the organization grew, he would need to bring in more managers—ones who might not share his belief in their limited usefulness.

After some more discussion, I asked him how he judged the quality of the managing going on. His answer was simple.

"We do a performance survey for each manager. The workers get to vote on any manager that they have interacted with. It is a simple score and just one question: Thumbs-up or thumbs-down, how well did this manager do in helping to make you successful?"

Wow, brilliant. "How do you use the results?" That's where the magic must lie, I thought.

"If a manager gets one thumbs-down, then we just have a conversation," Ben said confidently, pausing afterward, as if to let the idea sink in. But the silence dragged on—he was actually baiting me, I think.

I took it. "And what happens if they get a second one?" There had to be a challenge to solve here—like what if a worker was just being mean or whatever.

"Nobody gets a second one." Ben grinned wide.

Ben had turned the notion of managerial exceptionalism on its head. In effect, he said, if you, as a manager, fail at making our workers and teams better, then you have no managerial value to our organization.

THE FUTILITY OF MANAGERIAL RESPONSIBILITIES

Ben succeeded where many of us have failed: succinctly defining what managers provide an organization. He was focused on outcomes. When most managers are asked about their role, instinctively they rattle off a long list of *activities that they do* or *responsibilities that they have*:

- "I make sure the project schedules are updated."
- "I keep track of project status by holding the weekly status meeting."
- "I conduct one-on-ones and write the annual performance reviews."

- "I make sure we have enough resources for the work."
- "I make sure that everyone remembers the due dates for the work."
- "I approve everything before it gets launched, sent, or whatever."

This list certainly looks managerial from a traditional perspective, right? But does this mean that I should measure the manager by whether they do these things? Granted, these activities may sometimes be useful, but it depends on how they are done and what the outcomes are.

Consider that the team could still fail in their work while the manager "succeeded" at these tasks. What if a weekly status meeting turned into an hourly "What are you doing now?" interruption of the worker? Obviously, that would be highly detrimental to their productivity and morale. But the manager was merely executing their "responsibilities."

Responsibility lists really don't get to the core of why a manager is needed and why we don't just tell them to go home for the day. Instead, let's ask, "What is the measure of the manager?" Lacking that answer, how could we judge any choice of action by a manager?

My conversation with Ben taught me a lesson about the importance of clarity in how we measure managers in a project-driven organization. If we prioritize our teams' success because of their profound impact on productivity, we can only judge managers by a few measures:

- Are your people growing, building new skills, and overcoming their gaps and limitations?
- Do they feel acknowledged, supported, informed, and central to the organization's success?
- Are they happy, and do they feel engaged and appropriately challenged?
- Are they achieving their highest productivity while maintaining work quality and personal satisfaction?

Behind these questions is the most fundamental truth about workers and managers, what I have dubbed the First (and currently, the only) Law of Unmanagement.

THE FIRST LAW OF UNMANAGEMENT

Workers are the most precious source of productivity and capability in a project-driven organization. In their actions and design, managers and the organizational context can enable their workers' productivity—or they can define the workers' limits. The strongest organizations, from their structure to their preferred styles of managing, enable workers to the maximum productivity.

The productive speed of an organization is the speed of its workers and teams, not the speed of management. In fact, as you already understand at some level, an increase in the speed of management—that is, the frequency and intensity of managerial activity—is more likely to detract from the productivity of the organization. Enter the First Law of Unmanagement:

> The singular role of the manager is to be in full support
> of the workers and teams, enabling and unleashing
> their natural capability and energy upon the work and
> opportunities faced by the organization. In performing
> those duties, the manager shall not detract from
> productivity through any other actions or inaction.

This law shifts the burden of scrutiny—as Ben did with his thumbs-up survey model—onto managers. Are their actions making things better for workers and teams? This question provides a North Star for measuring managers, but it certainly is subjective. Any manager can claim they intend to support the team, hence the genius of Ben's survey: workers get to report on how supported they feel.

Your workers can provide vital feedback on the health of your organization and worker success. Research bears this out: Noted management consultancy Deloitte, in its own internal research, discovered that the strongest factor in worker success was whether managers had optimally enabled workers, as judged by this affirmation: "At work, I have the opportunity to do what I do best every day."[26]

CHAPTER 6

The Manager of Metrics

(Grow Part 1)

Measurement is essential to team and
organizational learning and growth.

THE MEASURE OF A MANAGER lies in how they enable their workers and team members to succeed. Much of this book is dedicated to helping you understand how to manage the Why, What, and Go Moments, but an important first step is considering the fourth of our key moments, the Grow Moment with regard to metrics, measurement, and reflection.

Embracing an attitude of measurement and self-assessment will only heighten your ability to make wise choices, but this need not be daunting. In this chapter, I describe a few higher-level metrics you can start using right away to foster growth in your teams.

To start, let's revisit the stand-up meeting discussion from earlier, where my AgencyAgile team analyzed whether managers should interject new information at the beginning or end of the stand-up. To do this, we used measurements; we monitored how long each stand-up took and assessed some more qualitative aspects, such as how "settled" people seemed in their plans for the day. With these measurements, we knew to advise managers to introduce new information at the end of the meeting.

Working with metrics can sometimes be a bit tricky and have severe unintended consequences. For example, if we *only* tracked the number of minutes that the stand-up took to complete—which might seem like a good thing—there is a risk that the measurement would distort behaviors. If everyone knew that doing it faster was how they were being judged, then they might just try to go quickly, without regard for what is being accomplished. Success, using that singular metric, might be a five-minute stand-up, but that would also probably result in an almost complete failure of one of the goals of the meeting: to ensure that coordination happens effectively.

In fact, one of the most common failures of stand-up meetings is when teams (usually project managers or scrum masters) overly focus on the stand-up duration as their primary metric.[27] So, in general, we always want to use a set of metrics that have a counterbalancing effect on each other.

METRIC: THE MANAGER-TEAM RATIO

In chapter 4, we discussed the growth of managers in a growing project-driven organization, using four pyramids as an illustration. One of the first questions we discuss with new clients is just that: What is the ratio of managers and workers?

If you have a roster of everyone in your organization, you can do this yourself. Identify the managers (they may or may not have *manager* in their title) and then the team members and workers.

Some people may fill both roles, which is common when there are a lot of managers. Not a problem: you can adjust your final count to tell you how much time your organization spends managing versus producing work for clients (this does not include administrative functions, like producing a project status report).

For the most accurate ratio, identify the amount of time spent as a percent of each person's responsibilities:

- **Count whole and fractional workers/team members.** Fractional team members are managers who also do productive work. If they do the work less than 25% of the time, then don't count them here. Total the number of workers for your team number.
- **Count whole and fractional managers.** Fractional managers always count due to the multiplicative impact of additional managing and fractional managing of workers. Double the number for the fractional managers (e.g., someone who is 25% manager counts as 50%) up to 100%. Total the number of managers for your manager number.
    - Remember: this count includes all types of managers, including project managers, client managers, and other types.
    - Clients can count too, especially if you have teams that work closely with clients or other stakeholders. A person is a manager if they feel they have at least some right to direct what a worker or team is doing.
- **Determine your raw manager-to-team ratio.** This is your manager number and team number separated by a colon (e.g., 6.5:14.25).
- **Divide both sides by the manager number**. This shows how many workers exist for each manager (e.g., 6.5:14.25 becomes 1:2.2).
- **This final score indicates your intrinsic manager tax, a very basic measure of your organization's managerial complexity.**
    - 1:6+ is a very low intrinsic manager tax, found more often in non-project-driven organizations.
    - 1:4 is a common ratio for project-driven organizations and indicates a moderate intrinsic manager tax.
    - 1:3 is a common ratio for complex and multi-stakeholder projects and indicates a high intrinsic manager tax.

- 1:2 (and worse) is found in high-volume creative and innovation organizations and indicates a very high intrinsic manager
  tax.

While many of this book's techniques can be valuable for organizations with low intrinsic manager tax (1:6+), they have been optimized for
the more challenging ratios. Many of AgencyAgile's clients are in the 1:3
category or worse.

METRIC: THE VOICES OF SATISFACTION

A great pair of qualitative metrics are the satisfaction metrics for teams and
clients—essentially, how happy they are with their workplace and the work
delivered, respectively. For reasons mentioned above, they work better as a
pair because optimizing only one of them—making clients very happy, for
example—can lead to teams that are completely burned out from unrea-
sonable schedules, work, and client behaviors.

One of the most well-known qualitative measurements is NPS, the
Net Promoter Score. You have likely seen it in many contexts, including
follow-up on a customer service experience, like I just had with my TV
service provider:

> *"On a zero to ten scale, how likely are you to recommend X (their
> service) to a friend?"*

You can compile the scores of multiple clients (and/or your internal
stakeholders) and arrive at an overall score that ranges between −100 and
+100 using the categories detractor, neutral, and promoter.

You can use the same basic model for workers and teams, as follows:

> *"On a zero to ten scale, how likely are you to recommend a friend or
> colleague to work in your job in our company?"*

We call this eNPS, the "e" standing for employee, but you should focus on workers and teams for your data, not managers. You can find a free, brief guide that we wrote for our clients on our resources page (https://unmanagedbook.com/resources/).

There are lots of tools out there for this sort of survey work, but here is what I like about NPS/eNPS:

1. **It is simple to use.** You don't need to hire a consultant. In fact, we tried to get an NPS consultant to sponsor our little NPS guide, but he replied, "It stands against everything that my business stands for. If they read that (your guide), then they would never hire me."
2. **It's free.** And you don't need to hire that consultant.
3. **It's simple (part 2).** You will get high response rates. Simple surveys get more responses than complex ones and place less burden on the respondent.

I am always amazed at how few companies track these basic measurements. Just get them going.

METRIC: WORKER CAPABILITY DEVELOPMENT AND UTILIZATION

In future chapters, I'll help you implement a few other key metrics supporting the key measurement stated in the First Law of Unmanagement. With them, you'll be well equipped to measure whether your teams are working better because of the managers supporting them.

At this point, though, just have your teams and workers answer one simple question:

"How well is the organization utilizing my skills and helping me grow professionally?"

This is a *sentiment*, not an NPS score, and should be measured on a simple one-to-ten scale. What you hear may surprise you, especially if you ask an open-ended follow-up question like this one we describe in our NPS guide:

"What are the most significant reasons why you gave that score?"

These capability questions, when combined with the eNPS score, effectively mimic Ben's thumbs-up and thumbs-down survey but with much better data.

SUMMARY

Section 1 was aimed at giving you several core concepts both central to the book and is also central to your understanding of the Why behind unmanaging.

- **Managers are more costly than we managers realize.** The cost is both a bottom-line impact and a net productivity impact. Adding in more managers raises this cost precipitously. One of the most costly forms of the manager tax is when managers manage poorly.
- **Taylorism left us a cultural legacy of bad managing.** The Industrial Revolution created a technological and workplace discontinuity that all but eliminated artisanal or craftwork done at scale. Machines were more efficient than workers, whose managers enforced rigorous time standards. Many Tayloristic notions are embedded in our societal perception of what managers should do and be.
- **The type of work drives both the best way to organize and also the best choice of management styles.** Increasingly, our work is knowledge work of a unique nature. Automation creeps out from the standardized, repeatable middle. The epitome of the unique knowledge work organization is the project-driven organization.

- **Project-driven organizations often lean on the old Tayloristic model.** The use of strict hierarchies and merit-based promotions of deep specialists tends to create a firefighter meritocracy, a challenging and biased culture of management.
- **Better managing is possible, but it requires a shift in thinking about the role of the manager.** The singular role of the manager is to be in full support of the workers and teams, enabling and unleashing their natural capability and energy upon the work and opportunities faced by the organization. In performing those duties, the manager shall not detract from productivity through any other actions or inaction.
- **Measurement is essential to good management and understanding the impact and effectiveness of change.** We discussed four new metrics you can use:
  - Manager-Team Ratio
  - Client/Stakeholder Satisfaction (NPS)
  - Worker/Team Satisfaction (eNPS)
  - Worker Capability Development and Utilization

Understanding and Opportunity

In this section, I focus on two of the most basic, yet important and often underserved moments, the Why and the Grow Moments. Understanding both of these moments will aid you in ensuring project success, of course, but they probably have a more profound effect on engaging with and developing the potential of your existing workers and teams. I touch on the What and Go Moments, but they will get a much more detailed treatment in their own sections. In doing this, we'll also explore the Theory Y shift in behavior, the release of control, and a few other cool topics.

TWENTY MACGYVERS TO THE RESCUE

I was traveling back on a cross-country flight, enjoying the rare privilege of a free first-class upgrade. It was the last flight from New York to LA and filled with businesspeople like the guy sitting next to me.

We both had our laptops open and were engrossed in our work when he decided to introduce himself. After a moment of politeness, he got to the point.

"I'm guessing you know about Agile, right? I saw your logo on the slide you were working on."

I nodded and described my AgencyAgile business to him, and he quickly cut to the chase: "So, I have a problem at my company, and I'm wondering if Agile can help. One of my friends said maybe I should try it."

I figured, what the heck, let's see where this goes.

He proceeded to describe to me his smallish company of twenty or so MacGyvers. He was in a custom electronics design and installation association (CEDIA) business, working in high-end homes.

If you want to be able to wake up in the morning, sit up and clap your hands, and then watch as the curtains open, music comes on, and a small fridge with champagne and orange juice magically rises out of the floor, then you should call this guy. No two jobs are the same, and he gets some pretty crazy requests as well.

At this point, I was stumped because I had no idea what Agile had to do with any of this. He went on to explain his "real problem."

"We are very successful, but what's killing me is that every Sunday I spend a lot of time trying to figure out the schedule for my installers for the coming week. No matter how hard I try, my plans seem to be wrong, and by Wednesday, chaos reigns. Everyone, clients and installers, is complaining. And I just killed my Sunday as well. Can Agile help me?"

I did have work to do, so I decided that I would just skip the whole "Here's what Agile really is" and "You don't really need Agile" speeches and just focus at helping him be a manager of a project-driven organization. I gave him a very simple instruction:

"On Sunday, or even early Monday morning, write out each job on a card or a Post-It note. Monday morning, put them all out on the conference room table and invite your installers in. Tell them to figure it out, and if they have questions about a job, they can ask you. Otherwise, get out of the way."

He said that sounded crazy enough to work. He thanked me, we traded email addresses, and I got back to work.

About a month later, I got an unexpected email titled "AGILE WORKS!" In it, he described how he followed my directions, and everything was going really well. His people are getting all of the jobs done every week, without any crises (at least not any that he needed to deal with), and they are much happier.

I wasn't at all surprised by that outcome. The only failure point in my instructions was whether he could muster the courage to stop managing something others could handle quite well without him. What he needed to master was probably the most important move of Unmanaging: releasing control. This idea is at the core of what Likert discovered between the X and Y styles of managing and their impact on team and organizational performance.

CHAPTER 7

Unlocking the Magic of Unmanaging

Each of us has a managerial battle within us, where the Angry Rancher and the Humble Gardener fight to control our perceptions and actions.

The Angry Rancher sees a world that needs to be controlled and driven, for it moves too slowly and wanders without direction. Disappointed by lazy, unhappy people who produce shoddy work, the rancher prods, yells, shouts, and drives his herd of dumb beasts that will never learn. The rancher chuckles at the idea of what a mess the world would be without him and the other ranchers that give it structure.

The Humble Gardener sees a world that needs nurturing and patience. All the ingredients are there—sun, water, and good earth. The garden just needs tending and love. Feeling blessed to be in the position of caring for such talented people, who strive for excellence and have a passion for what they do, the gardener knows that only a careful, light touch is needed to help them grow to their best. The gardener dreams of a day when the garden needs only appreciation for how well it is growing.

WHICHEVER MANAGER RULES YOUR THOUGHTS and actions determines your results. You may recognize this as a rip-off of the Two Wolves parable, but it reflects a reality of managing: we will have to choose, and those choices define us.

The Angry Rancher reflects Taylorism's militaristic origins: the superior manager controls with an iron grip. The Humble Gardener reflects the ideas Likert so vividly showed: that managers who allow workers to participate in managerial processes have better outcomes. You probably get this as a general idea, but the harder part is knowing what this actually looks like when engaging with workers and teams.

You could, of course, take collaboration to its extreme and just make the organization a cooperative where everyone participates in every decision. I know of companies that tried to completely eliminate managers, and they have had some success. But while success is *possible*, I also think it somewhat improbable that most companies sustainably integrate such a change. It might not even be the most efficient way to run the organization—the speed of production does matter, and group decisions can be costly from a time perspective. Organizations that function as cooperatives still tend to have someone in charge, and the most effective ones hybridize communal and hierarchical models.[28]

So, organizations do need some hierarchy, and you probably could not get rid of it anyway. But how can you know which managerial functions should be retained by managers, and which functions can be shared with or passed to the wider community of workers and teams? An easy way to think of this is ACE, an acronym for Authority-Control-Empowerment. These are the three core managerial functions—though they need not always be fulfilled by managers.

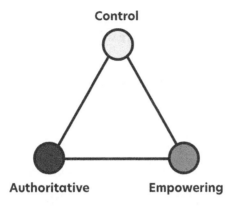

Figure 22: The ACE Managerial Functions Triangle

Each of these functions has a relationship with the other two, forming a sort of triangle. Two of these, authority and empowerment, are largely retained by managers, and the third, control, which you probably figured out already, is the one we will shift.

We'll explore how control becomes a team-centric function in the context of the other two functions. For the most part, things go better when managers separate themselves from the control function.

The *authoritative function* is primarily associated with defining or introducing the flow of work into and from the team. It's about being authoritative in terms of what needs to be produced and in defining acceptable levels of quality for the deliverables.

I'll discuss other aspects of authority, but the key idea actions include identifying the work, ensuring clear priority, and defining the desired exit conditions like timing, quality, and aesthetics. It's about establishing the "factual" aspects of the work and the resultant product, limiting conjecture, solutioning, or directing.

Typically, coordinating managers (e.g., client managers and requirements managers) fill the authoritative function, though clients and stakeholders also have a say.

The second function is the *control function*, which is primarily associated with defining how the work gets done, doing the work, solutioning, and many other pieces. This is where we involve and even transfer ownership to workers and the team. The control function makes sure the work gets done as well as it can in response to the "challenge" presented by the authoritative function.

Do teams need managers? Most small teams (under five people) need very little managing and perform no better with a manager "embedded" within them. The control function is very self-manageable given that the team is otherwise well set up.

The relationship between the authoritative and control functions, regarding the definition of the work, is an important but subtle one:

- The authoritative function represents the work from a business or customer perspective, which includes aspects of what the result of the work should look like when completed by the team.
- The control function further defines the work by determining solutions, tactics, execution strategies, etc. It also includes doing the work.

The third function is the *empowerment function*. As the name implies, this function is about supporting the team through coaching and mentoring and also protecting the team by making sure it has what it needs to succeed, including adequate staffing, skills, tools, and training. Department managers, project managers, and resource managers typically fulfill the empowerment function.

Those fulfilling the empowerment function must be servant-like at times, which may involve facilitation and support activities, such as making sure key discussions and reviews happen, providing the team with dashboards and reports, and doing basic housekeeping of project information and assets.

The authoritative and empowerment function also have a key relationship in terms of work. The empowerment function protects the team from being overwhelmed by too much work, overly aggressive due dates, interruptive activities, or work for which they have no capability or understanding.

VISUALIZING THE ACE SHIFT

Today's organizations, stuck in Tayloristic assumptions, tend to default to a manager-controls-all model. The illustration shown here portrays that configuration, which also isolates the client or customer from the team—this was a bit more acceptable in a factory setting but is a huge negative for project-driven organizations. This is called a *vertical management model*. One of the challenges of this model is that all managers—especially deep specialist managers—seem to gravitate toward the control function.

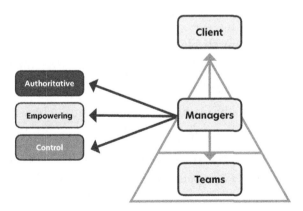

Figure 23: Traditional (Vertical) ACE Management Model

It is the release of control, but not the utter abandonment of it, that enables the correct balance of managerial behavior, which also corresponds to the Theory Y framework of good managing.

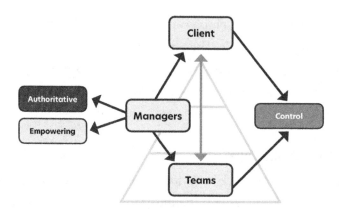

Figure 24: The Unmanaging Of The ACE Control Function

With this in mind, let's return to the story that opened section 2. When the electronics installation company owner told me his story, I immediately recognized that he was trying to perform the control function. Here's a little replay:

- The owner was probably in charge of sales, or at least had an authoritative view of what work needed to be done. So I told him to write out all of the jobs on note cards and . . .
- Pass *control* to the team. They had to figure out how to respond to the authoritative challenge and arrange their schedules accordingly. Whatever disorientation they might have experienced on the first morning likely dissipated quickly. Most teams love the feeling of taking control of their work.
- The owner needed to fulfill the empowerment function as well. He was already doing this with his rough capacity calculations: "Hmmm, how many of these jobs could the team get done this

week?" He likely also filtered work for how doable the work would be. Last, I suggested that he be available to them if they needed anything in support.

The CEDIA company owner had one other thing going for him: he didn't want the job of being in control of the scheduling. That's not necessarily always true; many managers enjoy the feeling of competence that comes with "managing." As a manager, you need to both be willing to release control and have a method for it. The company owner had the first piece, and I gave him the second. You can think of this as being the fasting and waiting of young Siddhartha, letting go of your hunger for control and waiting for the moments in which you must support or empower.

But what of the team? Why did I not worry about whether they would actually claim control and solve their manager's weekly vexing schedule challenge? And likewise, why should you as a leader assume your managers stepping back from "Control" will mean that workers and teams step forward?

WHERE WE ALL CAME FROM

One could argue that all the variations of hominids that preceded us *Homo sapiens* were good at working together and solving problems. The fossil record bears this out, but the characteristic that distinguishes us *Homo sapiens* from our predecessors, despite our mere half million years of existence, is that we work terrifically well together. Our superpower of collaboration is a key factor in how we outsurvived the other, often physically superior branches of the hominid tree.

That's how essential and fundamental the team is to humanity. We are tribal, and we are cooperative. Even in cultures where rugged individualism is a mark of pride, we need to step back and be honest with ourselves: we are all team players under the skin. Individualists typically exist only in the context of an awesome team of people that enabled them.

One of the best illustrations of our amazing skills at working together comes from describing the extinction events that eliminated other prehistoric life forms from the planet. Most people think of a cataclysmic event that ravaged and darkened the earth, killing off megafauna like the great dinosaurs—and this may have been the case. But that was sixty-five million years before our hominid ancestors came along.

When researchers look at extinction events that happened for creatures that coexisted with early humans, animals such as woolly mammoths or saber-toothed tigers, it wasn't an ice age that wiped them out. It was us. Their demise coincides with a massive expansion of *Homo sapiens*, human beings who had become very good at hunting.[29]

Hunting fifty thousand years ago was likely a team effort, not an individual activity. Our ancestors didn't have weaponry like we do now. Back then, we were barely clothed, often cold, and frequently on the edge of starvation. We used basic tools like sharpened wooden poles or rock-tipped spears. We had to work together, and by doing so we persisted and became the apex predator of the animal kingdom.

Research and our experience support one profound conclusion: when engaged in complex and interdependent tasks, we are much better together than we are as individuals.[30]

The good news is that we like being with each other. We are distinctly prosocial, and we are drawn to each other in ways that we often don't see because they are so fundamental to how we evolved and live. We have an innate desire to gather together. To explain how that works, let's take a trip way back in time, to when we first started getting clever.

THE HANDYMAN SOLVER

One of our early ancestors, *Homo habilis*, is also known as the handyman, the maker of tools. *Homo habilis* walked the earth around two million years ago—no small stretch of time for our skill sets and our brains to evolve significantly. Everyone you work with has a brain that has been tuned up by millions of years of evolution.

At some point less than one hundred thousand years ago, we *Homo sapiens* evolved from being a foraging species to being very capable hunters. That's five thousand generations ago. By then, we could solve problems really well. The modern world of technological convenience we know today is the product of that relentless push to make better tools and find better solutions.

There are other factors, of course. You can credit capitalism if you want—and there is evidence that capitalistic self-interest does *accelerate* innovation. You can credit education, language, writing, even YouTube. But regardless of the medium, context, or moment, we humans just can't stop trying to solve things. We are solvers.

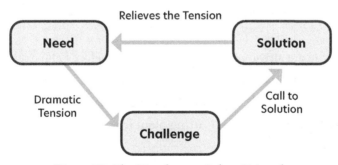

Figure 25: The Handyman Solver Triangle

Like blinking our eyes or swallowing, our solving instinct is so deeply woven into our behavior and the way we organize thought that it is virtually invisible until you stop and watch it happen. I often use a simple model to illustrate this: a triangle of events, starting with the understanding of a need, which links to awareness of the challenge that needs to be overcome to satisfy that need. Here our innate, nearly irrepressible urge to resolve that challenge drives us toward a solution.

Further evidencing our relentless solver-minds, we can do this sequence backward as well, starting with a solution itself and searching for a new need. For instance, we might create or have access to a tool or app that we then look to use to solve new problems.

But let's look at a more concrete example. As humans, we need water to survive. If we have no plumbing or water sources except for water from frequent rainfall, we have a challenge to solve.

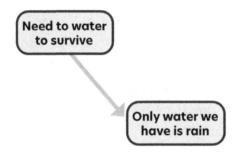

Figure 26: The Handyman Water Problem

And you are already trying to solve it, even before I can explain it!

My solution might be a bucket with a large funnel. But having used this exercise with hundreds of people, I have heard a wide range of solutions, the most common of which is using plant leaves to capture (presumably tropical) water.

When we are properly fed a well-understood need and challenge, we jump to a solution.

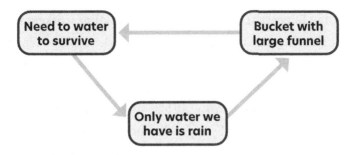

Figure 27: A Common Water Problem Solution

That CEDIA installer's team lives in that world all day long. You can't leave them with a challenge and not have them try to solve it.

Whenever a manager tells me that their people are their main limitation, I suspect that their people are not properly being given the challenge and opportunity to create solutions. And creating solutions is how we learn and grow.

Some of you might point out that not everyone is a MacGyver and that putting a complex problem in front of highly skilled workers and getting a stellar outcome is not really all that surprising. But then you would be helping me transition to the next topic.

THE HANDYMAN TAKES ON TAYLORISM

In the 1950s, a battle raged across the Pacific. Not in the Korean Peninsula, nor in Indochina, now called Vietnam, as you might be guessing, but in Japan. The Japanese auto industry struggled to compete against the much larger US auto industry. Back then, Japan was the underdog in this fight, both in terms of how many cars they produced and even more so in terms of quality. Japanese cars were, to put it mildly, a bit of a joke, or at least fit the cliché of a cheap, unreliable car.

Most auto production looked like classic Taylorism—long assembly lines producing vehicles at a prescribed cadence. Keeping the machines fed and the assembly line moving was the only way to compete on price and still make a profit. But cars are complex, and assembly-line workers, driven by Tayloristic time-standard managerial behaviors, were more encouraged to keep the assembly line moving than to make sure that everything fit perfectly.[31] All cars back then had quality problems that we would find unacceptable today, but the Japanese cars were legendarily bad in that regard.

US car companies generally focused on how to scale, build bigger factories, build more cars, and make new models and brands for new buyers. In a very real sense, they were invested deeply in Tayloristic thinking, so much so that significant unionization occurred in the US auto industry, with the United Auto Workers and other unions fighting for better wages and more-humane working conditions.

In the 1950s, W. Edwards Deming, a quality assurance specialist and project manager, went to Japan and started working with Taiichi Ohno to build a concept called the Toyota Production System.

They were industrial engineers, and like Frederick Taylor, Ohno and Deming valued quality and consistency over the speed of the production line. In fact, they defined quality as the ultimate measure of a company.

This was the first notable departure from the widespread tenets of Taylorism. At the heart of it lay a different way of thinking about the workers themselves. Rather than treat workers as part of the problem, they decided to enroll the assembly-line workers as partners, giving them *control,* if you will, of quality. With this decision and its implementation, Ohno and Deming shattered Tayloristic assumptions about workers and the relationship between workers and management.

Their innovation was paired with the implementation of the Andon cord, a cable that stretched along the length of an assembly line. Workers, who were always within easy reach of the Andon cord, were instructed to pull the cord if they saw quality suffering when assembling a car. This would stop the assembly line, and they could not restart it until they addressed the problem.

In committing to this concept, Toyota basically said, "No matter what we (the managers and higher-ups) might think about how good our machines and the parts we are using are, or how highly we think about our process and the way the system is designed, we are giving each worker the power to improve the way we do things." They surrendered control of production to the workers. In a very real sense, they traded the few pairs of managerial eyes that looked at the (complex) problem from a distance—those of the managers—for a much larger set of eyes (managers plus workers) that could observe and assess every single aspect of putting a car together.

That put more brains to work on creating solutions too. With the Toyota Production System came another innovation called quality circles, which were opportunities for workers to discuss ways to improve the assembly line, production processes, and vehicles. It was a forum for them to come up with better ways of doing things. Rather than having one engineer or some managers overseeing processes, Toyota embraced the problem-solving power of one big team committed to better quality and better vehicles.

One could argue that quality teams and the Andon cord were more easily implemented in a cultural context (Japan of the 1960s) that was less obsessed with exceptionalism than workplaces in the US, and that would probably be correct. Most notably, though, it proved the point: some managerial activity need not be done by managers.

THE UNEDUCATED TEAM

When you compare the enlightened approach of the Toyota Production System to Frederick Taylor's notion that workers are like oxen, it is important to keep the state of the worker in context. Taylor's idea of the "oxen worker" was in part driven by the fact that most workers had little education and language proficiency. They were rural farm workers, the uneducated poor, or immigrants who did not speak English. Few had any notion of what a factory was.

But while the Japanese auto workers of the 1960s shared some of those attributes, it is also important to note that they were nothing like today's highly educated knowledge (or even factory) workers. Literacy and workplace survey data from that time suggest that most Japanese auto workers had, at most, a seventh-grade education. They had only basic reading, writing, and language skills, and most had never even reached high school. But they did have socialization skills, four hundred thousand years of skill-building evolution under their belts, and a desire to do good work.

Over twenty years, these fifth-to-seventh-grade-educated Japanese workers helped Japan surpass the US in first-time quality of new cars. By the 1980s, Ford Motor Company, in response to falling market share and the success of the Japanese brands, changed its tagline to "Quality is Job #1." Even today, the Japanese auto industry has higher quality scores than those of the US.

The success of the Toyota Production System and its democratization of the control function to workers is, in my opinion, the most vivid repudiation of Taylor's dual idea of the oxen worker and superior manager. It portrays a way of thinking about releasing managerial control and enabling learning and knowledge sharing across the management-worker divide. Toyota (like Ford) is very much a product-driven organization. Unleashing workers can help almost any type of business, and this example is still an inspiration today, more than fifty years on.

CHAPTER 8

The Four Moments and the Release of Control

LET'S CONNECT SOME DOTS HERE so that you can start envisioning what happens differently as part of unmanaging. We've explored a few stories and vignettes that we can use to do that: "The Project on Fire," the CEDIA owner and team, and the story of Toyota Production System's enabling of workers via the Andon and quality circles. Each of them touches on one or more of the Four Moments, and the idea of releasing control.

1. **The Why Moment.** Here the manager must ensure everyone, individually and as a group, understands the reasons for the work. The natural human reaction after being told to do something is to ask, and even need to know, why it's needed. Because of that, it is almost always associated with one or more What Moments.

2. **The What Moment.** This is the moment in which the manager ensures everyone knows what the work entails. In a project, one form of What is often called scope: what is needed for a successful delivery. Another key detail is how to do the work and who should

do what. If the What Moment is not managed correctly, then the Go Moment often falters.

In the Project on Fire story, I sequestered the team and largely removed all management. My diagnosis was that the team didn't have a full picture of what needed to be done, and the misery of the project came from the team discovering this lack of understanding one painful failure at a time. To address this, I instigated a What Moment, a session in which I asked the team to take ownership of the scope of the project.

To my surprise, a dozen ridiculously smart workers who cared deeply about this project had lived up to and possibly exceeded what their handyman heritage had gifted them. In one day, they solved the project's What almost completely. At the end of the day, we had only a short issues list and just needed to confirm that we had the scope right with the client.

Like our CEDIA owner, I had one advantage in this situation: there was really no way that I, as a newbie to this project, could have figured out the scope. I had no other choice but to give up control of the scope to them. But even if I'd had a clue, giving them control would have been the best choice.

A few things also happened in the days that followed that tie directly to ACE:

- **Authority.** We met with the client, and I had the team walk through the scope. The control-shifted ACE diagram shows this direct relationship; managers need not be in the middle of the very valuable team-client scope discussions. For many reasons, this shift is more important than you might imagine. Having such a great description of the scope also enabled me to "lock" it, through direct agreement with the client. I established myself and the client as the owners of the resultant authority of scope. Before this moment, something like five or more managers had felt they were free to say what the scope and even the why behind it was.

- **Control.** We had a new spreadsheet filled with this scope, and I made the team the owners of it. Brian, the PM, was to be their facilitator, but *nothing* was to be changed on that sheet unless the team agreed to it. I wanted this project to be theirs.
- **Empowerment.** I set rules for how the department managers interacted with the team. The DMs are needed, helping and advising the team on their craft within the work, including things like judging quality or discussing potential solutions. But as can happen when multiple managers get involved, they were often opining on scope itself. The main rule was that anything they found that might adjust the scope had to be discussed with everyone, including me. There is often a fine line between advising on technique and approach (which is okay) and deciding that the scope should be different or reinterpreted, which is a common problem with firefighter managers.

This proper allocation of managerial responsibility (or the failure to do so), especially when transferring the control function to workers in the Why and What Moments, is one of the greatest influences on team and project success. Most projects need not be as difficult as they turn out; the failures in Why and What usually make what should be fairly straightforward, the Go Moment, a big challenge.

3. **The Go Moment.** This is what it sounds like, the moment when things get done. In an organization with managers and workers, the Go Moment includes both the moments of active coordination and the doing of the work. The Go Moment is when productivity happens. If the Why or What Moments have been poorly managed, then the Go Moment will struggle.

The Project on Fire and the CEDIA stories have this moment in common. When a What Moment is structured so the team can take ownership, execution typically requires very little management. More than ten years after I discovered this, it still seems strange to me, though I understand why.

The simple way to think of this is that if understanding (the Why and What) is owned by one or more managers, then the team will forever bounce back and forth between the work and the managers, never completely understanding until they are done. This can account for a large drop in worker productivity, and it also ties up the manager with answering questions, reducing whatever contributions the manager might have been able to make elsewhere in the business.

4. **The Grow Moment.** The Grow Moment is when managers make things better. Here an effective manager will encourage and enable moments of learning, measurement, reflection, opportunity, and mentoring. Too often, managers today, laser focused on managing the Go Moment, ignore these opportunities.

The Toyota story illustrates the release of control by the managers in two different ways: they released control of the Go Moment by implementing the Andon cord. This also then transferred control of the Grow Moment to the team because they were empowered to act when things needed fixing or were not going correctly. Additionally, quality circles further included workers in the continual process improvement.

All three of these stories illustrate the powerful and innate problem-solving talents within us, as well as our willingness to accept the challenge of solving things when they are presented to us in a way that engages us.

CHAPTER 9

The Manager of Understanding

(Why Part 1)

IN THIS CHAPTER, we're going to explore how and why the Why Moment works. I call this the "sushi rice" of all of the techniques because many aspects of it should impact everything that leaders and managers do. The Why Moment is the start of transferring understanding.

Transferring information is not the same as transferring understanding. I can send an email to attempt to transfer information. But understanding is different. It's born from a generative process, where information is assimilated through interaction—an effect that is amplified when done as a group activity.

- **Information:** Facts and other related data that describe a need, a product, a process, a something
- **Understanding:** A process by which knowledge workers incorporate information to create their own (subjective) model of knowledge that can lead to planning and formulating action.

THE WHY AND WHAT FAILURE: THE PROJECT BRIEF

Fifteen years ago, in my role as a client manager (CM), I was leading several different teams that were working on different projects. In came a new project, and after some prep, I assembled the team that would work on it. I had met with our client multiple times, and I understood what they wanted; the solutions were not terribly complex, at least according to me. A few side discussions confirmed for me that it was a very solvable problem.

Out of respect for the team's valuable time—and my schedule as well—I had arranged for a high-intensity "download" of the project to the team, scheduling only thirty minutes of our valuable time.

I had a slide deck with some of the key points, but I also figured conversation is better, so I had also prepared notes of the things I wanted to cover.

I started the meeting on time—well, a few minutes late. People were always busy with other work, so one or two— the most important people—straggled in five to ten minutes late. As was the norm.

I worked methodically through my mass of information, telling people about the client, their business context, the players, the project, its goals, our schedule, and the budget.

At the end, I unveiled an Excel spreadsheet with the hours allocated for each of the roles and people in the room.

With only a few minutes remaining, I asked, "Any questions?"

There was only a question or two. I was that good at briefing—only one or two questions!

After all that, I was amazed when, two weeks later, the questions started flooding in. I felt frustrated, thinking (but thankfully not verbalizing), "Didn't you hear what I said? Why don't you remember, or did you just not understand in the first place?"

As a manager, have you ever wondered whether workers are really listening to what you say? I have. Why couldn't they understand what felt like the most obvious concepts? Why even bother briefing them if they aren't going to retain much of it anyway? Turns out I was coming at this all wrong.

SPEED DIVIDES US

As Steven Pinker points out in *The Blank Slate*, we humans are largely equipped with the same cognitive faculties. Except for a very tiny set of outliers, most of us have pretty much the same innate ability to reason and learn. Granted, this capability gets developed more in some than others due to a wide range of influences, including environmental and social factors, access to higher education, as well as the opportunity to just, well, use it.

But underdevelopment does not particularly divide us. As our handyman heritage suggests, we are perpetual learning and problem-solving machines. We all are capable of learning pretty much anything; it's just that some of us learn faster than others. Yes, you can teach quantum physics to pretty much anyone; it just takes longer for some than others. Through this lens, you can see how our school systems actually divide us based on the velocity of their curricula. You are deemed "smart" if you can learn a subject within the allotted fifteen-week window. The famous bell curve says little about whether someone can actually learn the topic, but rather, how fast they are able to learn it.

In that way, what we call smart is often a factor of speed, and societally, we view the person who answers first to be the smartest. Really, they're just the fastest.[32]

THE SPEEDS OF KNOWING VERSUS UNDERSTANDING

If you recognize any of the headaches in "The Project Brief" above, then you have seen how speed can affect understanding. If we substitute the idea of *handing off control of understanding* for the word *briefing*, then it may be clearer that I screwed up. If I had been handing off better, then the number of postkickoff questions would have been tiny and also mostly focused on what was not talked about, rather than a rehash of things I had tried to say.

In the relay race of knowing and understanding, the runner with the baton of knowing often hurtles past the baton's recipient, failing on the handoff because of their mismatched speeds, metaphorically leaving the recipient wandering and looking for the baton, with precious time passing away.

If the team manages to win, the runner that possessed the knowing baton will claim it as a great personal victory, and if they lose, then the laggard recipients are to blame.

If there is a speed of knowing, is it faster than the speed of understanding? Yes, of course. Once we know something, we can recite that information much faster than it took us to first understand it. So, when briefing a team—that is, doing a handoff—it is highly probable that you will go faster than even you could have handled when it was explained afresh to you. And even if you were able to go at *your* slower speed of understanding, it might not be at the speed someone else needs.

But the whole story is even more complex than that.

THE MANY VELOCITIES AND STYLES OF UNDERSTANDING

We have different speeds, yes, but probably more important is that we have different styles—ways we are best able to (or even need to) collect and process that information and achieve understanding.

In her seminal book *Human Dynamics*, Sandra Segal identifies five different processing styles that also have different apparent velocities.[33] A person with one style may seek out "adjacent" information as they learn, drawing connections to what they already know and what they are learning. A person with another style may learn best when presented with long chains of questions and facts. I always find it fascinating to see people with this style in action.

Maybe you can see yourself or others in my descriptions below.[34] The first two styles tend to represent the majority of managers and leaders, while the latter three, especially in knowledge work organizations, tend to be the workers.

- **Style AV (The Executive).** A very fast processor, often not terribly concerned with details and prone to fast decisions. The AV likes to quickly jump to action. In some ways, AVs learn by trying or directing others into action before all of the available information or analysis is done. There is research that supports this idea—the speed of an executive or organization's decision-making can be a significant factor in overall performance and is referred to as decision latency.

- **Style AK (The Coordinator).** Also a fast processor, tends to be concerned with lateral linkages, how things connect to other things. Often these people have project management–type roles where spotting these linkages and dependencies is a gift. AKs tend to aim for a shallow understanding of the topic and be satisfied with a good lateral view. Most AKs also jump to a solution quite quickly, also before a thorough exploration of the information has been done.

- **Style VK (The Seeker).** A slower processor who seeks the essence of the situation and typically wants a very clean answer. The VK will ask questions in a linear fashion, focusing on one topic at a time and only moving on once the "correct" depth of that topic has been explored.

- **Style KV (The Architect).** A slower processor who seeks a structured systemic view and wants to construct a solution that has a good foundation and level of objective perfection. The KV tends to explore by referencing existing and previous solutions.
- **Style KA (The Builder).** The slowest processor who seeks to build an organic and full-function view of the project. The KA will often ask questions that don't make sense, at least at first, but often tend to be deeply insightful.

When I look at this list, two things come to me, the first of which is, "Wow, what an amazing set of skills available to us when examining or learning a new topic! A team will come at any problem or situation from a bunch of different angles. What a gift."

The second is a bit less enthusiastic: "How could a manager ever expect to succeed at explaining a complex topic to a group of people with different styles at the same time? Five different sessions, one for each style and velocity? That sounds crazy, right? This will take forever!"

There is only one possible way to do this: put the workers in charge. Yes, it's as simple as that.

To see how, let's rewind for a second to our opening vignette, "The Project on Fire":

The next morning, everyone was there on time, sitting at a U-shaped table, looking at me, wondering what the heck was going on. I was at the front of the room, sitting on a stool. My opening words were, "I think you all know that this project is in trouble." Everyone nodded. "So, we need to fix it." There wasn't much reaction to that, but I'm pretty sure they were girding themselves for a verbal flogging ("How could you possibly let this project fail?") or some form of managerial rah-rah, including the obligatory Mike Tyson or George Patton quotes.

Instead, I asked, "So, what do we need to get this done?" Blank looks on their faces. Dead silence.

I waited.

I'm pretty sure they figured this was some devious or torturous form of managerial rhetoric to command them to do work they'd already planned to attempt. But I had no idea at all what they should do. I had no idea of how to fix the project, save for what I had already done so far. So, I waited. I repeated my question and fiddled with the dry-erase marker in my hand.

Transferring understanding of the work follows a process that's the exact opposite of what Taylorism requires. Instead of "You only need to know what I tell you," you will take the posture of "Please tell me what you need to know in order to solve this, and I will tell you at your speed, not mine." The best unmanaging happens when we embrace the fact that workers are natural learners. They know best both the speed and sequence in which they need information to gain understanding.

This approach is a huge shift away from Taylorism and some of the trappings of meritocracy. Meritocracies breed managerial thoughts like "I know more than you" and "I *should* know more than you," as if knowing is a wealth ranking or a property that can be owned by a single person.

If you have become accustomed to being the dominant "knower" or enjoy sharing what you know, you likely will find this approach easy in concept but challenging in practice. I often remind the managers I coach to ask themselves questions like these, should they feel challenged in making the shift:

- Do I need to prove what I know (by telling) even though that will not help them in gaining understanding?
- How much am I holding my teams and people back by hoarding this information?
- How much better will this information get with more people knowing it?
- How does it serve me to feel like an expert or know-it-all at the expense of my people learning and doing better work?
- Why do I think they don't deserve to know as much about this work as I do?
- How have I felt in the past when I didn't know as much as I wanted about the work I was doing, why it was needed, or whom it was for?
- How did it feel to have understanding withheld, hidden, or metered out to me?

What follows is a basic model and some rules for how to shift to an unmanaged approach. Even in its simple form, this model is wicked effective when done well.

EXERCISE #1: BASIC UNDERSTANDING

This simple exercise is all about helping a group achieve a shared understanding. It follows the Japanese *Ba* model—the practice of getting together and seeing what needs to be talked about to arrive at a "common place" (the *Ba*) on the topic. Here are the basic steps:

1. **Determine your topic(s).** Maybe it is a new project. Maybe it is a decision you need to make in your department. Maybe you are just having a "town hall" meeting.

2. **Determine your audience.** This should include the learners, the people who you need to gain understanding, as well as at least one "knower," someone who understands a good bit about the topic (e.g., someone with the authoritative ACE role).

3. **Determine how you will capture information.** I recommend that this be a physical (or virtual) mechanism, like a wall, a whiteboard, index cards, or Post-It notes. It needs to be done in a way everyone can see it. Someone else needs to record everything that is learned as it happens. The group needs to be able to see this progress. Don't use a spreadsheet but instead write on the whiteboard or a virtual whiteboard if you're online. Importantly, you should pause the process until all notes are taken. This recording will go faster if you do it, but part of the reason for you not doing it (and having the learners write their own notes as well) is that it will signal that they, by virtue of writing notes themselves, are taking ownership of the process.

4. **Have the learners take turns asking questions.** Make sure you have a model that ensures everyone takes their turn.

5. **On their turn, a person gets to ask three questions.** As you make additional rotations, this number can change. I would start with three, as people with certain learning styles will want to connect the dots. Once they have one answer, it is better to let them get one or two more answers as well.

6. **Completeness is an option, not a requirement.** Keep going until you feel enough has been done or until all questions have been answered.

GROUND RULES FOR THE MANAGER OF UNDERSTANDING

We typically teach teams how to do this through hands-on, interactive training using real projects. We do that because explaining, even in writing, as I am doing here, is rarely sufficient to enable mastery. Nonetheless, here are a few additional tips:

1. **Avoid bundling information and concepts together.** One of the most common ways to fail at this technique is to shift back to "telling" mode—that is, responding to a question with a string of answers and information.

   I once asked a client manager to kick things off by telling the team (of ten people) a few things they should know about the client. I listened to her with my MBA ears and was impressed by the seven facts she chose to relate to them. After her stellar recital, I asked the whole group how many of the points each of them could recite. One person could name three. The rest did worse.

   So, we started again. I slowed her down, constantly having to pause her because she was overdelivering. At the end of that brief session, each of the workers had a great list of the most important things they needed to know. Each of their lists were slightly different in their focus, as you might expect.

2. **The manager makes sure everyone becomes a learner.** This means making learning (and participation in it) mandatory. I am always amazed when leaders and managers of knowledge worker teams are very passive on this topic, doing little or nothing about workers who shy away from engaging in discussion and understanding of scope. The job description "knowledge worker" means they should be constantly seeking to improve their skills, and understanding,

in order to help themselves and the team grow.

A very simple way to make this happen is to require that people take turns asking questions or participating in the conversation. Having no questions is not a sign of intelligence but of indifference; smart people get smarter by searching for what they don't know.

3. **The knower disowns the learnings.** As a knower, you will be naturally drawn to become part of the team—a growing mutual level of understanding and the thrill of progressive discovery can be energizing, and you may become inclined to join in. Don't. One of the best things I did in "The Project on Fire" was leave the team to discover and solve on their own. You may think it is not fair that you don't get to "play" with them, but you need to realize life is not fair. You get to be a manager, and they don't.

None of this is easy, but all of it is learnable and can be fun once you get the hang of it.

HOW TO TELL WHETHER YOU ARE GETTING IT RIGHT

When this starts going well, you'll notice some significant changes:

- Questions asked during the session will get richer. You will start to see people develop their thinking.
- People who are quiet will find their voice and participate more. Initially, this happens because you are pushing them; later, they'll find it feels natural.
- After the work begins, the nature of questions you receive will shift from remedial (things that they probably should have known or remembered) to solution oriented (what to do about new information and discoveries).

- Work quality will improve as people have a better grasp of what is being asked for, enabling better self-solutions. This will also reduce the tendency of teams and workers to just "do something" and then, when it is determined to be not correct, ask to fix it.

CHAPTER 10
The Motivated Worker
(Go Part 1)

THE GO MOMENT is when the work gets done. But like the work itself, it's not that simple. This is the first of several chapters that hone in on this specific managerial moment, and for now we're going to focus only on the core of the Go Moment: teams and what makes them go. You'll learn about the major influence of motivation on performance, what internal factors influence it, and how much of a difference those factors can make.

THE MOTIVATED WORKER

Motivation is at the core of our beings. The ability to envision a desirable future state and connect that vision to actions and choices is deeply innate for us. We are very motivatable, we humans. An essential part of shifting away from Tayloristic managing includes understanding how motivation can be unleashed in knowledge workers. The good news is that we're all wired that way anyway.

There are two styles of motivating factors, extrinsic and intrinsic. Extrinsic motivation is motivation that is driven or controlled by an external party. Intrinsic motivation is the opposite: it arises within the individual and through their perceptions. Being told that you must finish your project by the weekend (or else) can be extrinsically motivating but does not really make you work better, nor usually feel better. Receiving a new, cool project that you have always dreamed about stokes your internal fires, makes you more engaged with the work, and naturally inclines you to work better. That is the power of intrinsic motivation.

As a general rule, intrinsic motivators are the only ones that create lasting change, growth, and happiness in workers. For example, bonus schemes, which are a form of extrinsic motivation, tend not to impact average performance. I remember hearing about a legendary military study at RAND that discovered that giving people a $10 arm patch in recognition of an achievement had a far more lasting impact on attitude and performance than a $3,000 one-time bonus for that same accomplishment.[35]

But the opposite dimension—demotivation—is worth mentioning as well. Famous researcher Fredrick Herzberg found that certain motivational factors and demotivational factors operate independently of each other. He referred to the demotivating factors as being hygienic factors, things that a worker expects from the workplace, without which they will view it as deficient.

As an example (playing on the word *hygiene*), we could say that access to bathrooms is a hygienic workplace factor: a workplace that lacked bathroom access would be extremely demotivating (insert joke here). But having the opposite condition, a plethora of easily accessible and amazing bathrooms might not be all that motivating, especially compared to something like getting to work with people you like. Herzberg found that, in general, people complain about extrinsic factors (find job dissatisfaction in them) but find reward (and satisfaction) in intrinsic factors.

Keep in mind that every person assesses their workplace and work differently. For example, someone might put up with a workplace that is otherwise somewhat toxic (e.g., harsh managers or working hours) because they feel like they are learning things (e.g., building skills and experience) that will take them elsewhere, presumably somewhere better. Someone else might not have that kind of tolerance.

SELF-DETERMINATION (SDT) DEFINED

Probably the richest model of workplace motivation is self-determination theory (SDT). While much of the literature defines SDT as being about (intrinsic) motivational factors, what we've seen in more complex organizations, where they are suppressed by incorrect managerial behaviors, is these factors can start to take on a hygienic quality that's capable of demotivating workers when they are absent or only limited in their quantity.[36] SDT is also nicely simple, consisting of three worker perceptions:

- Their sense of *competence*: Josh feels he is, and that others believe him to be, highly capable, motivated, and able to master multiple skills. He believes the organization expects him to be competent.
- Their sense of *autonomy*: Riley feels they can, and are empowered to, choose their work and the way that the work is performed. They believe the organization expects them to do this.
- Their sense of *relatedness*: Nitya feels she does, and is encouraged to, collaborate with others, feel camaraderie with her team, and share in its experience. She believes the organization expects her to do this.

The wording here is very important. It is the *sense* of competence rather than competence itself that has the primary value. If you hold constant the actual value of the underlying factor, such as how competent Josh is, the thing that really matters is whether he feels he's competent. Even this idea of sensing is a rich one, as it encapsulates whether he believes he is competent, whether the organization expects that of him, and whether others encourage it.

SDT is especially interesting because it has such a strong research basis. As noted in many studies, increasing a worker's sense of competence, autonomy, and relatedness can create significant improvements in three other factors:[37]

- Productivity (how fast good work is produced)
- Quality (the error rate in the work)
- Attitude and engagement

A significant portion of the productivity improvements our clients see (which can range as high as 30%) has its origins in just having a better managerial style, one that shifts away from Angry Rancher behaviors. Probably most telling is that engagement scores go up as well, which would indicate that intrinsic factors like the SDT factors are being triggered.

So, the good news and the bad news:

- Your posture as a manager can influence worker motivation and performance significantly. Using the techniques in this book will help you create a positive impact.
- The posture of other managers can influence the motivation and performance of those same workers. From what we've seen, if this is a negative influence, it will "count" more than your positive influence.

The methods we'll explore in this book will help you shape how you and other managers interact with workers and tend to create positive SDT effects. Here's a quick overview of how they relate to each other:

- **The Why Moment.** The inclusion of the worker in group activities that are done inclusively and democratically gives them a greater sense of competence (that their understanding is important) and also relatedness (chapters 9 and 14).

- **The What Moment.** Giving workers the responsibility of shaping and owning the What drives their sense of autonomy and competence (chapters 15 and 16).
- **The Go Moment.** Enabling worker planning, coordination, and Flow allows workers to experience autonomy in its fullest form (chapters 10, 18, and 19).
- **The Grow Moment.** Extending opportunities also reinforces workers' sense of competence and also decreases perceptions of cultural and bias-based boundaries, which will increase relatedness (chapters 6, 11, 25, and in the metrics discussions at the end of sections).

The Go Moment, in its most simple form, is easy if you have fixed the What and Why. That was the point of the CEDIA business owner vignette: your people are not only natural solvers, but also highly (intrinsically) motivated doers. With a proper Why and What, managers often only need to move (and stay) away during the Go Moment. That will, as we'll see, be more difficult than it sounds.

Let's connect the dots to the ACE model, so it is clearer what your managerial roles might be:

- **Authority.** Make sure (require) your workers gain understanding of the Why and What. Embrace missing information and risks and hunt down answers, sharing what you find out.
- **Empowerment.** Make sure (require) they have the tools, time, and focus to do the work (the Go). You are there if needed.
- **Control.** Step back. Let them know they are in charge of getting it done. Yeah, this is the hard part.

CHAPTER 11

The Manager of Opportunity

(Grow Part 2)

It had been many months since the Project on Fire ended, and I was working with a new team for a new client. The requested build was bigger than anything the client and the agency had ever done before, and we were a bit more than halfway through the year-long project. The team had a good understanding of their target, so now it was just a matter of getting it all done.

The team seemed slightly understaffed; there weren't as many senior people as I preferred. The youngest and least experienced was Eric, who was just learning this technology and, in fact, did not even have any formal technology training. Eric was highly skilled though, we all had to admit, and as he showed us several times, his winning a state-wide yo-yo championship the previous year was not a fluke. Yo-yo.

We had been using Agile to manage our process, but when it came time for them to choose work for the next sprint, we encountered a dilemma. Our mobile expert, Joe, was also the platform and database expert, and we had a massive amount of work pipelined for him. In addition, the rest of the team, save for Eric, had a pretty solid backlog of items, at least several weeks' worth.

Then the client requested approval for the mobile app very early. We could just speed up our work on that, but the answer felt like a no. All we had was Eric. I mean, how could we possibly give that job to him? He would certainly fail, right? Everyone in the room just sort of shook their head at the idea, staying silent to the obvious but unspoken.

But I said it: "I guess then we have Eric do it." I didn't have to wait long as the objections piled on. Even Eric responded, leaning back in his chair, with a deer-in-the-headlights look.

"I know that Eric is not anywhere near as skilled as you guys, and probably not even 'ready' for this, but all that means is you'll need to help him get there. You all have done things for the first time. That's how you got here. Let's give Eric the backup he needs to get this done."

Within moments, the team shifted from viewing the plan as an inevitable failure to being cool to embark on an adventure with our team's yo-yo expert.

Six weeks later, Eric was presenting the first pages of the mobile app to the client.

YOU CAN GROW THE MACHINES!

In Taylor's time, machines were the means of production, and all they did was gradually wear out and require replacement or repair. If you wanted more machines, then you had to buy machines. What a gift it is that today's machines of knowledge work—your workers' minds—actually get stronger if properly managed! As the Humble Gardener knows, you can help them grow. They want to grow! You just have to give them the opportunity.

In theory, all of your people have opportunity. But in reality, that's not how it typically shakes out. In the race to excellence, each team member may seek to learn new skills and gain experience that will make them happier and more productive.

But the race is not a fair one. For one, team members will start from different starting lines; everyone's talents and experience levels vary, even if only in small, but meaningful ways.

One of the most important factors, as discussed earlier, is the velocity of learning. Some learn faster than others, and this can create a sort of *pecking order* effect. The term comes from the studies of chickens who aggressively defend piles of food, pecking as quickly as possible, while muscling other chickens out of the way. The biggest, strongest chicken (the top of the pecking order) gets more food than the others, which then makes it even stronger than it already was. If there is enough food, the other chickens eventually get to eat. But the first ones always get stronger and more dominant.

The same can happen when a team is trying to gather information: those with the faster learning velocities climb the pecking order. In a conversation, asking and answering questions can reinforce the separation between the "more-skilled" and "less-skilled" workers. Unchecked, the more-skilled workers with faster learning velocities will answer first, which will suppress others from trying to answer. Growth and learning come from trying to answer and asking questions. Even if those answering fastest don't answer correctly, they will still learn more because the act of trying to answer engages them in the learning, spurring their growth.

Other behaviors, like verbal dominance, add to this, making it increasingly unlikely that others will participate and get the chance to learn. Over time, this creates a stratification of talent, and various in-groups form, including the firefighter in-group, managerial in-group (largely promoted firefighters), and "A-team" in-groups. But the tragedy of the pecking order effect is the self-reinforcing zero-sum game it creates: winners win more, and losers lose more.

> *Stacy realizes that the project is in trouble. They had thought that Josh would be more than adequate to get the work done, but the work turned out to be more challenging than any of them realized. Stacy needs to put Lena on this problem and move Josh to one of the simpler projects. Lena's superior skills and speed can probably put things back on track, allowing Stacy to stop worrying about this.*

In this vignette, Stacy mistakenly treats this situation as a simple one, believing the only solution is to trade Josh for Lena. As a result, the gap between Lena and Josh grows, and Josh will likely not try as hard next time, which will further the cycle of Lena getting better by dealing with the challenge and Josh losing the opportunity to gain skills. Eventually, Lena gets all the hard work, again increasing the distance between her and others.

For Josh, being pushed aside is tantamount to being assigned to the out-group, the B-team, which is just as demotivating as you might expect. The many losers in the opportunity game represent a managerial failure and a loss to the organization's productivity.

GROW YOUR TEAM, MAKE A BETTER WORLD

The cool thing is that you can fix this. Even better, SDT puts growth in your control. The problem you need to deal with is that you are biased—horribly so, actually. Nothing personal, of course, as we are all subject to a huge number of biases, literally over 170 different biases, including the ironic belief that we are less biased than others.[38] Your best move is to doubt your exceptionalism in this matter.

I'll give you an example of how just two biases can make any of us managers horrible at making decisions involving other people. The first is in-group, out-group bias, of which racism is but one of many. Our minds, for probably some very good evolutionary reasons, are amazingly good at assigning people to categories or groups. Our value judgments about people in those groups, however, are incorrect more often than not. If my brain assigns someone to a group that I am also part of (the in-group), then I think of them more highly than if I assign them to another group, especially if what distinguishes that other group (the out-group) is unfavorable.

The second force is confirmation bias amplified by the pecking order effect (the phenomenon where winners win more, and losers lose more). Confirmation bias causes us to cherry-pick information that confirms my preconceptions. In that way, I tend to notice the positive things that someone from my group does and, contrariwise, to notice the negative things that someone from the out-group does.

Because I choose people to handle work items, I will tend to prefer those who are in my group and give them more challenging work because I believe they can handle it. Likewise, the out-group workers will get less challenging work. This invokes that same pecking order effect, where working on more challenging work, and being viewed favorably, will tend to accelerate the development of the in-group worker when compared to the out-group worker, who only gets easy work and is judged to be not that good at it. The lack of challenging opportunities will tend to exacerbate my original bias, creating an actual talent difference where none may have existed prior.

That's just two biases. You have more. I have more. Trying to avoid them is a fool's errand. If, instead of assuming that we are not biased, we assume that we are, what does that suggest in action? One thing it might suggest is that we should abandon the managerial act of choosing whenever possible and, instead, replace it with a "blind" or mechanical function of sorts. In the vignette about Eric, the situation served this mechanical function, ensuring that nobody else could be chosen because they were all too busy with other important work. Over the years, a few good habits in this regard have emerged from our work.

GROUND RULES FOR THE MANAGER OF OPPORTUNITY

1. **Accept your bias and avoid it.** There is nothing you can do to not be biased—the behaviors and perceptual models are so deeply ingrained in us. You'll need to find a way to mechanically invoke opportunity through rules rather than personal assessment.

   One of the best rules I know of is, "Take turns." It literally disables the pecking order effect. Follow it rigorously, or its capricious or occasional use may become another form of dominance.

   Bias can also crop up when special-purpose "squads" form to tackle a special project, present a sales pitches, and so on. It is fair to want some of the most knowledgeable people on a squad, but they shouldn't be the only members. I often suggest that a squad have at least 30%–40% of its members from outside that circle of most experienced. Doing this will allow those underestimated, out-group workers the opportunity to learn how the more-talented people think and work. You can further define rules for how these squads create learning/growth opportunities for the less experienced.

2. **Give up your "God as a chooser" role.** This is probably the ultimate surrender to the inevitability of your own bias. Avail yourself

of the contrarian posture, as I did with Eric the yo-yo master. There are a lot of ways to choose who works on something, and you can even just think of who you would pick and then construct a contrarian approach.

"Normally, I would say that we use Lena on this project, but I'm wondering whether this is an opportunity for one or more of you in this? Thoughts?"

One of the most-common God as a chooser behaviors comes from skill-to-work matching decisions, where achieving a perfect fit is especially precious to the manager. Creative directors seem to be particularly drawn to the idea of "putting people in the right spot." Phrases like, "Eric really isn't ready for something like this yet," are giveaways. (Eric's ancestors called by the way, and they they've been waiting four hundred thousand years for his chance to take this project on!)

3. **Measure yourself by your biggest challenges.** If the measure of the manager is the growth and success of their team, then measure the hard parts, not the easy ones. Your best people will get better, faster, even without you doing much of anything. The thing you need to focus on is how to get the other 50%–90% to grow quickly. There's a great side benefit to this: if you raise the bar from the bottom, then your high performers will strive even harder to be at the top.

4. **Create a culture of "team wins" from individual growth.** This complex technique involves you redefining the dialogue within your department or team. One of the best times to do this is in a periodic monthly review, or even a sprint review activity.

   ▪ Have people define goals for themselves and others. The horizon for this planning would typically be three to six months.

- As a group, choose which goals are top priority, with a weighting toward "closing the gap." These goals can be larger than would fit into one review cycle. Maybe refresh these quarterly. Include at least one big challenge for each worker.
- Keep these top goals in mind throughout the process of assigning work, even using them in group discussion as suggested in #2 above.
- The hardest part is sustaining this. That's your job as a manager/leader: to establish the team culture (a set of behaviors) and, in an ironically Tayloristic twist, ensure that it is followed.
- Celebrate the wins and analyze the misses.

HOW TO TELL WHETHER YOU'RE GETTING IT RIGHT

- You get surprised by what people can accomplish.
- Other workers step up to help each other succeed.
- Workers ask to be challenged in ways that you did not expect.
- You start seeing where your biases would have produced a different outcome.
- Your team gets stronger and more self-sufficient.

SUMMARY

Section 2 introduced new ideas, such as ACE and SDT, as well as some ways you can use the insights from the previous sections to put the key moments into action for workers and simple project team situations:

- **Release control.** The single most important shift that managers can make is to reduce their level of control over items related to production, including the Why, What, and Go.
- **Give up Angry Rancher behavior**, which overcontrols the Why and What and makes the team starved for understanding, creating

a dependence on managers as the team struggles during the Go.

- **Teams can learn and solve problems.** Managers who falsely believe otherwise often incorrectly assert control over the understanding of the work. Their belief that things are too difficult for their workers to understand creates a self-reinforcing set of behaviors that include hoarding and siloing of understanding.

- **Releasing managerial control of understanding requires patience and process.** The simple exercise presented is multipurpose and will help you go at the speed of the slowest learner so everyone gets to learn.

- **The Go Moment is easy in simple situations.** Teams can do the work without much managing if they understand the work. Believing in their competence, autonomy, and relatedness will make them believe in it as well and boost overall quality and happiness.

- **Being fair in enabling growth is hard for managers.** Opportunity and inclusion create growth. Your perception-based biases are the biggest obstacle to fulfilling your highest managerial function.

- **Follow the ground rules.** I have introduced several ideas that reflect excellent behaviors in an organization:
  - Go no faster than the slowest.
  - In turns, share the opportunity to learn.
  - Ask questions. The unknown is what you need to discuss.

- **Use metrics.** In addition to those discussed earlier, some new metrics in the list include surveying workers around how well they understand the work that they have been asked to do (on a one-to-ten scale).
  - Organizational Metrics (existing)
  - Manager-Team Ratio
  - Client/Stakeholder Satisfaction (NPS)

- Worker/Team Satisfaction (eNPS)
- Team (longer-term) Metrics
- Worker Capability Development and Utilization
- Team (near-term) Metrics
- Team Understanding of the Why and What

SECTION 3

Scope and Alignment

In section 2, we looked at how managers can better serve their workers and teams by making basic shifts in their mindset and behavior. In today's complex organizations, however, management problems and solutions are rarely so simple. The impact of overmanaging gets worse as size and complexity balloon, birthing multi-manager behaviors that can amplify negative outcomes. Nowhere is this more apparent than in a large, complex, and uncertain project.

These large projects, because they have fairly clear boundaries, are one of the best places to demonstrate some of the more advanced uses of the Four Moments. In practice, we have found them to also be great starting points for organizational change, in no small part due to how profound of an impact the techniques can have.

A BRIEF GLIMPSE INTO THE CHASM OF DESPAIR

Ahsan's gaze drifted across the computer screen; it was already past 11:00 p.m. So much for grabbing some of that great Thai food on his way home. When he took the job at Ingenious Quantum (IQ) Solutions, the new, hot tech consultancy, he knew he would be working hard—they had been on a win-streak for most of the year, and his former employer had been struggling to win against them. Better to be on the winning team, he thought.

In the relative quiet of the empty consultancy offices, he had spent the last several hours reading through a sample renter's contract from their client, a storage unit rental company called Bottomless Bins (BB). The contract was mind-bendingly complex, more complex than anything he had heard mentioned during the kickoff.

It was time well spent, though. Now he better understood why the client was irate earlier in the week when his team had shown off some of their work, the new "control panel" for renter contract management. When the client asked, "How does it handle our thirty-day 'Upsize or Out' guarantee?" it drew blank looks from Ahsan and the rest of the IQ team. And then things went downhill when the client described several other aspects of their marketing—some of which Ahsan had even seen on late-night YouTube ads. Nobody had any answers.

"How are you going to meet the launch date you committed to, if you don't even understand our business?" The client raged. It was, of course, a very good question, one that Ahsan was asking himself now.

Ahsan had been grateful when IQ's client manager jumped in, deflecting what felt like an attack on him and his hardworking team. Trying to use a voice of reason, the CM said, "You know I've spent a lot of time learning your business, and I am aware of the many ways that Bottomless Bins makes clever propositions. As you know, I led the franchisee interviews and even spent time with your contracts team, something that none of our competitors did. We're committed to making this a great solution for you and your team."

But nobody had seen this coming. The software "rental engine" they had chosen early on, upon which several thousand hours' worth of work had been done already, did not support the complexity of what Ahsan had just read in the renter contract. Much of Ahsan's night was spent digging into the many documents that had been traded back and forth when IQ competed for the business. When he searched through IQ's internal requirements document, he saw nothing that matched either. But BB was good at contracts, it appeared, because the appendix of the work contract between BB and IQs clearly named twelve sample renter contracts whose clauses all needed to be supported by the system they were building.

Ahsan thought back to the end of the meeting. The PM interjected that the GANTT chart clearly called out which modules they were building during this release, and none of them were intended to support "Upsize or Out," so "of course" the client would not see those features at this time. The client was smarter than that though and simply asked, "Okay, then show me where it is in your plan." The PM replied, "It's not, but we'll have to fit it in."

The client's last words as he and his team stormed out of the meeting: "Yes, you will."

That launch date was long gone, Ahsan reflected. What the new date would be, nobody could really say. He had just read the tenth contract of the twelve and had two more to look at. He wasn't sure that he wanted to see what was in them.

Ahsan's moment above may sound or be familiar to you. Over the years, large projects have, for us, been a sort of microcosm in which a narrow set of managerial interactions have outsize impact on project success.

Using this lens, we can dissect the motivations for many types of over-managing and illustrate how inducing a shift in managerial postures (ACE) and focusing on the Four Moments can create dramatically different results. This fuller view of a project environment will also allow us to develop an even richer set of metrics and reveal the often-elusive reasons why project success is challenging to achieve.

In this large-project example, we'll examine several key moments in the early parts of the project life cycle, including the selling of the project, and multiple Why and What Moments. I'll also do a deep dive into project management, which ironically often creates managerial blindness and unintended chaos in complex projects. This last point is a fun one for me, as I was a project manager for many years and now can see very clearly how well-intentioned project managers often lead projects, managers, and teams astray. Beware the project manager who says everything is under control.

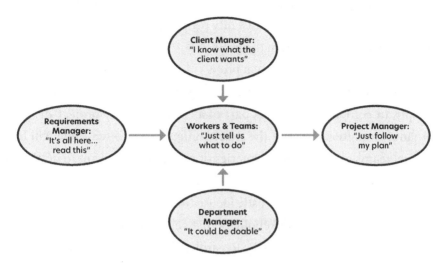

Figure 28: The Siren Songs of Overmanaged Projects

The above diagram shows the common siren songs of the managerial chorus. They instill the team's fatal dependence on input from the managers, who often say they know more than they do and are at times incorrect.

LARGE, COMPLEX PROJECTS HAPPEN EVERYWHERE

Large, complex projects are the province of many project-driven organizations, but not exclusively. Even a more traditional organization will need to conduct the occasional complex project, whether for a client or for itself. It may even hire a project-driven organization for help.

For example, one of our clients (a technology solutions vendor) was hired by a large automaker to implement a new capability, an app, that would connect consumers, social media, and the auto client's databases and systems containing new car information in a way that would seamlessly integrate with their nationwide dealer network. The project size was several million dollars. The resultant project organization was a mix of the managers and workers from the automaker, its information technology department, the internal users of the capabilities, the vendor (our client), and several other vendors whose scope of responsibilities contributed to the work product. All told, at least fifty people felt they should either have a voice or a hand (or both) in the project!

Even if your business is not a project-driven organization—our technology vendor's client wasn't—you still may get involved, possibly quite deeply, in complex projects as part of a cross-company project-driven organization. Regardless of the exact configuration, often there will be several teams of workers and coteries of managers who want to do their own versions of managing. Yes, a bit of a circus.

Although what follows mostly focuses on the vendor side of this, we'll also consider the other stakeholders that get involved and the complex managerial dynamics that ensue. Regardless of where you are in that sort of mix, you'll be able to leverage these techniques.

Complex projects, while often necessary, almost universally underachieve and fail more often than you probably realize. This is a business tragedy, the drama of which starts with hopeful moments and good intentions. The result is an *Alice in Wonderland* sort of experience in which the project unravels once its realities are discovered through trial and error.

By the end of this section, you'll know two proven techniques for clearing the fog of misunderstanding early in projects, and you'll see how a methodical reduction of managerial actions actually creates better outcomes for teams.

CHAPTER 12

The Large, Complex, and Uncertain Project

THE PROJECT IS THE STAGE upon which the actors play. There's a good chance you've encountered a few or many of these projects. You'll recognize many of these factors:

- **Size**, which has multiple dimensions, including the number of workers and teams required, the duration of their involvement, and the size of the managerial cohort across all organizations involved with the project.
- **Complexity**, typically because the project involves a complex problem requiring a complex solution or interdisciplinary team.
- **Uncertainty**, typically in the form of organizational size, which includes the team, the stakeholders, and the target users; the level of innovation or number of activities being done for the first time; and creativity, which may involve avoiding obvious approaches and solutions to create a novel solution.

The most important aspect of these large, complex projects is that they are largely doomed to face crises and tremendous challenges. Consider that, in the high-volume project organizations that AgencyAgile works with, which are usually typified by smaller yet still very complex and uncertain projects, they almost uniformly have a high rework rate—the actual number of hours required to finish the project versus the number of hours planned. For example, if the project manager planned ten thousand hours for a project but the team actually needed thirteen thousand hours, then the rework rate is 30%. As far as we've seen, that 30% is pretty much an industry standard.[39]

But rework is just a financial metric. A better view comes from asking what actual success looks like. Thankfully, we can use the following model of project outcomes adapted from the Standish Group:[40]

- **Success.** The project is on time, on budget, feature and functionally complete. Everybody is really happy, and your team has met the "promise" under which this was sold. I heard that gulp noise you just made.
- **Challenged.** You got it done, but one, and usually many more, of the "success" items above did not come true.
- **Failed.** One or both of the key parties (client and provider) decide to abandon the project before it is done.

Here's what Standish Group reported in 2015, a chart that looks like every semiannual chart for the ten years that preceded it and the ten that will follow it.

Figure 29: Overall Project Outcomes (All Projects)

If you haven't seen this before, it can be a bit shocking. What should scare you even more (and, yes, you as a manager should be at least humbled by this or worse) is that in the twenty-plus-year span that these charts have been made, the professionalization of project management and new and fancy software tools *should* have increased our ability to manage projects— yet they've had almost no impact.

You need to read the Standish reports in detail to learn why: as projects get larger, complexity and uncertainty go up, and—drumroll, please—the number of managers and stakeholders grows in size. This, as you realize, will increase the complexity of coordinating all the parties. This manifests as a steep increase in managerial coordination cost that the Standish Group calls "decision latency," the measure of how long it takes to make managerial decisions. Decision latency is highly influenced by the size and complexity of the manager and stakeholder group and their level of mutual understanding of Why and What.

The chart above accounts for projects of all sizes. As you might guess, it looks much worse when you filter out the small ones: failure rates rise to 30% or more, success rates plummet to between 8%–12%, and the challenged projects remain dominant. Shown below is data from Standish's 2022 report for large projects. It is because of the "long odds" of being successful (one out of eight projects) that these projects are such a great learning ground (albeit a painful one) for the many effects of overmanaging and the pervasive manager-on-manager taxes that occur.

Figure 30: Outcomes for Larger Projects

If you've been around these projects for a while, you know that only two groups see this phenomenon through somewhat sober eyes, being the most skeptical of promises of project success: workers and clients.

THE ILLUSION OF PROJECT MANAGEMENT

All large, complex, and uncertain projects use project management techniques and have project managers. But how well is that working, really? Is there any other service profession where you would accept a 12% success rate? Project management does not provide certainty and control in the way many people think it, and its misapplication can trigger a spiral of bad managing.

Project management is a somewhat formalized body of practice.[41] You can earn a master's degree in it at some universities, adding to its aura of presumed effectiveness. The project-driven organization, because it lives (and dies) in high levels of complexity and uncertainty, is drawn to project management methods because common wisdom says they make projects run well.

But it's time to peel off the misleading branding. Project management sounds like the panacea for project challenges, but in reality, project management has increasingly been "standard practice" for twenty years and has had little or no impact on quelling the effects of the managerial swarm.

Because of the work-style mismatch between PM techniques and actual project-driven work, project managers tend to make schedules based on low levels of scope understanding. That's not totally the PM's fault: there's no good way to incorporate unknown scope, nor the processes needed to uncover it into a schedule. The result, however, is schedules that appear complete even though they are not.

This mismatch in perception versus reality has its roots in the broad use of the word *project* (doing my laundry or building a bridge both count) versus the more-rare and challenging types of projects found in a project-driven organization.

Project management has its origins in construction management—the practice of building houses, buildings, roads, and other tangible projects.[42] You might be thinking, "Hey, those sound complex too!" But you would be wrong in a very important way: by the time a project manager becomes the core of one of these projects, the project is already fully defined, blueprinted, specified, etc. It may be a big project, yes, but it is not uncertain, and its complexity is more like a massive bookkeeping problem than a creativity or innovation puzzle; in general, all of the innovation is over by the time the PM is given the project.

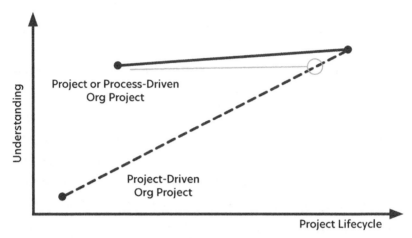

Figure 31: The Futility of Planning with High Ignorance

In contrast, the projects in the project-driven organization have much lower understandability at the onset—that's an essential characteristic of this kind of project. You can't write a project plan at the start of the project-driven project—you just don't know enough. Later in the project when your understanding is comparable to one's understanding of more traditional projects, the complex project is almost finished.

This simple fact means that writing a plan at the start of the project has the potential to make things worse in the long and short term, especially if you insist on believing it and behaving as if it is true and accurate.

WHERE PROJECT MANAGING WORKS WELL

It probably sounds like I don't think project management works at all. You, as a project manager—as I was—may suddenly feel like you need a backup career. But project management does work well in many situations. It's just tricky to use it in large projects and, to a degree, project-driven organizations.

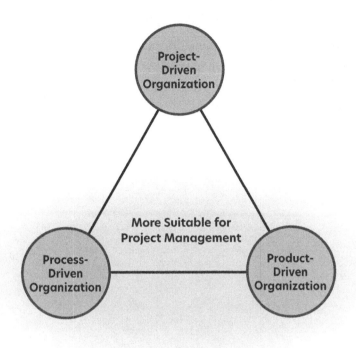

Figure 32: Project Management Versus Project-Driven Organizations

Project management works best when you have clear activities and dependencies, the most common being a stop-start. For example, the drywall cannot be installed (started) until the plumbing is completed and inspected (stopped). PM techniques work well in these situations and reinforce the idea that the PM should be the master of all disciplines. In construction, the PM is the integrator: the plumber and the drywall company do not need to coordinate with each other; the PM does that for them. They don't need an all-hands-on-deck coordination meeting to get their work done.

This highlights how project management works better when dealing with more standard processes or products. It can also work well, I believe, when not used prematurely in large projects. Most PMs, however, create plans too early, seeing it as a way to remove uncertainty in the project. But this doesn't work, and in fact, premature planning often does the opposite, hiding the fact that much is still not known.

CHAPTER 13

The Glorious Moment of Untruth

The curtain comes up and . . .

Wow, you did it! The project is about to start, and the beautiful flowers on the Plateau of Optimism are in full bloom. Life in Projectland includes all four seasons, so let's enjoy the flowers while we can.[43]

Everyone involved shares in the celebratory banter. "Don't worry, the client or stakeholder gets it." "This is just like that other one that we did." Although that project was last year and those people are gone, everybody has conveniently forgotten how bad that project was.

Others pipe in: "It should be simple to do quickly." "How hard could it be?" Even though you're dealing with new technology and work the team has never done before, you all know you've got this.[44] *No need to ask the hard questions. "What couldn't we do for a budget like X dollars?" you think.*

But suddenly there's a hint of doubt in your mind. You know that question usually answers itself quite well. There always is a limit to what can be done. In almost every project, you and everyone around you have brushed up hard against that line.

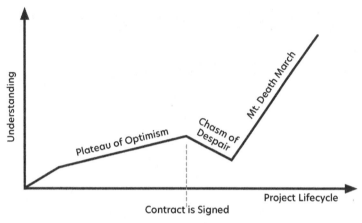

Figure 33: The Ignorance Gap in Large and Complex Projects

With the project kickoff, the plateau cuts abruptly. Here at the Chasm of Despair, the early summer turns into a harsh fall and winter, sending the flowers to the frost. You can still hear the dopamine-addled sales team celebrating, but you're there when one unlucky team gets assigned the work. The crows come home to roost, darkening the sky as the team slides into the Chasm of Despair. In the chasm, the hard questions are finally being asked, and few answers are available. Every time the team thinks that they have found a good starting point, more questions arise. The team struggles with unexpected scope choices and unforeseen obstacles, reaching up in desperation to those who originated the project, pulling them into the chasm as well. Managers blame the team for its lack of skill, vision, or basic competence. There is good news though: the chasm itself is the crucible from which true scope and understanding emerge. But the long winter is only starting.

You know most projects reach completion, but not without costly trial and error.[45] *With contract-mandated doggedness, the team climbs Mount Death March on the other side of the chasm. With a heart-wrenching tenacity, the team pulls itself up that mountain, clinging tightly to the ropes of understanding they managed to unearth. The climb feels steeper than it ought, however, because of the optimism in the project plan written on the flower-bedecked Plateau of Optimism. But there are no flowers here on the Mount. Here, past and future wrongs are spoken of candidly, and to the climbers, the plateau is but a fairy tale. They'll get to the top eventually, discovering scope through failures. Budget, schedule, and scope—probably all of them—will take a hit in the process.*

THE MYTH OF THE PLATEAU: SALES SCOPE

Virtually every complex project starts with a "sale," often between a client and a vendor. If it is an intraorganizational project, then the sale was probably a budget negotiation. In many cases both are true: the client had to make an internal sale to get the budget and then converted that to an external purchase.

But the negotiated deal is fraught with ambiguity and misperception. It starts with the idea that the "deal" or "bargain" was good or fair. That can only be true if we know what the deal was: what the client bought and what the vendor sold. But we don't. Nobody knows the real scope at this point. That isn't what happens on the plateau.

Because of the complexity and uncertainty in the various forms of scope, nobody can really know what was sold. But that's a scary truth to either party, so they agree to not agree to much beyond the very obvious pieces.[46] To avoid clumsy sentences, I will typically use the vendor-client metaphor, but you can substitute the details for an internal-only, interdepartmental project, and our story pretty much works the same.

Here's a sampling of the many reasons why Sales Scope is not very valuable:

THE (ACTUAL) SCOPE IS FAR MORE THAN WHAT WE KNOW

The terms we use for these projects, *complex* and *uncertain*, should tell you everything about this. At its start, the project has a sort of Johari window of scope, including:

1. Scope we think we know, and really do (known scope)
2. Scope we think we know, and don't (false scope)
3. Scope we know we don't know (missing scope)
4. Scope we don't know that we don't know (hidden scope)

We've never seen a client even get number 1 right at the outset, and of course there is a good percentage that fits number 2. When numbers 3 and 4 are systematically explored after the sale, using techniques like what you'll learn here, there can be anywhere from 30% to 400% growth in Project Scope. A multimillion-dollar project at an auto company was canceled because the project cost went from $2 million (approved budget) to over $8 million during our two-week project scoping workshop. We didn't even finish the workshop. One day during the lunch break, our customer came in and said we were done. They would pay us in full, and we could fly home. Without their company having an appetite for that budget, further scope development was pointless.

GETTING TOO SPECIFIC CAN TAKE A LOT OF TIME

As in the auto company example, getting specific has the downside risk of a failure to even start the project or get the deal. Often, one or both of the parties can't afford to *not* start the project or are in a hurry to get the project going. In this way, it becomes more expeditious to only talk about the known scope. If you want to sell the project, whether you are a client or vendor, managers are disincentivized to explore (and expose) the many reasons why it will be ridiculously challenging.[47] That means . . .

THE CORRECT PRICE CANNOT BE KNOWN

The result is a very business-like haggle until both parties can find a number that works well enough to justify moving forward. That number is *not* scope. It is just a number.

- For the vendor delivering the project: the best answer when asked about pricing is "How much can we get?" They may know some minimums or a floor price, but the best pricing often comes from focusing on the value created by the project for the client.
- For the client: the buyer likely hasn't ever bought one of these before. Sometimes the actual buyer has completed a similar project with a prior company, so they understand the value and much of what they need, but that is far less common. Most buyers don't understand what they are buying, nor how difficult (expensive) it will be to deliver.

THE MARKET/BUDGET OFTEN DETERMINES PRICE

If multiple parties are bidding on the project, then it's usually a buyer's market where the buyer's procurement organization will often seek to use the minimum price as a lever for negotiation with all parties. Because of this …

THE MINIMUM MARKETPLACE PRICE IS OFTEN VERY LOW

We see this all the time in project deals small and large. Some suppliers will price aggressively due to a combination of factors:

- **Marginal cost.** The floor price is calculated as the cost of the people, no markup. This sounds crazy, but bidding at this amount is a decent "portfolio" strategy for a seller with other profitable projects and spare capacity, or a seller who wants revenue growth without concern for profit.

- **Penetration pricing.** "We'll make it up on the next project." It's an approach that can work but often doesn't. If you price low, you are probably underfunding a project that has a bigger scope than you know. An increased probability of project challenges (or failure) decreases the chances that this client will hire you again after they see the mess you created in the first project.

Sometimes market price is but a simple, brief conversation at the base of the plateau, as in this example dialogue between Angela (client services) and her client (Arthur):

Angela: "Hi Arthur, I would love to learn more about that new project! Thanks for letting me know about it!"

Arthur: "Great. Here's the deal: I have $600,000, and I need it done by November 15."

Angela: "Exciting. Let me get a team on it, and we'll see what we can do for that $600,000 . . ."

Arthur: "I'm sorry, let me say it again: I have $600,000, and I need the whole thing by November 15 . . . do you want it or not?"

Angela: "Um, I don't know. Probably."

Arthur: "Because one of your competitors calls me every Friday and asks whether I have any projects they can work on . . ."

THE POISONOUS POPPIES AND THE YELLOW COLUMN OF DEATH

As all the Angelas run back to the office with their verbal approval from Arthur, they pass through the part of the Plateau of Optimism that contains a field of poppies like those in *The Wizard of Oz*. Instead of making Angela sleepy, they instead convince her to craft a story to justify the deal that she is bringing in. Someone will ask, "Yes, but does it make sense?" Here all the Angelas of this common moment find a way to say that it will be okay. Or at least that is the only explanation I have for what follows next.

Imagine, if you will, a simple spreadsheet. Each role on the project gets a row, and the columns to the right show how many hours are needed for each role in the successive weeks or months of the project. Someone builds this spreadsheet, presumably after a brief, incomplete discussion of scope with department managers to get their guess (yes, it's a guess) of how many hours each person will need. From there, you just multiply the billing or cost rates for each role in the spreadsheet times the totals on the far right, giving you what should be the price of the project. Except there's a problem. The dollar number is more than the contract size, more than the budget.

We have arrived at our glorious moment of untruth. Do we walk away? Of course not. There are many ways that denial will manifest here and propel the organization into signing the deal. The one I like most is a yellow column to the right of all of that. Years ago, I saw it in two client projects in a row. In one case, the header on that column said, "Use these numbers," which essentially meant that those yellow numbers, though blatantly incorrect, would add up to a price that made it look like a decent deal. And in that moment, the project was doomed.

The yellow column of death will suppress argument from any department manager about scope. "I know you said you needed twelve thousand hours for your workers, but you only get ten thousand. Everybody got cut. Make it work." In the firefighter meritocracy, this edict is both a challenge and a threat.

You wouldn't be a manager if your brain wasn't saying right now, "Okay, yeah, we're underfunded, but what about all those great scope documents we have?"

THE MYTHS OF REQUIREMENTS DOCUMENTS

Our client landed a large project. They had even gotten their client to pay for a "discovery" phase in which they would explore and detail the project requirements. We were there because the COO of this vendor had learned to distrust the yellow columns and all of the hopium-filled assurances of the managers. We had saved his bacon before.

We started with the techniques you'll learn in a bit, but the next day, we pulled out the large requirements document, a hefty two-hundred-plus pages, to double-check and refine the scope that the team had defined on the wall. The document was working well, until it wasn't.

The team had come to a section, two-thirds into the document, which only contained blank "boilerplate," an outline of what needed to be written there but without any project-specific content. This was a document signed by the VP of technology of the client company, a large, publicly traded company. Shocked at this, the requirements manager insisted that they must have printed out the wrong version. We broke for lunch, and while we were away, a search ensued. When we got back, it was confirmed that their client had signed off on a requirements document that had twenty-plus incomplete pages inside of it.

Never count on people reading or understanding requirements documents. The only people who understood it were the ones writing it, and even they did not get it right. But that pile of paper got the contract signed.

Don't worry, you can use those specifications when you have them, but starting with them tends to shut people's brains down rather than waking them up. In the end, the other 180+ pages were useful, enabling us to be thorough in the team's work to create a richer scope.

Communicating scope through detailed requirements documents (and systems) tends to result in high information loss. This is especially true when using single-use documents that expire at the end of (or during) a project—they are only written once, rarely updated, and often not understood very well by the reader. Information loss can run as high as 50% between the author and reader if they are in the same discipline and up to 80% when read by a cross-discipline reader.

> Information loss on single-use documents can
> run as high as 50% between the author and reader
> if they are in the same discipline and up to 80%
> when read by a cross-discipline reader.

I recall a different vendor with a requirements manager who had worked very hard to get their requirements document under ten pages in length.[48] We had discussed creating a requirements document prior, and I was dubious that one would be helpful, but I relented, cautioning them to keep it short. We had the team read it at the start of the scope session, and one of the team members stopped after maybe five minutes of reading and just set it down. I asked why, and he replied, "I'm sorry, I just can't understand this at all." Ten pages, wow.

Just to be clear, I'm not saying you shouldn't do work on defining requirements while you are selling (or starting) the project. It will certainly help you think about and also justify the sale. And it will have some marginal utility in the project. But requirements documents are not the definitive descriptions of scope that many claim them to be. They create an illusion, a managerial myopia, that scope is already understood. Regardless of their completeness, their utility as a tool for communicating scope to the client and the team is quite limited.[49]

The client has tremendous power over project specifications but not in the way that you think. I noticed this when managing large projects where we would write a set of assumptions into the contract, usually a list of opaque (to the client) statements like, "The platform implementations will be rolled out assuming the client is responsible for all deployment roadblocks." Whoever wrote that, and I certainly wrote my share of these over the years, had no clue that it was both incomprehensible to the client (a client can't agree to something they do not understand) and effectively unenforceable.

The reality is that the client doesn't need to pay if they're not happy with what the vendor has delivered. Welcome to the golden rule of business. "I don't care if I signed off on that," they will say. "It is your job, as the vendor, to get it done. You don't finish it, you don't get paid." Contract assumptions, scope documents, specifications, and so on are only useful to the degree to which they are truly understood by the client. That's not something that usually happens on the Plateau of Optimism.

R.I.P. SALES SCOPE. LONG LIVE THE NEW SCOPE!

Throughout this chapter, we've looked at the work of the sales team, which often overlaps with client managers. Whatever their title, that person does their job of brokering a deal that starts a new project. It is an imperfect process, but the best ones balance the various forces and costs. I can hear the client manager saying, "Okay, maybe not as much money (and time) as we had hoped for, but how bad could it be?" That question does eventually get answered, of course.

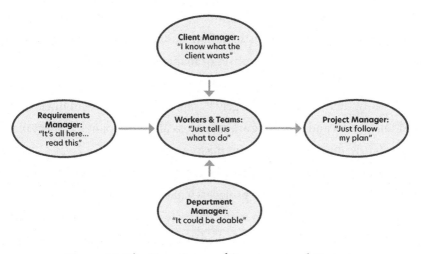

Figure 34: The Siren Songs of Overmanaged Projects

The requirements manager creates a large specification of sorts, which helps to bolster the client manager's rationale for the sale. In actual practice, the specification has very limited utility, yet the client also will embrace it, if only to demonstrate their own diligence.

Add to this that a project manager likely has taken that specification and built a project plan crippled by incomplete and missing information. These plans should have a tobacco-products style warning label that says, "Caution: the numbers, dates, and scope within these plans commonly have a margin of error ranging between 30%–600%. Use of these documents for the purpose of project delivery is highly contraindicated, and may cause project failure or illness."

"Caution: the numbers, dates, and scope within these project plans commonly have a margin of error ranging between 30%–600%. Use of these documents for the purpose of project delivery is highly contraindicated, and may cause project failure or illness."

But the existence of voluminous specifications and a conjured-up plan that matches the unrealistic staffing budget in the yellow-column-of-death spreadsheet sparks the onset of managerial myopia: *We must have it under control.* They all imply correctness and completeness, and almost universally, neither are true, largely because of a high level of uncertainty and unknowns and poor alignment across all participants. Project plans are *palliative* for the management masses.

It is for all these reasons that we must both celebrate the win and also forget what it took to sell the project—what you had to tell yourselves or the client, what you had to do to the estimates to feel okay about quoting a price for something that defies detailed pricing. Kill the Sales Scope. Dispel your illusions about the project plan: it is wrong. You have no idea, so just embrace the certainty that it will be very wrong. I'm not saying to forget everything, but just don't try to use the Sales Scope for anything. It will do you no good.

The good news is that if you follow my guidance and create a rich delivery scope, you'll have a more realistic picture of the work than the horrible Sales Scope paints. Yes, you will discover a much bigger delivery price and a longer schedule, but that ship has already sailed. You're going to live with the painful truth now, but you and your project will be better for it if you address it right away. Enjoy that glass of champagne. Tomorrow, we start the real work.

CHAPTER 14

The Distant Why

(Why Part 2)

Atop the Plateau of Optimism, a figure emerges from behind a tree, a Merlin-like conjurer, a wizard. The rejoicing crowd falls quiet. He speaks, "Your journey will be a noble one and much like those I have seen before. I have come to be your guide—to share what my legendary vision, as shown in this project plan, foretells. With me as your counsel, this journey will be, unlike so many others before it, a truly wonderful and successful adventure."

IT IS ALMOST AXIOMATIC that mere moments after a project is sold, someone conjures a project management document built on yellow-column calculations and disregard for the unknowns. It always looks official and well thought out. All but the savviest of managers who see it will feel assured that things are actually *not that bad* and feel optimistic that *things under control.*

We've covered many of the challenges that come from relying on Sales Scope. We've looked at the narcotic effect of various managerial actions in the sales cycle (on the plateau.) Fortunately, teams offer an even more powerful antidote for another of the failings of the firefighter meritocracy: firefighters can be quite poor at defining scope, especially uncovering what wasn't spoken of.

So, as touched on in "The Manager of Understanding," the best way to expand our understanding of scope is to start with the team. Since the team has not been involved prior, then they, and possibly many others in the process, will need to revisit the Why, which we at AgencyAgile also refer to as the context, before they can do an effective job on the What, which is the scope.

In this chapter and the ones that follow, we'll explore key moments in a four-step process for using the team to uncover the most valuable scope, that which is unspoken, unknown, or unknowable:

1. Contextualizing the project (the Why)
2. Building scope (the What)
3. Using managers to improve and clarify scope
4. Using clients to verify scope

At the end of this process, your organization will have a much richer scope and better understanding of the challenges that may arise.

THE IGNORANT EYES OF THE TEAM

Why would we not rely upon our "more talented" people? We probably have a bunch of senior workers who are either firefighters or have already been anointed with the crown of manager in recognition for their talents. Why would we trust this project to a bunch of people who are, well, somewhat lesser in status, and by definition decidedly ignorant about the project?

The answer: because it works better. You knew that was coming. Let's take a quick trip through the Why of that.

When I first started untangling why managers and firefighters get scope so wrong, I drew on some behavioral theory and research and then verified it by putting it into action with our clients.[50] The big ideas can be summed up as follows:

I. Firefighters are more comfortable with risk, uncertainty, and complexity.[51] This is a different orientation than most workers and teams, who are very uncomfortable with the unknown. If I'm looking for missing scope, which of those two groups should I rely on? I want people for whom leaving things unknown is very uncomfortable.

- Firefighters are more optimistic about how well a new project will go. Workers and teams have a more pessimistic view. In real life, we see this in conversations where managers talk about how well things will go, while workers and teams talk about what can go wrong. I think part of this is that firefighters are more confident that they can figure out the unknown or handle the surprises.[52]

- Firefighters are more optimistic about past projects, believing them to have turned out better than they, in fact, did. Workers and teams have a much more accurate assessment of past projects.

- Firefighters are prone to "shading" their assessments to be socially acceptable within the manager cohort. If you want to play on the plateau, then you need to play nice. They will give estimates they know are more optimistic than they should be, but they do so because they want to give people an answer that they like.[53]

For those reasons, the catchphrase of department managers and fire-fighters is, "Yeah, that should be doable." I want you to pause and really look at what is being said. I'm going to first push it a bit further and see whether you can hear what is going on. Try this, "Yeah, with Eric working on it, it should be doable by Friday." Hear it? Here's what I hear:

- It could possibly get done by Friday, but maybe not.
- Friday, unless we get surprised by something.
- If Eric is not available, then probably not.
- What else won't get done because Eric is needed on this?
- There are probably a dozen things that need to go right for this to be true, for Eric to have the focus, and for other elements of the work to happen just right, none of which are present in the statement.

The probability that it will get done by Friday is probably less than 50%.

Do you think that Eric would have answered differently? Maybe with those caveats and details? Whose answer would help you make better managerial decisions?

When we need to see what we're not seeing, we need fresh eyes, *especially* ones that are fearful and skeptical about what lies ahead. Fresh eyes reveal things that those who have stared at the problem for a while do not even notice. That's why having the team examine and elaborate upon the scope can be so powerful.

DISCOVERING THE DISTANT WHY: THE PROJECT CONTEXT

Most projects are conceptualized without help from the team. Typically, a project progresses like this: client needs surface, some discussions were had with some combination of business development or sales people, client managers, and maybe a firefighter or two, and then all of a sudden, things got serious, and we're hiking up the plateau. In most cases, the people working on winning the deal, having those early, pre-plateau conversations, are not the people who will deliver the deal.

Time can be a challenge as well. It is common for months or even years of conversations to pass before a project becomes a reality. The conversations and the valuable contextual information are typically lost (or hidden) from the team by this passage of time and the distance between them and the client. We call it a keyhole effect, where the team looks through an old-style keyhole, peering into the past in order to understand where this project came from, what preceded it, what else was spoken of, and so on.

Every organization is different, but in most cases, client services and requirements managers typically insert themselves between the team and the client well before the deal has closed. They do this under the auspices of "taking responsibility" for the client relationship (client services) or the client's needs (requirements). Most commonly, these roles become purely intermediary, meaning the team has little or no contact with the client.

The idea that managers should know the client and their needs better than the team—the origin of which may be exceptionalism or even something so simple as a false belief that they are more effective or efficient—is a self-reinforcing prophecy, causing teams to become more and more ignorant of what the client wants. Working in ignorance, they are forced to rely on what these managers *believe* the client wants and use frequent and inefficient inquiries ("What do I need to do now?") to gradually gain understanding and navigate the project and their work.

Often these managers can be heavily invested in the need to be seen by others as knowing and in control. This drive for factual superiority creates a breeding ground for verbal dominance. As illustrated in my personal vignette in "The Manager of Understanding," where I spoke constantly and authoritatively while delivering a less-than-thirty-minute briefing, any suppression of information transfer to the team will hamper their ability to ever gain understanding.

It is probably worthwhile to note that the intermediation of managers between the team and the Project Scope can happen for other reasons. One of these can be tied to the mistaken belief that Sales Scope documents are thorough and correct—why do we need the team to work on scope when it is already worked out and just requires supervision? Another challenge can be that the vendor organization has a way that they staff projects, and that approach (and possibly the project plan) doesn't really make room for the idea that there is a need for better understanding in a broader group that includes the team but also the stakeholders.

The unmanaging remedy is one you're now familiar with: team members must ask questions (rather than being told), and the somewhat amazing result is that a lot of new and missing information is uncovered. Managers are often surprised at the massive increase in information uncovered when the team leads.

As a manager of this process, you will need to be hyperaware of your and other managers' desire to be factually superior and that verbal dominance will often propel you or them into areas where facts are not evident. Here's what this looks like:

Client manager (CM) addressing a question raised by the team: "I'm pretty sure that what the client wants is X, and we need to . . ."

Me: "Hey, sorry for interrupting, but I have a quick question!"

CM: "Sure, what?"

Me: "When you said, 'I'm pretty sure,' does that mean you are sure, as in the client has told you exactly this? Did you ever speak directly with the client about this exact point?"

CM: "Uh, no, not directly."

Me: "So from what else do you draw such a strong conclusion?"

CM: (fidgeting uncomfortably) "Well, I feel like the team needs an answer so they can get going."

Me: "So they can get going in the wrong direction?"

That's harsh, yes, but the behavior, if unchecked, can lead to some disastrous consequences. The cost of early project mistakes is often compounded by the work this is built upon their faulty foundations, and the correction of these mistakes can be quite costly.

Be aware that the pressure is quite high in many managerial roles; the territorial claim to be "in charge of the client" implies they should have all the answers. That's neither true nor fair, of course, but the firefighter organization requires that everyone has control of something.

EXERCISE #2: THE CONTEXT (WHY) SESSION

One concrete step toward creating greater understanding in complex projects is rethinking the traditional project briefing. I don't like that term because it implies a speaker-to-listener exchange. Instead, I call this a context session because the goal is to help those who must learn about the project (e.g., the team) "draw out" the context with questions.

The term "context" refers to the many things that you could say about this project, without getting deeply into the details of its scope.

Here's the choreography, based on the Why technique that we used in Exercise #1:

I. **Identify your discussion topics.** Here's a list of some topics that you can use:
    - **Business context:** Why is the project happening, what are the related projects, and who are its sponsors?
    - **Project purpose and goals:** What are we trying to accomplish, and how will we measure that?
    - **Project approach:** What do we know about who and how this will happen, technologies, etc.?
    - **Risks:** What could go wrong, what do we need to prepare for or manage, what do we know we don't know?

- **Open Issues:** This is sort of your Andon cord for what needs to be answered, what is missing, what we don't know, etc.

2. **Your audience is the team and managers.** Most of these will be learners, the people you want to gain a common understanding. You'll need at least a few knowers and make sure they know their role.

3. **Determine how you will capture information.** I recommend that this be a physical (or virtual replica of) mechanism, like a wall, a whiteboard, index cards, or Post-It notes.

4. **The learners take turns asking questions.** Make sure you have a model to ensure that everyone takes their turn.

5. **Each turn a learner gets three questions.** You will have a choice as to how many questions the learners can ask per rotation—yes, you will go round and round. Always start with team members. Always. You can even let them go for a round or two until you open it up to manager-learners.

6. **Capture it where everyone can see it.** Write it on the whiteboard or a virtual whiteboard if you're online. We use Post-It brand sheets, one (or more) for each topic. Have the learners write their own answers so they take ownership of it.

7. **Completeness is an option, not a requirement.** Keep going until you feel like enough has been done or until all of the group's questions have been answered.

8. **Time limits can help, but beware.** You can put a time bracket on the session, for sure, but beware that the goal is transferring understanding, so time limits can result in incomplete scope or yet-undiscussed issues that still need attention.

At the end, you will have an "open issues" list with a bunch of unanswered questions and any other topics that need resolution, and for those, answers need to be found. This is something that managers can manage.

Once the answers are found, reconvene everyone to discuss and capture them on the board or wall.

Last note, resist the urge to "clean this up." The messy and mutually developed nature of this is far more memorable than a highly organized and sanitized format. Changing the wording in any way is absolutely forbidden, as it will destroy the memory of the discussion that surrounded it.

WHAT HAS BEEN ACCOMPLISHED

We have pried the historical-contextual understanding of the project from the clenched hands of the managers and effectively conveyed it to the team and others who were unknowing. This has several knock-on effects:

- We have removed managers' possessive control of information, enabling the team and others to make more efficient use of it.
- We have started the process of helping other managers break through the myopia that comes from the Plateau of Optimism.
- In the form of the open issues list, we have started the process of finding missing scope and identifying uncertainties.

The difficult path of driving this project to success will now benefit from having a much larger team of solvers who, engaged early on, can think about the challenges ahead. These clever solvers will be the foot soldiers in this battle.

After what is usually less than four hours of shifting ownership of some information, this project will run far better than a project that has not done this.

A ray of light emerges from beneath the clouds in the distance.

CHAPTER 15

Team-Based Scoping

(What Part 1)

The wizard waves his plan around, claiming it to be the map for a successful journey. "You must first travel into a dark chasm, from which all knowledge will come. And then you will climb a great mountain. Once you reach the top, victory shall be at hand."

A brave team member speaks up. "But what hazards do you see on this journey?" To which the Wizard replies, "One can never tell what the fates may present, but my map is true and shows no great challenges, save for those I have mentioned."

Someone in the team comments quietly, "Yes, but that's what you said last time too, and it was an epic disaster. We lost many good people as a result." Others nod.

You speak up. "Why don't we take a few minutes to capture what we do know and seek out what we don't yet know? Even if the wizard's great plan is correct, this would make us feel more confident and be better prepared for the journey."

There are three reasons why scoping with teams is a better way to do things:

- Their pessimistic eyes and strong memory of what didn't work well or was poorly defined in previous projects will enable them to uncover scope that managers have not noticed.
- The very act of building scope becomes an act of taking ownership of the scope.
- The act of constructing something together activates a prosocial capability in our brains, the magic of intersubjective dialogue.

THE MAGIC OF INTERSUBJECTIVE DIALOGUE AND ALIGNMENT

It's one hundred thousand years ago, and two people live on the banks of two different rivers. They don't know each other—they are each from different tribes. One day they happen to meet up on the banks of one of the rivers. Although they speak different languages, they find a way to communicate through motions and gestures. They both know how to fish, but they fish differently, which means they each have something to teach and learn.

Despite not having a language or a tribe in common, they are drawn to learning from each other. They will both get better at catching fish, feeding their tribes, and making sure their tribes survive another day, another week, another month, a year, a decade, a millennium. Through shared learning, they'll live on.

This ability and innate drive to learn from each other is wired in us, but workplaces often don't enable it as much as they could. Department structures, for example, separate workers, limiting this intersubjective communication and, in doing so, limiting the individual and group learning that comes with it. Let's add some "departments" to this story:

The tribe that lives on the first river is very open to learning and sharing. All its members like to talk and share information among themselves and with anyone else who comes along. The tribe that lives on the second river has no such desire.

The first river tribe members are so drawn to sharing and learning together that their innate fascination helps overcome their fears of competition, of being killed, and of being near other humans whom they do not know. The people on the second river have always been outcompeted. They learn more slowly simply because they do not talk with others, either inside the tribe or outside.

You might describe the first river people as being curious, but the truth is much richer than that. They want and need to understand something that the other person understands—something that they understand in their own way as well. This idea is known as intersubjective dialogue.

With time, the second river tribe fades into obscurity, unable to compete with the growing first river tribe. The process of evolution ensured that we all have a prosocial leaning, that we are wired to engage in intersubjective dialogue.

I believe we are aware of this at some level, but few of us understand its implications. As I illustrated with "The Handyman Solver" in chapter 7, we are natural problem solvers. But we are also very drawn to intersubjective conversation. While solving is something that many creatures do, especially primates, the predisposition to solve *together* and progressively integrate our solutions, is uniquely human and arguably the fundamental component of our ability to build tools upon tools and innovations upon innovations.

Intersubjective dialogue is not merely a thing that sometimes happens, but rather it is the core of how we create great things together. Viewed through this lens, a team without intersubjective dialogue is a team that is asked to succeed without access to its best superpower.

Intersubjective dialogue is not merely a thing that sometimes happens between people, but rather it is the core of how we create great things together.

Intersubjective dialogue is the best way to increase team alignment: the mutual understanding in a team of each other's understanding. Knowing where everyone stands is critical for effective team self-management and group solutioning. Alignment is what enables mutual adaptation, the ability of the team to adjust to changes, challenges, and discoveries, without high levels of supervisory management.

Team alignment is the mutual understanding in a team of each other's understanding. Alignment is what enables mutual adaptation, the ability of the team to adjust to changes, challenges, and discoveries, without high levels of supervisory management.

Teams, of course, need to become adept at creating alignment, but the good news is that this can be quite easy to accomplish because we are so predisposed to it. Knowledge workers are quite drawn to alignment from intersubjective dialogue as long as it is a game that everyone gets to participate in. We'll see this in the next exercise, which is all about helping the team develop scope.

PRODUCT SCOPE IS WHAT MATTERS

Scope has many meanings, so let's address some key assumptions and distinctions. First, nobody really gets aligned in the first place—not prior to the sale, not at the kickoff. The most important and also most basic form of scope is what the client needs and what they think (or we think) they have agreed to pay for. If we don't know what we're delivering, the climb up Mount Death March will always be painful. That's why we want the team talking about Product Scope, not Project Scope.

- **Product Scope** is what the customer will receive. It is described in terms of the utility or value provided or what it will accomplish. It does not include anything about how it is done, people, teams, time, resources, etc. It is just what they will get—a feature, a function, a thing, or a valuable (to them) activity. If you cannot break your project down like this, then you will never have alignment in your teams, nor among managers, much less with a large or complex client or stakeholder group.

- **Project Scope** is what it takes to get the Product Scope done. All that project management stuff: people, time, dependencies, and so on. Software Agile, of course, taught that it is far too easy for people to get carried away with saying *who*, *how*, *what*, and *when*, especially early in the project. When the project was sold, every-one focused on Project Scope because that was the easiest thing to assign a price to. But without a solid, aligned version of Product Scope, you're still on the plateau. The quality of your project plan (and Project Scope) is always limited by the quality and complete-ness of your Product Scope.

Beware of wizards with maps for a journey that is not yet understood.

EXERCISE #3: TEAM-ALIGNED PRODUCT SCOPE

Like most of our clients, this client was learning how to use teams to scope projects. Over four-plus days, the team had grilled Adrian (the client manager) and Jerayne, who had led the tech feasibility investigation.

Up on the wall were hundreds of colored index cards, stretching like a mural across twenty-five feet of wall, some sections of it so high on the wall that the team had used a rolling ladder to place the cards there.[54] Each card detailed an important element of the scope.

The deal had been signed a few weeks ago: $2 million to design and implement a new installation at one of the most prestigious museums in the world. Mobile apps, kiosks, signage, designs for all of the visual elements, even parts of the launch plan, were included.

The colored cards included greens, yellows, blues, and even some purples; our two thousand yellow cards hadn't been enough. But the remaining cards, the red ones, mattered most.

The red cards were what identified unknown scope—open items like missing information, risks, and other pieces that were not in the Sales Scope. There were a lot of red cards, somewhere between $600,000 and $800,000 worth.

Over the years, we've developed all kinds of fancy tweaks for team-based scoping. But at its core, scoping is quite simple, and because workers are solvers, there is virtually no training except to just explain the format.

THE PROCESS

Starting with a blank slate makes teams and workers revert to their natural thinking and learning styles. It gives them room to think.

Here's a simple three-card version of the choreography:

1. **Gather your tools: index cards or stickies, sharpies, and so on.** Use markers so people can read the card from a distance. You'll want different color cards; here's a starting point:
   - **Blue (story).** This is a deliverable that marks the creation or delivery of value to the client. It is a thing, a piece of functionality, or a service that you provide on behalf of the client. The client should be able to say, "Yes, I would pay for that."
   - **Yellow (criteria).** This defines a criterion for judging whether the blue card was done correctly. If the blue card is a testing report, then the yellow cards would say things like what format it is in, how it is delivered or reviewed, how many pages, what information is contained within it, and so on. Each yellow card is associated with only one blue card.
   - **Red (risk or issue).** This is what it sounds like: any question, concern, risk, or problem associated with a blue or yellow card.

2. **The team builds the scope.** In general, even though you have managers in the room, all of the cards should be written by the team. Beware that there are often dominance problems, which we will discuss just a few pages from now.

3. **Remember, you have already done the Why with this team.** If you have not done exercise #2 with them already, then you need to do it now. Make sure everyone has a copy of those artifacts prior to this exercise. If it has been a while, consider having the team walk through the results of that exercise (as a group) again.

4. **Write some blue cards (only two to twelve words per card).** Give everyone ten to twenty minutes to write as many blue cards as they

can. Everyone should do it on their own. They can also write red cards as well at this time. Keep the ideas simple, with only one per card.

5. **Gradually reveal them.** Take turns putting cards up on the wall. Start with two cards per person, and after a few rounds, make it four or five cards per person. I prefer to just have people put them anywhere on the wall. The point is to just get out ideas.

6. **Scope is bigger than just in-scope.** If a card being put on the wall is likely to be out of scope, then congrats, you have just defined some of the hidden scope that is out of scope. It's a good thing. Do not throw it away or exclude it. Earlier, I mentioned that it is the scope that people don't talk about that gets projects into trouble. That unspoken scope takes two forms: in-scope work that we didn't talk about and out-of-scope work that we didn't agree is out of scope.

7. **Dedupe and organize.** Once you have all of the blue and red cards out, take turns deduplicating and organizing them.

8. **Add the details (yellow).** You can divide to conquer with this one, allowing individuals or small groups to just walk around and add yellow (and red) cards. This goes pretty quickly in comparison.

9. **Sweep the details.** When everyone is exhausted—rather, when they have exhausted their cards—then you need another walk-through so everyone can understand the yellow cards and add to them per the process above.

10. **Time limits are dangerous.** This is typically high-payback work. We figure that teams get a ten-to-one return on the time invested, in terms of project average.

It is a long process, for sure. It works pretty well as long as you can keep the team driving it. That means you'll need to deal with the managers and possibly yourself.

MANAGING DOMINANCE

The team stood facing a wall of blue cards with ideas on them, each card taped there with a piece of blue painter's tape. There was no order to them yet, just a random cloud of cards, as they had just started the exercise maybe ten minutes before. Each member of the team held on dearly to the stack of five to ten blue index cards they had each written, awaiting their moment in the rotation to put up one card, a single idea that might be a good contribution.

Standing just behind them was Brad, an amazing talent. He had risen quickly through the tech ranks as the company grew and was legendary for his broad knowledge of how things worked and what clients needed. Of course, he was good at rescues as well. Brad was also a very likable guy, with a quick smile and pleasant style.

We had trained them all a few years ago in how to do this technique, a sort of variation on inductive grouping, where random ideas are brought together to build stronger ideas. The company's CEO had asked that I pay them a visit, as she felt they just weren't getting the good results that they used to from the technique. A lot of people even felt it was somewhat pointless and time wasting. Brad disagreed with all that, but he was happy enough knowing he could pick my brain on some other topics during my visit.

It didn't take long to see what was wrong. I was standing sort of behind them all, just off to the side of Brad, when I saw someone take their turn, showing their card to everyone, and describing it with a bit of pride. As they turned toward the wall, card already taped, Brad suddenly pushed through the crowd and grabbed the card out of the person's hand, saying, "There is no way that the client would ever do something like that." He added the card to a thin pile of cards he had already collected.

I watched for a bit longer. After a bit, another card went up, and though Brad did not take it down directly, he started talking about what the card should have said on it, then wrote out a new card, which he taped on top of the other card. I recognized right then that Brad thought he was being helpful.

The quality of the learning and insights within a great scoping session are entirely a product of how well you can suppress the dominant urges inside of the more talented (or more entitled) people in the room. It is a well-intentioned but misguided behavior, of course. Brad, a sincerely charming guy, just wanted to help the team. But he wasn't. Being a firefighter or just being a manager among firefighters seems to bring out a myriad of dominant behaviors. Here are a few things to watch out for:

- **Avoid the overlayers, modifiers, and summarizers.** As seen in our vignette with Brad, a whole host of dominant behaviors can come up in these situations, including:
  - Putting one's similar idea on top of or over another person's idea. Ideas should be kept separate; organizing them is a later task, if needed.
  - Deciding to rewrite someone else's idea "correctly." This is massively different from asking them when they present their idea to explain whether they really mean X.
  - Coming up with a summary/category idea that "includes" other people's ideas. A simple example is when there are already three cards on the wall naming different types of reports, and someone writes a card that says, "Reports," and suggests that the other cards are not needed. Meet the summarizer. Some

people's brains just work that way, often managers, as they are used to summarizing things. Summary-style cards don't add information; in fact, they usually remove information if they are used to replace more-detailed cards.

- **Hold off debate.** One of the favorite tricks of the dominant is to attack ideas early on. When cards are first presented, be sure to only allow discussion that expands everyone's understanding of the topic. The only way someone becomes great at coming up with ideas is through a path that often starts with not being very good at them. Don't cut off this learning journey.

CLOSING OUT THE SESSION(S)

This is where we start bringing much of the preexisting information and tacit knowledge within the manager group to bear. The act of the team *trying* to define scope, at this point, has activated their problem-solving skills. From here, other scope topics can easily be added and assimilated.

An important postscript to the earlier discussion on requirements documents: something that we have seen with some regularity is that people (especially team members) who would have struggled with a two-hundred-page specification at the start of this will be able to browse through the document, scanning for information as if they had written it themselves, once they have learned and built the Why and What. In some cases, they will even start correcting the document's problems. This is the difference between using a single-use document to create understanding, which I think they do poorly, and using it as a reference tool for someone who already possesses a good level of understanding.[55]

- **Only the Team Touches the Scope**
- Since we also want to start the transfer of ownership to the team, it must remain theirs. As you and other managers bring up additional information, or raise questions regarding the scope they have assembled, let them solve it and make the changes.

HOW TO TELL WHETHER YOU'RE GETTING IT RIGHT

- The team connects dots that were not obvious.
- They find problems, gaps, risks, and so on.
- They think of the project in ways that you wouldn't.
- Even the most-talented people in the room start reacting to other people's information.
- During the actual project, you will see things happen that were speculated on, and people will know what to do.

WHAT TO DO WITH THIS SCOPE

Through the process of you unmanaging the Why and the What with the support of managers, the team can uncover the Product Scope, a scope that describes what the project must deliver. The value is the uncovering of missing scope, getting the team aligned on the project, and having them take ownership.

With all of the information from this section, you can formulate the needed Project Scope:

- **Add internal Product Scope.** If it does not already include it, scope should include internal Product Scope—things that must be done in order to make the project successful that may not be a client-facing scope element. This can include a wide range of managerial-supportive activities like weekly status reports, project management tasks, and any project-end activities.
- **Estimate resource (labor) needs.** The team is the best starting point for this, and the process of doing this typically results in some further elaboration on the scope items, such as how the item will be delivered or tested or whether there is time for refactoring and revisions.
- **Perform sequencing.** This will also advance you toward a more

solid project plan. While this technically could be done by department managers with PMs, it's best if the team takes a crack at it. Having them take some ownership of project flow only helps.

There are many next steps from here, the most important of which is our next chapter, which closes the loop with your client and stakeholders.

CHAPTER 16

Client-Team Scope

(What Part 2)

LARGE PROJECTS, BY THEIR VERY NATURE, invite problems. The previous two techniques will help you massively with defining the Project Context and Product Scope, but with the dismal success rates of large, complex, and uncertain projects and the trials of Mount Death March, they are hardly magic pills. More than 30% of project challenges arise because of a lack of alignment between clients, vendors, and teams. For all of your scoping efforts to succeed, ensuring client and team alignment over the life of your project will be key. This, in the end, is the heart of the Why and the What.

After your scoping activities, the team will be feeling pretty savvy. Managers will probably be feeling more confident as well. But the Product Scope is not complete until the client understands and agrees to it. There's the rub because you may be returning to your client with a scope that is too large for their budget—a budget that you have already agreed to. But there is much more at stake here than just the money:

- You still don't know whether you have the right scope.
- The client probably doesn't understand scope very well.
- This re-scoping and re-quoting happened because everyone agreed not to get into too many details in order to get the deal done.

Because the client is the ultimate authority, they can say the scope is pretty much anything they want as long as it doesn't overly conflict with the often-hazy Sales Scope. They hold the gold, so they rule. Even when managers feel the client changed the scope, it's more likely the client is trying to fill in the blanks within the Sales Scope. Are they good at doing that? No, of course not. But what would you expect when they're doing your job for you?

As you know, clients are mostly incapable of reading some big project specification, much less understanding a lengthy GANTT chart. But what they *can* understand—amazingly well, in fact—is the output crafted by your team in the context and scope exercises. Those outputs are the key to aligning your team with the client and, believe it or not, winning their trust early on.

EXERCISE #4: THE CLIENT SCOPE CONVERSATION

Whenever the scope changes, most managers go back to the client with a clean document and ask for their approval. You probably know that sort of approach rarely has success, but with a potentially massive change of scope in the works, you need this win. Here the principles of unmanaging will work for you.

Recall all our efforts to shift control away from the manager. Who owns the scope now? Yes, the team. So let them own it.

Instead of your leadership team visiting the client and giving them a management summary, have your leadership introduce the team to the client and have the team walk the client through all of the thinking they have done. Have them show the client all the messy outputs of the process. Ask the client to bring in some of their team as well so they can all also get anchored in Product Scope. By now you probably grok the basic mechanics of facilitating a conversation like this, so I'll just offer a few tips based on role:

- **The team.** They walk the client (and the client's team, if there) through the scope, answering questions and fielding discussions of other new information. Give the team some prep time so they can choose the parts they will brief, and even consider allowing them to do a dry run with an internal audience. Have them position themselves as experts who are willing to collaborate: "We believe that we will need to make an X, with the following attributes. Do you have any thoughts or questions about that? Are we missing anything?" Finally, keep in mind the facilitation suggestions from the previous exercises. Give the less-senior people airtime. The more-senior ones can chime in, but only if needed. Beware of their desire for airtime, and make sure it is truly an additive comment when they do it, then ensure they "sit back down."
- **Client manager.** They organize the event and kick it off by asking everyone to introduce themselves. Then they present the goal of the session: to improve mutual understanding of the scope and create a conversation about what needs to be discussed.
- **Project and requirements managers.** Usually, they just listen. They can take notes if they want. At the end, the PM can present the draft schedule, assuming it has been adjusted per the team's scoping work or, explaining that it was provisional, based upon this session.
- **Department managers.** These firefighters need to sit back and let their people struggle and shine. The DMs can contribute to the discussion but only as a safety net for when the team cannot answer with sufficient depth. Then they need to sit back down. Yes, I repeated that point.

You'll want an action items list as well, ideally one curated by the team with the support of the client manager.

What is the impact of this strange interaction? More than a decade later, I am always still amazed by the results:[56]

- **The client is blown away by the thinking of the team.** This is the first time they have seen someone dig and think deeply into the project.
- **The client will start to think that they have made a good choice.** On some level, they knew that it would be challenging. You are already making the project better.
- **The client gets connected to the team.** The sales promise is an amorphous one: we will give you a team, which is usually followed by the client never seeing much of the team. A team whose names and faces are known can feel like a gift, and the process of reviewing the scoping artifacts promotes the resilient bonds formed through intersubjective dialogue.[57]
- **The client may help you solve the scope "overage."** This happens about half of the time: the client will either volunteer some more money or help trim back some of the scope.
- **The client will be more likely to "trade" scope when they truly need to add something.** In many cases, they have no idea how far their money goes prior to this session, and the conversation makes even the largest budgets comprehensible. With a better understanding of the dollar value attached to work items, they become enabled to know when to trade or pay for an ad hoc change in scope.
- **You will not be so caught totally unaware when things go wrong during the execution and delivery of the project.** And they will go wrong because of the various forms of uncertainty and risk. Your team will be better at adapting. Remember, replanning and plan repair are easier to do if you have a good plan in place to start with. Your client will also be more understanding and supportive.

CHAPTER 17

The Hidden Cost of
Project Contagion

IT'S FUNNY WHEN I THINK OF IT. I've always felt that getting a project to go well, or at least to avoid the disaster of Mount Death March, should be plenty of motivation to invest in a new way of doing things. Yet the thing that really sells people on our trainings and techniques, especially the leadership, is best seen by taking a slightly larger view—the portfolio of projects that a project-driven organization has during any given period of time.

Project contagion is the idea that because all projects in an organization are sharing attention, resources, and so on, they and their outcomes are inextricably linked. Let's look at the true cost of a bad project, the one that runs over budget as the uncertainties unravel into a seemingly ever-expanding scope:

- You "win" the project thinking it is ten thousand hours (according to the yellow column), but it was really twelve thousand in your first, albeit not-so-informed, calculation.
- That twelve thousand was a guesstimate, given how little you knew.

If we factor in some of the project realities that we discussed earlier, the project will probably consume fifteen thousand hours.

- Going that far over budget won't kill the organization per se, but it will do something far worse: it will kill other projects.

Ask yourself: if this is your scenario, at what point in time will your organization discover that ten thousand is not correct and then later that twelve thousand was not correct? How many of those ten thousand hours will have been used when you learn of this?

I ask this question of virtually every one of our clients, and the answers generally are that the "missing hours problem" will become undeniable around the time that 80% of the project hours, in this case eight thousand hours, have been used up. If we assume that fifteen thousand is where we will finally end up, at eight thousand hours we are (only) slightly past the midpoint of Mount Death March, but we think we are almost at the top. With a mere two thousand hours in budget left, it is now clear we have something like seven thousand hours' worth (or more!) of work remaining. Who will fill those hours? Forget the budgets—this project must be completed—and let go of the idea of delivering on time. But where do we get the workers?

Adding new people at this point is very challenging and almost universally slows down the project.[58] We will need to just keep our team working. Whew, okay, that's a relief.

But what of the projects that those people were going to work on *after* they finished this? Those projects will suffer from late starts, suboptimal staffing, and other challenges. And they probably didn't have any extra slack in their schedules either.

This is project contagion: your bad projects make your good projects go badly. In this way, even a good project, one with a reasonably well-understood scope and a friendly client and timeline, will get damaged by the bad projects. That's because managers usually scavenge schedules and resources from those other projects that can most afford to give them; it is the good projects (and good clients) that suffer the most.

Smart leaders and managers realize that very few bad projects exist in isolation. In the chaos of the project-driven organization, there's no better rationale for all the changes I suggest in this book.

Project contagion means your bad projects
make your good projects go bad.

METRICS

We're now in the territory of relying upon teams themselves to help diagnose the system—the many-headed managerial project organization generally has a more-optimistic view of its own challenges. Because workers and teams are at the core of the production function, they, like the assembly line workers in our TPS (Toyota) story, can be an excellent barometer for how well (or poorly) things are going.

Here are some team-driven metrics, which can be surveyed frequently (every other week or monthly) as a group exercise. We'll typically just use a ten-point scale for all of these metrics and ask individuals on the team to score the metrics one at a time, with discussion when warranted ("So, Eric, everyone gave it a six or seven, but you gave it a ten. Why was that?"):

1. **Understanding.** How well do workers understand the project and work that they are being asked to work on? This would include the Why and What, of course. Also mentioned earlier.
2. **Team satisfaction.** This is a ten-point scale version of eNPS. How happy are they with the project and being part of the team?
3. **Client satisfaction.** It can be interesting to see how happy teams think clients are—their perception will color their performance.

Also use a one-to-ten scale. For fun, you can also ask the client for their number and let the team know after they have guessed.

4. **Quality.** Workers and teams have a pretty good idea of the quality of their work. This is typically more useful than a manager's assessment.

5. **Schedule.** You can define this however you want, but it can have several interpretations, of which you should choose one. Here are four:

   - How reasonable was the schedule?
   - Did we meet the schedule with sufficient quality?
   - How well did the planned schedule match the actual?
   - How much did the work impact my personal schedule?

Capture the summary metrics (approximate average for each metric) in a spreadsheet so you can look at how the numbers are changing over time.

MEASURE YOUR OWN THEORY Y FACTORS

Y-style organizations tend to be collaborative and intuitively follow many of the ideas discussed in this book. Measuring your Y strengths can help show you where your organization stands—and how you can improve. AgencyAgile has a proprietary survey for this, but the basic idea is simple. Whenever managers and workers interact, measure whether they perceive Y-style behavior (revisit our discussion of Likert in chapter 5). Here's an example using the topic of Project Context sessions in chapter 14:

How effective are managers at ensuring teams and workers understand the project background and scope by conducting a high-quality Project Context (Why) session?

1. Managers only rarely brief teams and workers, instead relying on project plans and specs to guide them

2. Managers sometimes brief teams, or teams only get some questions answered
3. Managers routinely brief teams but not much of the time is spent on questions and answers
4. Managers always brief teams, and are insistent about ensuring that all information is uncovered, and all questions are answered

Keep the manager and worker scores separate—the difference between them is often one of the most informative findings.

SUMMARY

Section 3 brought us into a seriously complex real-world situation where multiple managers interact with clients, teams, and each other:

- **The need for different types of managers arises from project and organizational complexity.** Many managers come into existence as a response to chaos and uncertainty, but few ask whether managers are the best people to address these challenges.
- **Large projects fail or struggle most of the time.** A good portion of this, while not avoidable, can be remedied postsale using team-based techniques. The largest problems include a very poor understanding of the unknowns and a resultant lack of alignment across all major stakeholders.
- **Most managerial roles underperform in these challenging situations.** Client managers understate risks and inadvertently hide context. Project managers create scope and schedule documents that end up having a narcotic effect on rational management thoughts. Requirements managers produce reams of information that go mostly unread or unfollowed. Worse, most information in requirements docs is incomplete or created without collaboration with the team.

- **Teams can rescue projects because of their war-weary and cynical eyes.** Unlocking a richer context and a better Product Scope are key activities that should always be driven by teams postsale.
- **Aligning clients and teams through discussion is key.** If this does not happen, then neither of these parties understands what is being delivered in a way that will create a high probability of success.

Productive Flow

In this section, we'll move on from our focus on the Why and What Moments, and shift to the Go Moment, when things really get done. Key to this will be understanding Flow, the state of superb productivity. In the Go Moment, we can release control by transferring the planning activity to the teams and workers and also limiting managerial interventions during their working (Flow) time.

MANAGERS UNMANAGING PRODUCTIVITY

Jeremy worked for our client in Midtown Manhattan. He specialized in front-end programming, writing software that makes a website or mobile app respond the way it does as you click and swipe. It is hard work, and since it often happens toward the end of projects—when a project is running late—Jeremy often works late.

His employer had implemented our Why and What techniques with some good rigor and had recently switched to our Go model as well.

We were there on a Friday to check in with everyone and lead a quick feedback session to hear how things were going and see what we could tune up if needed.

Everyone put their thoughts on cards and took turns putting them up on the wall. Jeremy put a card on the wall that surprised everyone.

"My wife thought I had been fired."

Nobody understood what he meant. As he quickly explained, his wife told him that she was concerned that he wasn't sharing something with her, that he had been fired from his job. It sounded like she had brought this up in a caring way.

We all laughed as he explained. He had been arriving home uncharacteristically early for several days in a row. She figured he must have lost his job. The reality was that he was getting things done much more quickly these days.

In section 2, we could see in the CEDIA owner vignette, that the Go Moment was the easy part once the team had worked out the What using the Post-It notes on the conference room table. Now you probably recognize that they were essentially building their own Project Scope, the last parts of the What. Go was easy for them because once they knew who was doing what, they just went and did it—it was naturally unmanaged. But things are more complex than that in most project-driven organizations.

Workers in a more complex, project-driven setting almost always have multiple projects to juggle at once, and often that means multiple different managers. Each of those managers can impact the productivity of the Go Moment for many workers, even if they are not currently working on the manager's specific project.

One of the most important first steps in remedying this is to transfer control to workers in (1) the planning and coordinating of their work and (2) determining the time windows needed for them to execute those plans (that is, do the work).

In this section, we'll explore how to enable the worker *Flow*—the state of doing things fluidly—in the Go Moment. We'll cover how to use the stand-up meeting as a frame in which to do this and then, of course, what managers must do to ensure the promise of Flow actually happens.

CHAPTER 18
The Flow-Planned Worker
(Go Part 2)

TODAY'S WORKPLACES ARE FILLED with computers that would baffle an early-twentieth-century Taylorist. Their most startling feature is how they represent a major shift in the relationship between humans and machines. Whereas in Taylor's world, workers enabled machines to produce, today, computers are machines that enable workers to produce. In this way, in today's project-driven organization, the real "machines" are the workers. Let's better understand how those machines work.

The answer lies inside a term coined by the famous Romanian researcher Mihaly Csikszentmihalyi and later elaborated upon by Nobel Prize winner Daniel Kahneman. It's called Flow. If you have casually heard this term before, you might equate it with the idea of focus, like when someone has their headphones on while sitting at their desk, staring intently at the monitor. While that person might very likely be focused, Flow is a much more complex and challenging state to achieve. It is the fragility of Flow that confirms the idea that managing is the opposite of productivity.

Flow is a state in which the worker has everything that is needed to do a piece of work. This includes some set of intrinsic motivators, such as Self-Determination Theory's worker's sense of *ownership* and *competence*, as well as a having a plan for doing so, and the actual time, space, focus, and the necessary tools to become deeply engaged in their work.

That's a pretty tall order!

Part of the challenge of achieving Flow is internal, certainly, since we humans are highly distractable beings. But a large portion of the Flow that we seek for workers is often derailed by avoidable managerial behavior.

People who do work in Flow experience massively higher amounts of productivity and quality in their work, whether that work is corporate knowledge work or, in the case of artists and musicians, creative, artistic production.

FLOW ALLOWS THE BEST WORK TO HAPPEN

Csikszentmihalyi focused his research on what happens when someone experiences Flow. As a manager, your job is to make it happen. Your first step is providing your workers understanding (through the Why and What). Once that is accomplished, you need to enable and even stimulate the process of a worker creating a plan for having Flow. This is, in essence, the worker taking control of what they will (soon) do by anticipating it, formulating it, or in some way envisioning it.

The Flow plan is an internal model (plan) that the worker forms to achieve a goal. It often is a general plan that leaves things to be discovered along the way.

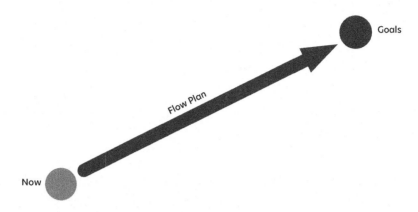

Figure 35: The Flow Plan

I don't know of research that discusses how to orchestrate Flow as I do below, but my work with AgencyAgile's clients and teams bears out its effectiveness.

The Flow plan is the worker's concept of how they will go from now to the completion of one or more goals. Here's a simple example of one with several goals:

Goal 1: Today, I want to finish the TPS report, get my dentist appointment rescheduled, and take a break from work and go out for lunch (which I don't do often enough). I know I have two things I should finish for Jason, and I also need to scan my old emails to make sure I didn't miss anything when I was so busy last week.

Goal 2: I think I can fit most of the TPS report in before lunch and also, at some point, call the dentist and wrangle up a lunch buddy.

Goal 3: If I have extra time before lunch, I'll scan my emails. Otherwise, I'll do them later in the day.

Goal 4: After lunch, I'll get going on Jason's work right away so I have time to get some feedback from him and wrap it up before I am done. Also, I will put the final touches on the TPS report and send that off before I go home.

Goal 5: I hope to get all of this done by four thirty so I have time to stop by the gym on my way home.

Having contemplated that plan, and being otherwise left to themselves, this person would be very likely to experience Flow. The key here is "being otherwise left to themselves."

Note that this is not a project plan. It is both more conceptual and more personal than that. It is the property of the worker.

The plan is probably not correct. For reasons we'll cover in just a moment, it is *highly unlikely* to be accurate when compared to the final work process that was used. This is okay, but it also adds to the futility of anyone trying to exert control over someone's day (i.e., project manage).

The overall goal (Goal 1 in the list) is where the plan begins, but it is not as simple as you think. But we need a whole section to explain that.

THE MULTIDIMENSIONAL GOAL IN THE FLOW PLAN

From what I can tell (and what I know about myself as a Flow lover), *goal* is probably too simple of a word for what it is. I use *multidimensional goal* because many simultaneous and interconnected goals can exist:

- **Process goals.** For the process that the worker envisions, there may be goals for *how* they do the work, both in terms of process, timing, and content.
- **Time goals.** Time is almost always a consideration in workplace Flow plans, so time may be expressed as part of the goal, as we see in Goal 5.

- **Optimization goals.** All of these factors may interact with each other because the plan is tentative, pending the act of doing the work. That is, depending on how one works toward a goal (there may be two solutions or pathways), the time goal may shift to be optimized.
- **Satisficing goals.** If the worker has multiple work items bundled together (e.g., what I will get done today), they may have interactions and trade-offs that are both known and unknown. Some goals may be tradable for other goals.

If this sounds kind of loose and challenging, you're right. But it is how most people like it, especially knowledge workers. Csikszentmihalyi called them *autotelics*, which roughly means those who are intrinsically goal-directed in their motivation. The Flow plan is a tentative set of actions aimed at a set of sometimes related, but also potentially morphing goals.

Csikszentmihalyi noted that the optimal Flow plan design balances familiarity with challenge or boredom with anxiety. Flow itself is a shifting dance through the plan, where an individual adapts to new learnings and adjusts their approach. Goal 5—"I hope to get all of this done by four thirty so I have time to stop by the gym on my way home"—is a great example of this, as it puts that extra little bit of overachiever challenge into the plan, which many find fun. Csikszentmihalyi would probably say this is just a way to ensure things are challenging enough.

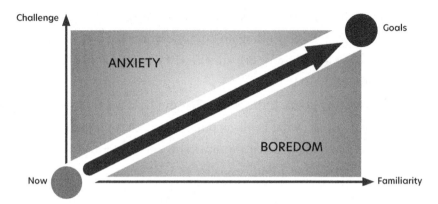

Figure 36: The Flow Plan Balances Factors

Goal-oriented Flow plans should seem somewhat familiar to you, as most knowledge workers already think this way. It's one way the handyman solver manifests within us all.

While the Tayloristic manager would tell workers what to do and when, likely to the detriment of Flow, the unmanager activates the handyman solver within their workers by ensuring they understand what the goals are and giving them a "frame" within which they can plan solutions.

Managers often interfere with the worker's process by going too far. Explaining goals such as deadlines, deliverables, and other versions of Why and What is a good managerial practice because it is truly authoritative, but telling them *how* and *when* they should do it is controlling. You may think you are a better solver for them, and the good news is you may be right. The bad news is that it will do you no good. Your challenge is to make them great solvers (and maybe accepting your feelings around not getting to do solving like you used to).

EXERCISE #5: ENABLING FLOW WITH THE STAND-UP

The stand-up meeting, a fairly brief daily meeting of the whole organization, can provide an amazing boost to daily productivity. Many people know it from Software Agile, but I picked it up back in 1982, nineteen years before Software Agile came along. I suspect the stand-up goes back about as far as we *Homo sapiens* do in history.

That said, most stand-up meetings today are done in a style that mimics the Software Agile scrum meeting. Most of these meetings are a mess, however, and much like scoping, they are misunderstood, and their key techniques misapplied.

The basic scrum format is that the team stands around and are expected to answer three basic questions:

1. What did you do yesterday?
2. What will you do today?
3. Is there anything standing in your way (also called a blocker)?

Over this last decade, we at AgencyAgile have fine-tuned the choreography of a high-performance stand-up. When well executed, it is a thing of beauty (no dancing required). One of the key components of our model is a format that induces Flow planning in the workers, both individually and as a group. If you can do this, you set everyone else up to support their needs and goals for Flow.

Here's how it works:

1. **Everybody attends, everybody reports, everybody is on time and prepared.** When done well, this will be the most important meeting of the day. When done really well, it will obviate the need for many other meetings.[59] The last point, showing up prepared, is very important: you should know what you're going to say before you get there.

2. **Workers and team members go first.** They are the productive core, right? Managers and leaders go last and must confine their comments to things that might immediately impact the team and the production of work during the next few days.

3. **The first question may be optional.** The question, "What did you do yesterday?" doesn't impact what we're illustrating with this exercise. We even have clients that skip it because they have Why-What-Go so dialed in that everything gets done, so why talk about it?

4. **The new version of the second question is, "What are you going to accomplish today?"** Clever, right? "Accomplish" is a goal statement. This switch requires that all workers state the goals they will pursue. That gets their brains working how they need to when creating a Flow plan.

5. **Be sure it is only accomplishments.** The problem with the old "going to do" question is that *doing* is not necessarily *accomplishing*. Partial accomplishments are fine, as in, "I'll get the first half of the TPS report done and send it to Jason for review."

6. **The new version of the third question is, "What do you need from others in order to get that done?"** This will make the team address the externalities they can anticipate before attempting to achieve Flow. A reasonable answer to this is something like, "I'll need to focus on TPS all morning, so if anyone has anything else new for me today, please wait until after lunch."

7. **Managers can and should ask questions but cannot direct or control.** Jason might interject, "Hey, I'm out tomorrow, so is there any way that I could get it earlier?"

8. **Managers can also express priority (authority) or support (empowerment).** Priority would look like, "Okay, thanks for the update, and yeah, Beringer called and asked if we can get it done sooner. Is there a way to do that?" Support might look like, "Wow,

Muthu, you have a lot on your plate, is there some way I or someone can help you out?"

9. **But nobody is in charge.** It is everybody's and nobody's meeting. Make a rotating roster so everyone gets a chance to be the first one to start.

This last point is at the heart of a broader application of the unmanaging style. You (or others) are entitled to be authoritative about the stand-up meeting, but the meeting is not yours. It belongs to everyone. The authoritative frame is quite simple and usually looks like this:

- The meeting must happen.
- The meeting happens at a certain time every day (or whatever period you choose).
- Everyone must attend.
- It follows the process above (or however it has been agreed to).
- It takes as long as it needs to take, but no longer.

HOW TO TELL WHETHER YOU'RE GETTING IT RIGHT

You can accomplish much more in a stand-up meeting than what the above exercise describes. In our trainings, we typically coach a group for four days in person with follow-ups over the next few weeks; like any form of dance, there are always additional aspects to be mastered, in this case, adding effectiveness along with the occasional elegance. Nonetheless, you will be able to get some good mileage from the above techniques, notably:

- Workers will start to create Flow plans. They will start thinking about what it takes to create a productive day.
- Workers and teams will coordinate through the conversation and shape their plans to work together.

- Managers and leaders will understand what is going to get done today. This is amazing in and of itself because this information is normally very costly to acquire and share. Even better, managers will understand the cost of distracting or interrupting their workers: some of the things discussed will not happen unless people are given the time and focus to do them.
- Managers will understand what they need to coordinate to resolve blockers, interdependencies, and externalities.
- The teams will be prepared to Flow and go, and everyone else knows what's needed to support that.

A FEW LAST TIPS FOR FLOW-ENABLING MANAGERS

1. None of this will work unless people understand the goals (the Why and What) of what they are going to work on.
2. As manager, you are only a "customer" of the Flow plans that you'll hear. Customer, not owner.
3. Oh yeah, and the bad news. You don't get to have Flow. Sorry.

On this last point, managerial activity is by definition chaotic. You're dealing with other managers, stakeholders, and customers—people, not deliverables. The needs of the workers and teams (Flow, questions, reviews, coordination, etc.) take precedence over your managerial efficiency. Since your most important goal is to enable them to maximize *their* productivity; they can interrupt you any time they want. Even if you are a partial or working manager (with only fractional management responsibilities), their work comes first. They are the machine. Keep the machine moving, even if your part is going more slowly.

By implementing this approach, you will have accomplished a lot of what it takes to enable workers and teams to really go. And we're only maybe thirty minutes into your workday. We're not done, though, because much can go wrong during the rest of the day.

CHAPTER 19

The Manager of Interruptions

(Go Part 3)

When I led Sapient's Los Angeles office, I wore multiple hats, and it often felt as if I was juggling many things at the same time. On a typical day, I played the role of group account director (CM), which involved monitoring and directing how we worked with the half-dozen clients in my portfolio, trying to find new things we could do for them, and on occasion, pitching a new client. Also, because of our relentless focus on margin, I doubled as a program manager (PM) for several of those clients' projects to avoid overburdening our already-scarce project managers.

But the role I worried about the most was leader of the office. I really had no idea how to do that, but I did know that keeping people happy was part of how I would be measured.

Most days, I would attend to my first two roles until 3:00 p.m. or so, when I felt a bit worn out and in need of a change of pace. On came my third hat, a sort of chief morale officer.

For me, lacking any better technique, the third role entailed surveying the office, walking around, and talking to people. A typical interaction went like this: I see Jonathan sitting at his desk, staring intently at his screen, and I think of what I can do to give him a fun mental break from his hard work. I walk up and stand next to him.

He looks over and pulls one side of his headset off his ear and says, "Hey, what's up?" His eyes flit back and forth between me and his monitor. I just jump into it. "Hey, I just saw Marla yesterday, and she said to say, 'Hi.'"

Jon just sort of nodded blankly and said, "Oh, okay, cool." He seemed restless, but I pushed on.

"So, Marla has a new product launching for the holiday season, and we'll probably want to use you on that when it lands! Should be really fun!!" I had sort of made up this one, as it was only partially true, but I know that he liked the work with Marla, and it really didn't matter that I didn't even have that deal signed yet. I wasn't majoring in the truth here.

"Oh, okay, that's great." Jon kind of smiled and glanced back again at his screen, which I took as a hint that maybe he was busy or even found me annoying.

"Okay, just wanted to let you know that and how much she liked your work. I'll let you get back to it." I smiled and walked away.

Mission accomplished. The wrecking ball manager strikes again.

THE KNOWLEDGE WORKER'S MIND

A good way to think about the knowledge worker brain and how it operates comes from the work done by Daniel Kahneman and Amos Tversky, as described in Kahneman's book, *Thinking Fast and Slow*.[60] It's a story of planning versus execution. Previously we discussed the Flow plan, a precursor to the actual Flow event. Kahneman's insights are geared to this latter part: the execution of work, the Go. Both Kahneman and Tversky agree that having the ability to focus is key for execution, but Kahneman puts a very fine point on it by describing how productive focus happens.

In Kahneman's model, the brain has two logical systems that support the two main types of thinking that we do: simple thinking that we use to navigate the world and deep thinking that we use to solve problems. He posits that we have two "parts" of our thinking brain, and he (cleverly) named them System 1 and System 2.[61]

System 1 comprises the restless scanning part of the brain that constantly assesses the environment and the situations around us. It is fast and can switch its attention quickly to effectively notice several stimuli at the same time. Many people believe they can efficiently multitask, and the behavior of System 1 is likely part of the reason. Although researcher Daniel Levitin likens multitasking to "ineffectual plate spinning,"[62] the fast attention switching of System 1 can feel pretty amazing in its own right because it can think of many things at the same time. I often notice my own System 1 mindset when I am delivering a presentation in front of a small group of people, say, ten to twenty or so, in a business conference room.

Standing with my PowerPoint slide on a screen behind me, I am speaking, reciting words I've said many times before. I notice people shifting positions in their seats, I see facial expressions changing, and I even notice events occurring outside thanks to the windows at the back of the room. Much of this happens without me looking directly at a particular person or event.

System 1 generally knows what's going on, automatically and peripherally. That's its job. Yet the usefulness of System 1 is limited because, frankly, it does not make the greatest of decisions and is very error prone due to its biases. For example, as I walk down the sidewalk and see a person walking my way, System 1 will construct a behavioral portrait of this person that is sadly lost in stereotypes and preconceptions. That person's momentary expression, posture, attire, and gait will all be assessed against a bunch of memories so that System 1 can quickly categorize and assign meaning to that person. Yet this person is still twenty feet away, and sadly, I know nothing about them. System 1 thinks itself to be deductive when dealing with things unknown, like a Sherlock Holmes, but really it is more like a loose-lipped cynic or critic who has had a few too many drinks.

One could argue that such rapid judgment would have been very useful in more primitive times, say, when walking through a dense forest filled with creatures both edible and deadly. Having a mind primed to restlessly scan the surrounding area would be a big help. System 1 is pretty good at doing that and at raising the red flag when potential threats emerge, even if those threats turn out to be false positives. Better safe than sorry.

You may have already connected these dots, but just in case, System 1 likely plays a role in some of our biases, especially in-group and out-group bias. Maybe a big role.

But searching for problems is a good way to think of its MO, and when System 1 does recognize a potential problem, it signals System 2. This is the brain system that actually solves things and where our genius resides.

It's where we think. System 2 is the slower, more contemplative system that thinks things through and is capable of more balanced decisions.

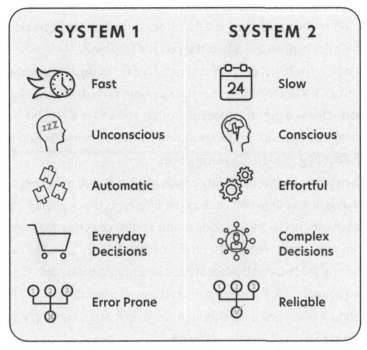

Figure 37: Kahneman's Two Systems Thinking Model

THE ELEPHANT AND THE RIDER

Imagine trekking through the jungle atop a ponderous elephant, your legs sticking to it in the hot, humid air. You wish to stop in the village you know is nearby, but your mount seems eager to lather itself in the mud pit nearby; it's been marching toward that well-known pool of respite for quite some time. As an almost helpless appendage to the massive strength of the elephant, you know the village will have to wait.

The *Elephant and the Rider* is a metaphor many authors have used to discuss motivation, emotions, and other things. Here, it usefully illustrates the relationship between our brain's two logical systems.

System 2 does the heavy lifting, as does the elephant. All the real work happens because System 2 did the thinking, the formulating, and the ensuring, as much as possible, that the answers are solid and correct. In this metaphor, once the elephant is engaged in a specific piece of work (e.g., cooling off in the mud), then it gets it done. Like System 2, the elephant's work does not happen quickly, but it gets the job done.

System 1, the rider, is a useful appendage for many things but not for getting work done. One thing that the rider can do is divert the elephant's attention. This is a gift that System 1 often abuses on a regular basis by redirecting the elephant in nonproductive ways, such as steering it away from the cooling mud in the searing heat.

When System 2 (the elephant) engages in a task with a clear objective it understands, it is in Flow. When the rider interrupts the elephant by yelling, grabbing its ears, or (sadly) whacking it with a rider's crop, then the work stops. The rider, in that way, controls the productivity of the elephant. The rider can give it helpful guidance on the task at hand or diminish the elephant's productivity by (constantly or repeatedly) distracting or redirecting it.

System 1 is dogged and, although not a deep thinker, is very good at interrupting System 2 any time it wants.

FIGHTING THE SYSTEM

Systems 1 and 2 work together, providing crucial functions that address the weaknesses of the other, but their interactions may hinder us more today than they did in millennia long passed. In the modern workplace, the context—the current topic of System 2's work—determines which managerial actions (if any) will enable a worker's Flow state. For example, when I walked up to Jonathan to delight him with some chitchat about Marla, his "context" was the work that his System 2 was doing on the screen, which had nothing to do with Marla.

But we're reusing a word, right? Didn't I complain about this sort of ambiguity with "project" and "manager" and several other terms? Yes, but in this case, we pretty much mean the same thing. The context of the work, which we also called the Why, is the frame in which the work is being done (the What). Likewise, we've observed that your managerial contribution to worker Flow (which is a System 2 activity) is best assessed by thinking of the context of the work being done at that moment. This even extends to other activities in the context of the worker's Flow plan. So, I'm "in context" when I interrupt a worker to discuss a topic that is being worked on or when my potential interruption is already part of someone's Flow plan.

Had I merely walked by Jonathan and given a simple wave, his System 1 would have seen a minor routine interaction, maybe signaled that he should nod back at me, but otherwise, Jonathan would remain "in context." If he happened to be in Flow, he would continue in that mode.

But when I caught (okay, forced my way into) his attention, the elephant came to a halt. It happened very quickly as System 1 signaled that something less trivial might be going on.

When we interact—and this can be via text, email, or in person—we experience a battle of focus. When we're in Flow, Systems 1 and 2 might be duking it out. But this war has an additional interpersonal dimension. When I interrupted Jonathan, my brain wanted his brain to start focusing on:

- The successful past work he did for Marla
- My appreciation of his good work
- His appreciation of me for saying good things about him
- That he might be doing some work in the future with Marla again
- His gratitude that I am working to arrange that future work

I was pretty intent! And how about Jon? I'm pretty sure he was doing what he wanted his brain to be doing. To some degree, my brain won, if only because I was so hell-bent on interrupting him. So how costly could that interruption be? As it turns out, people study such things, and the answer is surprising and complex.

THE COST OF AN INTERRUPTION

So, I visited Jon for about two to three minutes. How big of a deal is that? He has a whole day to work, so my guess would have been, "No big deal." Of course, that's wrong. The true cost is somewhat difficult to calculate, but in general, much of the research points to "strong" interruptions costing at least fifteen minutes of productivity . . . *after* the interruption.[63] A strong interruption happens when we force a context shift within System 2—that is, when we derail System 2 and set it on a new course.

How did that happen? Jon's System 1 was probably grappling with one or more of the following questions:

- What the heck does Jack want with me?
- Why is he mentioning Marla?
- What new project?
- Doesn't he remember what a disaster that project was?
- Were things better here before they hired Jack?

All valid questions, and System 1 can't answer any of them. So, what does System 1 do? It passes them to System 2, who likes nothing more than a good question or five. You've experienced this after a flyby or a quick, information-rich interaction. Try to get focused again, just try.

How costly is "Got a minute?" At least fifteen minutes, and that'd have been true even if I had asked Jon and he had said no. As I walked away, his System 1 would have started pondering some of those unanswerable questions.

Let's look at my awesome example of ignorant managerial behavior: I was walking around and interrupting anyone who was in the office! On any given day, maybe forty people were sitting at their desks, trying to get work done. Forty times fifteen minutes. That's ten hours of productivity that I was able to kill in twenty minutes. Maybe I should have just gone home instead.

Let's also consider Jon's day. How many more people were, like me, stopping by and interrupting him? Eight, ten? And would Jon get tired of that? Research says, yes! In fact, Jon will grow more fatigued with each successive interruption, and the recovery time after each interruption will go up.

THE BEST AND WORST OF INTERRUPTIONS

We all interrupt, but not all interruptions are the same, and not all interrupters are the same. Let's talk about what's better and the worst of the worst, which will set us up to talk about the needed managerial behaviors.

In-context interruptions have the lowest cost, unless you just count not interrupting someone at all, which is highly recommended. In our work, the lowest cost interruption is one that is expected. For example, that might happen when, at the stand-up, Ritesh mentions to Katrine that he might need to have her look at something this afternoon, and Katrine agrees to be available for that.

Coworker interruptions that are planned or in context seem to have only negligible impacts. Manager interruptions with those same criteria are probably a bit more impactful.

Once you drift away from in-context into out-of-context discussion, then it just gets bad. In our training sessions, we don't distinguish between types of out-of-context interruptions because we fear that people use any gradation as an excuse to interrupt; "I don't know why he got so upset, it was only a grade 3 interruption."

That said, it is probably best to talk about the worst of the worst. The worst interruptions introduce unknowable uncertainties, and at that far extreme is a little thing called gossip. "Did you hear that Jonathan was talking about it with Debra this morning?"

Gossip is negative information about you or someone you might know. The word comes from the Old English for godparent and referred to family relations invited over to attend a birth but who then descended into idle chat about other people.

Our System 1 survival mechanisms stay hyperaware of this type of chatter so we can protect ourselves from unwittingly being hurt or betrayed by someone in our familial or social circle.

When we teach about how toxic gossip can be during our Flow workshops, we hear some pretty great stories in response, like this one:

> *"The coffee and water station is on the other side of my cubicle wall. What struck me about your teachings on gossip is that I can work just fine if someone gets coffee alone. But if two people are there, then it is much more difficult—and even more difficult if they try to be quiet so I can't hear what they are saying. When that happens, I just stop working and wait until they are done. My brain is listening intently for gossip, yet I'm not really a gossip kind of person."*

This instinctive response to gossipy conversation demonstrates how a person could maximize their interruption effect by including some gossip. Consider if I had inserted this little snippet into my conversation with Jon:

> *"And with people doubting whether Marla is the right person for that role, it may be important that you, Jon, get involved again because she has suggested that a couple of our current people on the account are not that strong."*

That would probably wipe him out for the rest of the day, and as a bonus, anyone else within earshot. This most powerful type of interruption also creates ripples of interruptions inside the organization. Maybe Jon starts repeating what I said to seek out answers ("So, who do you think Jack was talking about?") or try to feel safe with others.

But even if you can avoid the gossip, you, like me, have likely obliterated your workers' productivity. It's not personal: the research suggests the most frequent and most severe source of interruptions in a workplace is managerial activity.[64] If you watch managers in action, you'll see that most are oblivious to this. Let's break the cycle.

EXERCISE #6: THE INTERRUPTIONS OF CHOICE

Obviously, the best thing you can do for your worker's Flow is to not interrupt it or their efforts to get in it. So don't. But when can you make necessary interjections? There are really just two different moments:

- When they are working in Flow on the topic that you will interrupt them on. This is more likely to be "in context" and less costly, but it is still costly because you are a manager.
- When they are not in Flow. This has the best potential to be low cost.

"Okay, Jack," you say, "how the heck do I know when they are in Flow and what their context is?" Great question.

RULES FOR THE MANAGER OF INTERRUPTIONS:

- **Have patience.** Don't treat your urges as more important than productivity. In general, your needs can wait if it means preserving someone's Flow. Consider collecting notes for most of the day and then choosing some good times to run through them with someone. Also, having a list allows you to "bundle" topics and create only a single interruption.
- **Look for the non-Flow moments.** The Japanese used to have a sort of business rule that went something like this: "Do not walk up to someone when they are sitting at their desk." Why? That is the most likely spot that they will be getting into Flow. So, what's left?

A lot of things. Going into or coming out of meetings. The start of the day or the end of day. Before, during, or after lunch. If you're in office, then they're heading toward the restroom—oh, maybe on the way back instead.

- **Understand their Flow plan when possible.** One of the reasons to use our version of the stand-up is you then know what is in everyone's Flow plan.

- **Recognize Flow on sight.** We were with a large client in Kansas City, and we had just returned from a session break when one of the managers told the story of seeing Flow destruction in action. Just moments before we all returned to the room, he saw a manager ambush a hard-working specialist in their cube. Stop and make sure you are not that manager.

- **Prioritize and narrow your workday conversations.** System 2 is also quite fond of trying to decipher vague information and uncertainties, and System 1 will pass them straight through for analysis. Limit your interruptions to topics of immediate and direct applicability: something that is being worked on now or soon by that worker (or team) is a good rule. Broader and farther future topics should be constrained to the end of the day or the start or end of the week.

- **Avoid the gossip effect.** Flow can be impacted well outside the direct conversation you are trying to have. Be conscious of your impact upon those who you are not speaking with but are within earshot. Be aware that the existence of one-on-one conversations behind closed doors also tends to trigger gossip reactions.

- **Be a gatekeeper.** This is what I used to have my PMs do—they were under explicit instructions to keep managers, regardless of their rationale, away from the team during peak productivity times. Or just report to me, and then I would come over and scold them, reminding them of our mutual commitment to worker productivity, and usher them out. Repeat offenders would have to come sit in my office in the corner.

HOW TO TELL WHETHER YOU ARE GETTING IT RIGHT

Here are some signals that may guide you:

- A productive day is often quiet. People know what to do and are doing it. At AgencyAgile, a few months before this book was finished, a new client called and said they wanted to work with us. That's nice, but it is quite rare—our sales process includes a lot of steps and works really well, but it does not include someone just saying, "Let's go!" at the start. They had visited another client of ours and seen how quietly productive the whole sixty-plus-person office was, and that was enough for them.
- People will be getting stuff done. Really good stuff.
- It is okay to ask how productive people are feeling. Flow is a feeling of productivity. We've added a metric below for this.
- People may notice "time dilation," a condition where one gets so immersed in the work that they perceive time passing differently. Often much work happens in a shorter amount of time than usual. The opposite can also be true when someone emerges from deep thinking and feels the world just went by.

METRICS

Let's add to the team-driven metrics in section 3 by incorporating Flow, which can be surveyed frequently as a team exercise or directly to individuals.

1. **Flow.** How much Flow time are people getting? Look at this score in conjunction with their understanding scores, of course. If understanding is low, then Flow will be low as well because lack of understanding creates a lot of interruptive activity.

Because it goes so well to the heart of worker and team productivity, you can also add follow-up questions to discover things like:

- What is the most common type of interruption you got this week?
- Who is the most-common interrupter?
- How many interruptions did you get today?

For your reference, the team-driven metrics presented earlier are listed here:

2. **Understanding.**
3. **Team satisfaction.**
4. **Client satisfaction.**
5. **Quality.**
6. **Schedule.**

SUMMARY

Section 4 was about the core moments of productivity: the Go Moments. Great managing comes from a mastery of how to enable Flow in workers and teams:

- **Fully informed workers and teams** get things done quickly and well, and they enjoy doing it. The Go Moment is easy if the Why and What discussions worked. Without a good Why and What, Flow cannot happen.

- **Flow is the target behavior and starts with planning.** Flow can happen naturally, but in a busy workplace, the seeds for it need to be planted. The first step is to ensure that a Flow plan can be structured by the workers and the teams. An effective stand-up meeting gives both of them a chance to share their Flow intentions for the day and work toward facilitating optimal coordination.
- **Flow requires periods of focus.** The biggest challenge to these periods of focus is the actions of managers and specifically the interruptive nature of a multi-project, multi-manager workplace.
- **Managers must limit and channel interruptive behavior.** This may require the force of policy to make it work. Chaotic managerial behavior is often the cause of unaligned priorities and massive interruptions during the working day.

Leadership Challenges and Opportunities

Alisa sat at her desk, her head spinning with all of the things that she needed to get done. It was almost impossible to keep track of. Before the meeting earlier in the afternoon, Ben had come by to talk about what was now a slightly overdue piece of work that Alisa had hoped to work on all day and was hoping to get done soon. Ben had given her plenty of time, and even let her develop the whole structure of it, which was one of the best experiences that she had ever had in her short career. But Nick, her department leader, had also been hovering this afternoon, asking about some of the work due later this week. Nick had pushed it on her without asking how busy she was, and when she voiced concern, he told her to "work it out." Alisa felt like she needed to show Nick some progress by the end of the day (or else), yet that didn't seem fair to Ben.

She wondered how everything got this way. She reminds herself that she enjoys working here, but some days it can feel like the organization is working against her . . . and itself.

In section 4, we focused on how managers can enable Flow for workers. One of the best ways to do this is to simply avoid manager tax #5, bad managing, which often looks like interruptions that break worker Flow at the worst times. But as organizational complexity rises and workers become subject to more managers (as touched on in section 3, complex projects), then the effect of one manager's correct managerial actions can be undone by actions of the other managers, who use less-correct managerial actions and styles.

Put simply, in a one-on-many "managerial fist fight" between an Angry Rancher and the Humble Gardeners, where the prize is the attention, priority, and precious productivity of a worker like Alisa, well, the Angry Ranchers tend to win. Even if you're doing everything else as taught in this book, the vertical, Tayloristic management style of just one or two Angry Ranchers can undo much of your good managing.

In situations like section 3's large, complex, project, a firm leadership hand can correct detrimental managing behavior by establishing a better set of behaviors and culture ("On this project, we're doing it this way"). But the more chaotic the organization, and the more it is truly project driven and burdened by a range of other complexities, the more likely that bad, top-down management by the few will overpower the actions of the many good managers unless checked by leadership. In our work with larger organizations that have a dozen managers or more that can impact any team or worker, the sad reality is that it only takes a few Angry Ranchers to obliterate many of the great benefits of unmanaging techniques and culture.

This is the heart of the leadership challenge. While managers certainly can start making a shift using insights and techniques in this book, a holistic implementation of anything at the organizational or company level presents a bigger challenge.

In this section, we'll focus on some of the challenges leaders must address to ensure that good managing gets a cultural leg up on bad managing.

Several themes emerged from AgencyAgile's 2023 analysis of past clients and their challenges. Our key insight regarding leadership was that the most important role of leaders is to ensure the creation and support of a culture of empowered unmanaging, both to enable an organizational shift in behaviors and, more importantly, to sustain it. This requires leadership's attention on the five different elements in what we call the "Culture-Alignment Pyramid," a framework that we use in our leadership workshops for understanding and assessing the gaps between how an organization *intends* to be versus the way it actually behaves and why.

CHAPTER 20

Aligning Your Culture

WHEN WE TALK ABOUT CULTURE, we again are facing a word with many different meanings. Despite being heavily used with much reverence ("Our culture is the most important thing about our organization"), it is also very misunderstood. Here is how I define culture in an organizational context: culture is the way the organization behaves in any given situation. It is the set, the collection of behaviors that *actually happen* inside the organization, not the ones we might *wish* were happening.

> Culture is the way the organization
> behaves in any given situation.

The dominant, culture-shaping behaviors in an organization are those of the managers. Everyone else, like Alisa in the opening vignette, largely behaves in response to the managerial behaviors that they experience;

managerial behavior is, in that way, the backbone of an organization's culture.

Figure 38: The Culture-Alignment Pyramid

Our coaches at AgencyAgile observed early on that leaders love to tout their organization's values, yet when our coaches look at the actual behaviors (culture) of the organization, the values and behaviors often do not align. For example, leadership would say, "We have an inclusive culture, where everyone's voice is important." But when we watched how managers behaved around teams in projects, we saw managers who dominated conversations, talked over others, and acted dismissively. The stated values (the talk) were not aligned with the actual behaviors (the walk).

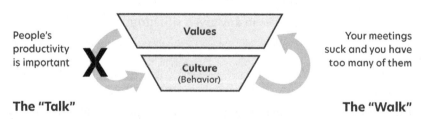

Figure 39: Actual Culture Overrides Hoped-for Values

This one idea illustrates an important aspect of the leader's job: ensuring that the promise of organizational values is realized through the culture (behaviors) of the organization. The key behaviors to look out for? Those of the managers.

If leaders want a values-driven culture, they do, in fact, have to put in work to make it happen. Do you, as a leader (or do your leaders), have a comprehensive set of values defined? Do they map to how those in your organization actually behave? A good way to start assessing the completeness (breadth) of your organization's values is to consider each of the following categories:[65]

- Our work
- Our teams
- Our organization and management
- Our processes
- Our clients, partners, facilitators, and mentors
- Our community and ecosystem
- Our selves

The next step is to address the most common challenges we see, which is a lack of specificity. For example, your values statement might say, "We are good people," but what does that mean in terms of behaviors (culture)? This is an example of a "Platitude" value, one which can be difficult to anchor in reality.

For example, how does "good people, etc." guide us when we interact with our vendors or our community? What is "good" behavior, and how can we know when it is happening, and how can people know how to do it?

That's why, in our leadership team alignment workshops, an important step is to create *tangibility* in the values, so as to drive the desired behaviors. Tangible values are easier to assess and less likely to become an abandoned or underserved platitude. Consider this difference:

- **Platitude value.** We empower each other.
- **Tangible value.** Nobody behaves like a jerk.

People not only cannot measure the first one, but it is hard for many to know what behaviors would make it true. The second one has a somewhat self-evident nature to it: we know what behaving like a jerk looks like and also know how to not do it. Tangibility in a value makes it easier to adopt and also monitor.

I'm always struck by how vacuous some organizations values can be in this regard. The platitude value above is a from a very large client that we have worked with over many years, where, sadly, we don't really have access to the people who came up with it. Once I understood how important tangibility can be, I found a new appreciation for words that can carry both sides of this, noble and tangible, like freedom or equality.

And values are just one aspect of the challenge of creating a great culture. I the pyramid shown at the beginning of this chapter, the three bottom layers are the "levers" in that pursuit: change any one of them, and it will generally change the culture.

That can be a two-edged sword, though, because unless you make wise choices in the bottom layers of the pyramid, choices that are aligned with yoru desired culture, they will choose for you a *resultant culture*, often not the culture that you want.

The third layer, that of the organization and its roles, arguably has the most direct influence on culture.

CHAPTER 21

The Chaotic Project Organization
(NOCO)

AS THE PROJECT-DRIVEN ORGANIZATION'S complexity grows, its operational chaos increases, increasing managerial complexity and the potential for bad managing to dominate. Examining this extreme form of project-driven organization is highly educational for leaders who lead one, but can also be useful for those whose organizations have symptoms discussed earlier in the book.

At this far extreme of complexity exists the most chaotic of project-driven organizations, which we call a NOCO, a naturally occurring chaotic organization. It is a special form of the project-driven organization where many different workplace factors are all running at or near their maximum settings:

- **Level of creativity or innovation.** How unique are the projects? How unknowable is the scope?

- **Team complexity.** How many different skill types are involved?
- **Client complexity.** How complex and unique is the client and stakeholder ecosystem and business model, and how many different types of clients are there?
- **Multi-project allocation.** Are workers and teams shared across a range of projects?
- **Multi-management.** Are there a multitude of coordination-type managers (CM, RM, PM)?
- **Client-team distance.** How removed is the team from the actual client and intended users?
- **Start-stop work.** Is the project done in pieces that can be delayed for approval or other reasons, breaking up team and worker continuity?

A good percentage of the organizations we've helped fall into this extreme NOCO category and follow what is often called an agency model. Typical agencies deliver marketing products and services, digital products, including software, or consulting services. Research organizations and more-traditional types of businesses, however, can often be categorized as NOCOs.

In a NOCO, chaos is legend. Executives agonize over vanishing budgets and margins, the churning of clients, and the roller coaster of staffing. Managers stress over looming deadlines, staff turnover, and the creeping feeling that if they don't push people constantly, disaster will strike. The productive core of the organization—the workers—struggles with a constant flood of unclear assignments, interruptions, and shifting priorities, creating days so riddled with meetings and vague communication that the productivity loss means that almost every project (and its deliverables) can become a Project on Fire.

Standing on the outside of these organizations with an unmanaging mindset, you can easily observe an invisible quicksand of managerial exceptionalism: the more you try to manage, the more chaos you create, so the more managers leadership hires. And as we know from Coase, each manager makes all the previous managers less effective and reduces overall worker productivity.

Their productivity loss—which comes in many forms, including lost clients, vanishing margins, poor morale or high attrition, and lower work quality—can approach 50%! Literally, the organization can be half as productive as it should be.

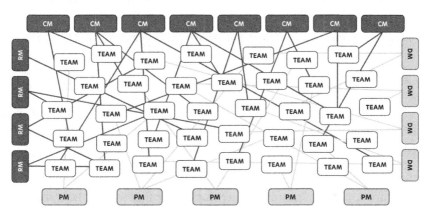

Figure 40: The NOCO's Overmanaged Workers and Teams

This results in two extreme organizational phenomena, one of which is the "spaghetti diagram" above, which shows the productive core trapped in a noodly mess of competing groups of managers, clients, "experts," projects, and timelines.

The diagram illustrates that the number of "managers" who can "touch" any team or worker can be quite large.

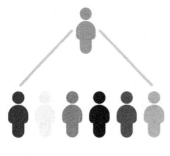

**Traditional Span
of Control**

**Inverted NOCO Span
of Control**

Figure 41: Over-managing Distorts Traditional (Vertical) Managing

As a result, we have a second phenomenon: the inverted span of control where a worker may have three, five, or even ten "managers" at any given moment, including department managers, clients, stakeholders, client managers, requirements managers, and project managers.[66] To understand the challenge of this, consider that each of these ten managers can believe they alone know the "number-one priority" for that worker. But who wins this battle?

> The bravest worker is the one who comes into work at a NOCO every day just seeking to get things done, learn a bit, and feel good about themselves, knowing that they will face the gauntlet of NOCO-based misguided overmanagement.

THE ORGANIZATION AND ITS ROLES DRIVE NOCO CULTURE

It is through this NOCO perspective that we can clearly see how an over-managed, overallocated workplace results in behaviors (i.e., a culture) that are not aligned with most reasonable organizational values. In the diagram below, we can see how the wished-for realization of the organization's value of "We want our people to be happy and productive" is undermined by the multi-managed organizational structure and the resultant overmanaging.

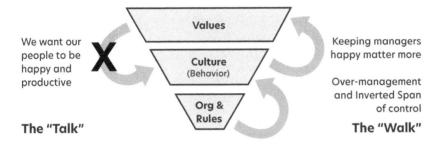

Figure 42: Structure Can Drive Culture, Destroying Values

But the battle for the worker's focus levies an even greater cost upon both productivity and worker happiness. Worse yet, bad managing and bad managers get amplified (and hidden). It only takes a few Angry Rancher managers to undermine the morale and productive capacity of workers, not only in that manager's projects but also for everyone else.

Working with NOCOs through AgencyAgile has given my coaches and me insights into these and other leadership-level organizational dynamics, but they exist in virtually every project-driven organization to some degree. The rocks are there, regardless of whether your water level is high or low, and they are making your organization less effective.

CHAPTER 22

Inclusion
and Diversity

THROUGH OUR WORK over the past decade, AgencyAgile has been a huge enabler of more diverse workplaces. We don't get involved with hiring or compensation decisions, but what we teach is at the core of a key principle: inclusion.

Diversity, equity, and inclusion (DEI) has been at or near the top of the list for corporate value statements for the last several years. Having had the opportunity to look at a series of proposals from DEI vendors, I am more than a little skeptical of top-down solutions to culture that involve non-actionable platitudes ("Hey, everyone, you need to be more inclusive!") or the outright shaming of people for what I've discussed earlier, our many forms of innate bias. Recent comments by key researchers in the field confirm what we have seen in practice: structural change in process can enable managers to avoid those failure points where bias creates negative outcomes.[67]

The biggest challenges in DEI lie not in trying to re-shape individual behaviors directly, but in re-shaping how the organization actually operates, its processes that then shape (or even proscribe) certain individual behaviors. The main leverage point for the organization is the third letter in DEI: Inclusion.Here's a quick overview of how I am using these terms:

- **Diversity** is about the social, demographic, and behavioral richness of the people in your organization. Defined this way, your organization's ability to achieve diversity is defined by a few somewhat rare point events: you have either hired them or not, and they have either stayed or left.
- **Equity** is about providing fairness in compensation, rewards, and resources. This begins with hiring, but more importantly, equity is supported by a periodic review (often annually or quarterly) to assess or measure people in the organization. Changes in equity are typically based on merit. Some research suggests that fairness in initial compensation decisions is a dominant factor in career-long wage disparities.
- **Inclusion** is about enabling everyone in the organization and encouraging their participation in the team. Throughout the book, I've used the term *opportunity* to describe this. Same thing. Back in section 2, we saw Eric the yo-yo master take on a tough new project—that was inclusion. Inclusion is what spurs opportunity for meritocratic advancement (equity) and growth in capability (as happened for Eric). Inclusion also spurs diversity of thought—workers who aren't included will never contribute their unique perspectives. Inclusion is what matters.

Creating and retaining a diverse workforce is probably the best way to grow one. But that requires your organization to both create opportunities for inclusion and see its benefits in action. In chapters 4 and 11, we covered the many biases that need to be overcome in order to level the playing field where manager and group preconceptions get reinforced through rituals of choosing the "right" or "ready" people.

THE OUT-GROUP TRAGEDY

Most managers and leaders spent plenty of time in the firefighter in-group. Their daring rescues and rise through the ranks put them in an elite club. But even if they work to compensate for their in-group bias, any lack of inclusivity can affect those outside the club. Research shows in-group bias impacts out-group members' perceptions of themselves. It starts with perceiving yourself as part of an out-group, a group that is contextually inferior to the in-group.

As you now know, if we ask someone in the in-group to compare two equally talented people (one from each group), they will perceive the in-group member as superior despite no actual difference. The ugly side effect of this is that out-group members *also* judge the in-group member to be superior, rating themselves less capable. The class distinction is pervasive and infectious. Consider a workplace where we create, say, an after-work group for female executives. The very existence of the group could very well trigger this effect. In this way, the more we create (group) distinctions, the more opportunities for negative out-group bias to erode team self-efficacy. Inclusion breaks this down.

As a leader, you set the tone for culture in your organization. To improve inclusion in the workplace, you must cultivate behaviors that reduce opportunities for in-group and out-group bias. Implementing the techniques for opportunity (chapter 11 and others) and mentoring structures (chapter 25) is where this can start from a practical perspective. Our other techniques, for the Why, What, and Go moments also contain similar forms of process "democratization."

Methods and structures can and do counter innate individual and entrenched organizational biases.

CHAPTER 23

Fixing Meetings

(Go Part 4)

FEW WOULD DEBATE THE ASSERTION that meetings are costly to an organization. Your workers certainly agree. The fact is, meetings tax productivity even more than the worst actions of an oblivious manager, and in the organizations we work with, they're the number one most-reported cause of productivity loss. Since their challenges are familiar, I'll use meetings to dissect the rest of the Culture-Alignment Pyramid and clarify how all of the pieces can fit together, giving you a more-complete view of how the "alignment" of culture happens whether you like it or not, based on choices made regarding each layer.

Let's start with a reasonable value to have regarding meetings: "Meetings should be valuable for everyone." That was easy. I think we can all agree on that. But it is rarely true. Let's explore.

A massive number of studies examine meetings and their effectiveness, most of which corroborate what people feel.[68] What they report is not pretty. In general, meetings are judged to be only about 50% effective—that is, about half of the time spent in meetings does not provide value.

Yet if we dig deeper into the actual cost and how it is distributed, we can get a better view of how meetings impact the effectiveness of an organization. For a few years, we studied our client's meeting effectiveness using a return on time invested (ROTI) scorecard. It's very simple: We asked each attendee to keep a diary for two weeks, rating how much time value they got out of each meeting and dividing that number by the duration of the meeting. The ROTI score is a percentage: a sixty-minute meeting with thirty minutes of value (for that participant) equals a 50% ROTI score.

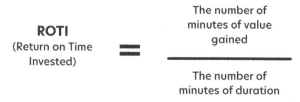

Figure 43: Return On Time Invested Calculation

In this case, the attendee defines "value" as the time spent on content or discussion that helped them do their work better or faster. Average scores came in around *20%–40% value provided*. Most meetings were one hour in duration, and it was not unusual for people to have three, four, or even five meetings in a day, which means that in four hours of meetings, people were getting only 48 to 96 minutes of value—a stunning loss of 150 to 180 minutes (as much as three hours) of productivity and value per day!

What we quickly discovered is that these scores are almost universally dismal. The data from managers and workers differed slightly, but in general, everyone rated meetings as less than 50% effective. Managers tended to rate closer to 50%, and team members rated it closer to 25%. That means that a six-person meeting with two managers that lasts for an hour would waste *three hours* (4 × 75% of an hour wasted) of team productivity in return for only *one hour* of managerial value (2 × 50% of an hour).

It gets worse when you consider Flow. Team members stop working for a bit before a meeting, and it takes a while to restart afterward. I would add fifteen minutes to each end, and when we multiply by that the number of team members, you get another two hours of lost team productivity. These should be frightening numbers, but most managers still think that meetings can boost productivity or are at worst neutral. They are not.

We found another interesting nugget in this meetings research: vertical meetings tend to have lower perceived value than peer meetings. That means when *teams* meet (peer-level discussions), the ratings go up. When there is a lot of hierarchy present (two or more levels of management), then the value of meetings goes down. This was also evident in the ROTI surveys we did with clients.

Here we have a basic culture-values misalignment: the hope that people would honor and value people's productivity is crushed by the sad fact that meetings are generally horrible at providing value to anyone involved.

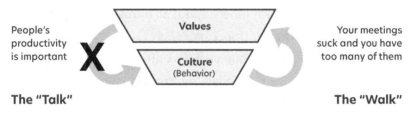

Figure 44: The Culture of Meetings Competes With Most Values

DIGITAL CALENDAR DYSFUNCTION

If you're an old dog like me who started work before digital calendars existed, you'll remember an era of fewer meetings. This did indeed feel less disruptive. In general, what I remember is that we would talk about the need for a meeting prior to having it, and this discussion would usually happen at a prior or current meeting. The *invitation* used to happen through conversation, but now, generally, it doesn't. How much difference could that make? Buckle up for this one.

With digital calendars like Microsoft Outlook or Google Calendar, there's newfound ease to roping people into a meeting invite. But digital calendar invites are a tool, and tools always have an implied process to them. As often happens with technology, its implementation shapes human behavior, when it should actually be the other way around: tools should amplify the aspects of culture that reflect our values.

Rather than gaining a person's consent first, today we find it easier simply to schedule meetings through their invitations. People's calendars fill up with meetings they never consented to attend. Now you may be thinking, "Hey, Jack, just decline the invitation." The problem is that now we have to explain why we don't want to go to your (stupid) meeting.[69] We essentially have to apologize for saying no.

I like to think of unexpected (or unwanted) meeting invites as an unwanted and surprise dinner guest who arrives knocking at my front door, wondering what we are having for dinner, and presuming that I will welcome them inside out of politeness. Yes, I should defend my evening and my privacy. But like many others, and as an introvert and frankly a nice guy, I feel I don't have the right. So, I say, "Okay . . ."

People face this same dilemma when confronted with meetings that impose themselves on their calendar and, consequently, upon their time and their privacy. And in most cases, it is a manager inviting them to yet another (stupid) meeting, and that is even harder to say no to.

WHAT MAKES FOR REALLY STUPID MEETINGS?

In addition to finding that vertical meetings are among the worst types of meetings, our ROTI experiments confirmed two key factors noted in other studies as making meetings worse:

- The number of attendees (this seemed obvious)
- The complexity of the mix of topics (i.e., how broad the agenda is)

To this last point, a meeting that tries to cover too much is said to be one of the worst meeting types. It even has a name: the compound meeting. It may be that compound meetings feel worse than they actually are. They can create low engagement, which means that they lose even more effectiveness. Single-topic meetings tend to do better in the same way that peer-group (flat) meetings do.

Clearly there's more nuance to meetings and meeting invites than we might assume at a glance, and this points to all the ways one everyday thing—the meeting—can affect an entire organization's Culture-Alignment Pyramid. Let's look at one with all of its layers:

- The **tool** is the digital calendar invite.
- The **process** is the agenda, date, time, attendees, etc.
- The **roles** are the meeting organizer (often a manager), who owns the meeting, and you, who must attend.
- The **behavior** (culture) is that the meeting is run for the benefit of the manager, not for the value provided to the attendees.

This, of course, obliterates the organizational value that meeting should be valuable to all.

Meeting Invite

Figure 45: Integrated Tools, Process, and Roles Creates Their Own Culture

Hopefully, this also illustrates to you how diligent leaders must be if they want to truly change anything. Small-scale attempts to improve meetings almost uniformly fail because they only address small pieces of this problem. But you have some options, one of which is doing a radical values-based reimagining of the whole use of meetings. The second is to find some strategies to reduce the need for meetings, and the third is to place some constraint on their creation. All three can work together, but the first case—the radical reimagining—benefits from a unique approach championed by Ricardo Semler.

MEETINGS ACCORDING TO RICARDO SEMLER

Ricardo Semler is a Brazilian CEO and author of two notable books, *The Seven Day Weekend* and *Maverick*. He is a successful manager, and his company, Semco Partners, is well known for walking the walk and practicing industrial democracy within its operations.

Semler states categorically that companies have too many meetings and that we need to change the fundamental rules behind meetings . . . and he did. His rules are really interesting, though definitely alien to the typical organization:

- Rule 1: Anyone can call a meeting.
- Rule 2: If you want to call a meeting, everyone has to agree to attend before you book the meeting. If they do not feel it would be valuable to attend, then they can decline.

In other words, a manager who calls a meeting cannot act as some unwanted provocateur, metaphorically knocking on a bunch of people's doors via email and saying, "Hey, we're having a meeting." They instead need to have a conversation with each invitee about whether this meeting is needed.

Now, one of the interesting things that happens when you do this is that if you have to ask everyone, "Do you think this meeting is needed?" then you probably have to explain why you're calling the meeting. In the course of doing that, you may end up having a string of small conversations that are actually far more effective than having that meeting at all, allowing it to evaporate off the calendar before it even appears.

By changing tools and processes, a change to culture occurs—we only have meetings that everyone can agree might be valuable.

> By changing tools and processes, a change to culture occurs—we only have meetings that everyone can agree might be valuable.

Now this evaporation-through-conversation process may work for some meetings, but there are others that may still need to happen regardless. But even these can be refined. For this, Semler gives us a third rule:

- Rule 3: If you're attending a meeting but you feel you are no longer getting any value from it, then you can leave. Bye-bye. Out of here.

This freedom to depart represents a significant shift in the power structure of meetings. In many situations, the invite to a meeting is as much a demonstration of tribal power as it is a functional element of workplace communication. By handing the worker the choice to attend or stay, they take ownership of their time and attendance.

This means it's up to the person calling the meeting to ensure it stays interesting, relevant, and valuable. If not, people can, should, and will leave.

This permitted attrition policy has double benefits: the first being the imperative to ensure the meeting has sufficient value to exist and to pay for itself. The second benefit to permitted attrition is the changing dynamic of the room when someone leaves. We have all experienced this in any group situation. When one person leaves, the shape and the force of the room changes. The focus and thought patterns change, and the event takes on a renewed and different identity. This can be extremely useful to the meeting's objectives, allowing for stringent refocusing each time a person voluntarily departs.

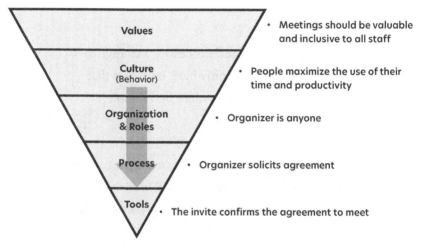

Figure 46: Values-Driven Alignment for Meetings

As his book title suggests, Semler is a bit of a maverick in his views on the value of managing. Much can be learned from him

DAY STRUCTURE AND THE EVAPORATIVE MEETING

One challenge with Semler's approach to meetings is everyone needs to actually follow these rules. If you're transplanting his method into an already entrenched meeting-free-for-all culture, compliance may waver since the rules and behavioral norms may feel foreign.

At AgencyAgile, we piloted a modified, distinctly unmanaged version of Semler's meeting concept with several of our clients, calling it the Evaporative Meeting. We did not constrain the creation of meetings like he did with his first two rules. Instead, we mandated a version of the third rule and a process for it. Meeting attendees would put their agenda items up on a dry-erase board upon arriving. Everyone would then agree on a "firing order" that would optimize people's time to value calculation. This allowed people to leave when the meeting was no longer relevant to their topics. In other words, when each attendee recognizes that they got what they needed from the meeting, then they can go. This turns large meetings into smaller, better, simpler, and faster meetings, and returns a sense of ownership to the broader group of attendees.

That said, it's often hard for clients to get this to stick. The existing culture was that managers wanted to run their own meetings and were allowed to. While some would try it, eventually people just reverted to what they knew best. What we have found to be more helpful is a stronger policy stance, which we implement through a workshop and process called Day Structure. Here's the basic outline:

- From a worker perspective, days are typically filled with a random mix of interruptions and, in their worst form, meetings.
- Usually this reflects a lack of policy on how and when interruptions and meetings should happen. Hence, they proliferate, and the day is noisy or, said another way, lacking in quiet time.
- Most organizations with some awareness of this problem implement "quiet times," but these generally have limited success.
- We implement a policy model that has a structure for the workday, Day Structure. The cornerstone of this policy is to solve the quiet time challenge by prescribing certain "noisy times," the times during which most of the random conversations should happen.
- When we conduct our Day Structure workshop, which assesses and optimizes all existing meetings and types of meetings that will happen during the week, we typically see that at least half of the meetings get optimized out of existence. Often there are obvious

other ways to accomplish the same function; some meetings really shouldn't be meetings.

Yet even when this works, there is always a need be vigilant in the fight against "meeting creep." All of this comes down to a question of how we counterbalance the ease with which someone can interrupt or otherwise destroy the productivity of another by simply sending a meeting invite—an activity that is relatively inexpensive for the perpetrator but costly to others and the organization as a whole.

A third approach to meetings is to just require that all meetings getapproved in advance by some sort of meeting executioner function, whose goal is to counterbalance the ease with which meetings get formed.

Any of these solutions would need to be, as was the case with Semler's changes, leader driven rather than the renegade act of a small set of managers.

CHAPTER 24

Mistaken Metrics
and Tools

Angela walks out of her project review meeting with the CFO, feeling like a failure. Her client's projects are all out of control, showing 5%–15% percent overages every week. She wonders, "How is it that, as hard as I try, I can't get people to stick to the plan?"

She walks up to Josh, who is at his desk with headphones on and engrossed in his work. He's a medium-level rebel to her well-crafted project plans, but one of their most talented designers. She and Josh started on the same day a few years ago, and for a long time, they jokingly referred to each other as "classmates at the asylum." But lately things have been more strained between them, with laughs few and far between.

"Hey, Josh, do you have a few minutes to talk about the Uomo Kitchens project?"

"Uh, oh, oh sure," he says, setting his headphones down.

She gets right to the point. "I know you're working hard all of the time, but I just don't understand why you keep taking longer than planned on this account?" Josh just blinks, so she continues, "Like last week, the revisions to the design were planned at six hours, and you came in at eight, that's like 33% over. How could that be?"

Josh looks down at the desk and thinks about how to answer. "I don't know, really. I tried, but that's how long it took."

"I know how long it took," snaps Angela. "I just had the CFO reminding me of that, along with ten other pieces of work that all went over budget."

They stare at each other for a second, and Angela continues, "I'm just trying to figure out what I need to do for you to come in on budget, for everyone to come in on budget."

Josh looks down again, somewhat ashamed, and says, "I don't know. I'm sorry, but I don't know what's going on. I'm doing my best."

Angela walks away.

TODAY'S ESTIMATES ARE NOT YESTERDAY'S TIME STANDARDS

Be careful of what you measure and the tool with which you do it. Much of what passes for managerial measurement—and this is a leadership policy question for your organization—is often arcane and applies poorly or not at all in modern knowledge worker workplaces, especially project-driven organizations and NOCOs.

At the heart of Taylorism are *time standards*: a way of measuring the worker that sat between the machines, essentially measuring whether that person could keep up with the machines. In our Culture-Alignment Pyramid, time standards are in the tool layer.

Taylor's numbers were useful, though at times their "enforcement" was degrading or even brutal. But the numbers did reflect a reasonable expectation of what a capable worker should be able to produce (e.g., two hundred widgets per hour). The time standard was typically empirical, based on "scientific" observation of a repetitive process. When a human works between a machine on the left and a machine on the right, there are a limited number of things that can or should be done between the two. In Taylor's era, this performance goal made sense. But not these days.

In the vignette above, Angela's question seems reasonable from a Tayloristic perspective of optimizing the people between the machines: "Why can't you achieve the time standard that I expected from you?" But here's where we hit a fork in the road, actually two forks: Was the time standard correct, and what is to be done about it?

But when we're working in a project-driven organization—where much of the work is unique, the workplace itself may be a bit complex and chaotic, we're doing something for someone we've never worked for before, and the team may be new. The equivalent in Taylor's day would be that the machines that the worker sits between are constantly changing. So, where do we get empirical, scientifically derived numbers?

There are none. We have only *estimates*, and estimates are not, in most project-driven organizations, remotely anything like a time standard.

There can be no time standard for work that is nonrepetitive. Estimates are not time standards.

We must then abandon the question that Frederik Taylor and Angela asked: "How do we make humans perform to the numbers?" Instead, we need a new and better question: "What are the best ways to judge how we are doing and assess what can go better?" Add to that, "And what do the numbers really tell us?"

In a project-driven organization, any numbers around productivity can only ever be rough guesses. The subjective nature of many types of knowledge work makes standardization extremely difficult. How long does it take to write a report? How long does it take to respond to an email? How long should a meeting be? It would be not only easy but also very accurate to answer each of these with a shrug. "It depends," isn't just valid, it's the most correct.

SHIFTING THE BLAME TO ESTIMATES

Angela confronted Josh with two numbers, an estimate of six hours and his actual time of eight hours. Let's dig deeply into these numbers.

Where did the estimate of six hours come from? Most often, it is either made by a PM or a senior expert (more senior than the worker performing the work). As you know now, both tend to be inaccurate because of missing information and optimism. The PM may have used some data from past work that seemed similar. But "similar" does not equal "the same."

Even if we assume Angela's estimate was not just a guess (which would be worse) but instead an average number, we're not much better off. Averages tell you nothing about any given number. Choose a random number between one and one hundred, and repeat that one hundred times. Your average will be around fifty, but few of the individual numbers will likely be anywhere close to it. In that same way, averages in knowledge work are somewhat useless because there are so many other contextual aspects to the work.

Managers tend to dismiss these contextual aspects, though they can have a great impact. Is the client the same? Is the worker the same? Is the other work being asked of the worker the same? Knowledge workers do not sit in a controlled setting like Taylor's workers, wedged between the same two machines making the same two parts over and over.

- Even if a manager accepts all of the above objections, they might be lured into thinking those estimates, though perhaps flawed, provide a "goal" for the worker to aim for. They're a way to ask, "Could Josh get it done in six hours?" Yet the answer ("No, it would take eight hours") is often not treated as the pure information that it is. Instead, it's a failure on Josh's part; Josh has failed as a worker to meet the time standard.

The estimate is merely a guess, and as we know from exploring project success rates, often a somewhat bad one.

LET'S LABEL OUR GUESSES CORRECTLY

So here's the shift: in Taylorism, the time standard is a correct number that has been proven. In project driven work, the *actual* is the correct number, and its proof is reflected by what happened. The estimate is the guesstimate.

This shifts the conversation from why workers are not performing to why our estimators did not do better. Why did they think it would take that long? Why did they not factor in the uncertainties, the unknowability, and the risks?

Usually, the answer is because that is a lot harder than just making a wish and hoping it will come true. And the correct form of an estimate is something many managers do not feel brave enough to use, often out of Tayloristic paranoia that workers are prone to laziness and shirking.

The "correct" estimate for Josh's work was probably something like "somewhere between five and nine hours, depending upon several factors that we have little control over."

The number six comes from a very optimistic view of the world. Often it is said like this: "Josh should be able to get it done in six hours. It is doable."

That last word is the clue. What's left off is the rest of the sentence: "Unless something comes up that we didn't think about, or it is harder than we thought." The missing piece is including probability in the number: "There is a 25% chance that Josh can get it done in six hours, so let's hope for that." Management by hope.

Inside this example of an incorrectly used tool and process (time standards and actuals) is a lost and confused manager who makes noise about incorrect information, taxing the attention of the organization with a flawed idea and driving lower morale in workers. Meet today's timekeeper manager. So severe is this influence of Taylorism that project management systems and timesheet/timecard systems reinforce this illusion of precise, time-standards-based control while destroying morale and causing perverse behaviors.

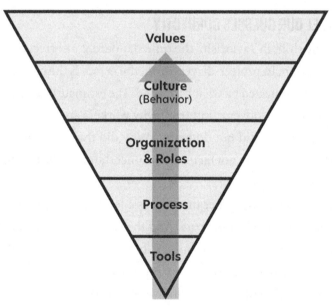

Figure 47: Tayloristic Tools Drive Tayloristic Values

THE TAYLORISTIC WORLD OF WORKFLOW MANAGEMENT SYSTEMS

Imagine Josh had to use a timesheet system showing he had six hours to do that job. Knowing that Angela might come see him about exceeding those hours, what number is Josh most likely going to enter on his timesheet, even if it took him eight hours to do the work? Six.

Josh resorts to lying to avoid an unpleasant conversation with Angela.

Hidden in this story is another lost reality: the odds that it takes *exactly* six hours to do some ad hoc project work is very low, maybe 10%. It may be close, like 5.5 hours or 7.25 hours, but we'll never learn that because once Josh understands this game, he will lie in both directions. If a job comes in with six hours allocated yet turns out to be very simple, Josh will also enter six into the timesheet. Why? Because if he enters four, then the next time, he may be allocated less than six hours for the work, and it might require more than that.

Tragically, the lies Josh is enticed to make give credibility to the bad estimates, a false validation that estimates work when, in fact, they do not, further perpetuating their legitimacy.

This gets even darker. Consider how Josh might react to the range of managerial behaviors that Angela might employ? If Angela is more severe (Tayloristic) in her reaction to his timecards, will he be more prone to lying? Does this lead Angela to a self-reinforcing behavior, where her desire to demonstrate prowess at forming estimates reinforces negative behavior toward Josh's truth-telling on a timecard?

DOES WORK FLOW WITH A WORKFLOW SYSTEM?

There are legions of workflow management systems out there, and we've seen and worked with most of them at AgencyAgile. Our conclusion: if you're trying to do what is taught in this book, a workflow management system, while useful in some ways, is a very mixed bag. It can lead you down paths like the ones we discussed earlier in this chapter.

In 2015, two articles, one written by me,[70] shared a message better stated by the title of the latter article: *Digital Taylorism.*[71] Workflow management systems use a production control model taken from factory automation. And if those words don't scare you enough, read on.

One of the great tragedies of software automation is feature bloat, which causes tools that promise productivity improvements to end up killing productivity, make process management more costly, and as you might guess, require more managers.

Feature bloat occurs when a basic software tool (like a simple workflow tool) enters the marketplace. Whereas it may have been built simply and elegantly to perform its basic functions, when it enters the world of software competition, market pressures cause the software manufacturer to engage in a seemingly endless set of feature additions. This happens because companies buying software tend to think that more features are better. After all, their competitors will certainly claim that to be true. Eventually, you have bloated software, one with so many features that it can do anything, and people blithely implement a lot of those features.

A long-known principle of software design is that the more features a piece of software has, the less people will be able to use it. The more complex the features are, the fewer people will understand how it works or even how to access it. And while software may make some aspects of what some people call managing easier, it does not necessarily make for better managing.

About 70%–80% of our clients implemented workflow management systems prior to working with us, and most of them were not happy with them. A large percentage of those were on their second or third system. To the best of my knowledge, none of those systems reduced their need for managers.

That said, we've seen (and helped) a good number of clients shift their whole way of thinking away from these false metrics (How many hours did Josh go over budget this week?[72]) to a better set of metrics.

One approach that seems to work well is to reduce the granularity of timekeeping, ignoring detailed task estimates, and shifting to a weekly or even monthly summary number per client. At the end of the day, this number lines up a bit better with another number you have: how much you charged the client that month. From there, you get a straight answer to the question, "How much did it cost us to deliver what the client paid for?"

A bonus to this sort of approach is that timecards are almost as despised as meetings in project-driven organizations, so you'll probably make some friends (and improve your culture) if you make shifts in both of these areas.

CHAPTER 25

The Mentoring Organization

(Grow Part 3)

Dan runs a great shop in one of the Melbourne, Australia, suburbs with a thirty-person design and technology team. He has no managers. His team members do not carry titles. They are all very happy and work collaboratively. When they decide to leave Dan's company, Dan says they can give themselves whatever title they want on their resume.

IN OUR VIGNETTE, Dan's organization has little use for titles, managers, and hierarchy. In reality, they can all be discarded, and often the organization runs no worse and can even run better.

For some reason, we conflate the hierarchy of the org chart with power, control, superiority of being, and class, to name a few. Collectively, we like these distinctions, and yet they divide us. It rewards a few and punishes the rest. You may have noticed that your workers or team members get a little preoccupied with using the idea of climbing the organizational pyramid as a way to measure accomplishment.

In that way, the organizational pyramid itself has become a problem, a metaphorical managerial garage filled with an odd assortment of activities and attributes that are there for no other good reason than it's a convenient place to put them:

- Seniority
- Skill level
- Managerial responsibility
- Span of control (how many people under you)
- Performance reviews
- Skills development
- Goal setting
- Discipline

This conflation has its conveniences, but it causes way more problems than the benefits this convenience suggests.[73]

Your organization's structure reflects and greatly impacts the behaviors and norms of the workplace—that is, its culture. It can encourage overmanaging, firefighter meritocracies, endless days of meetings, and relentless time-tracking—but the opposite can also be true. If you have leadership and decision-making power in an organization that suffers from any of the above, you have a grand opportunity to reimagine your organization's structure from the ground up. You might even break free of the traditional vertical management model and, as Semler did with meetings, shift to a less manager-driven model. In this chapter, we'll explore ideas to help you change the organization itself to support the principles of unmanaging and provide a rich environment for team and worker growth.

Creating the right environment to implement the mentoring part of the Grow Moment relies on two shifts: separating the acquisition of skills from the managerial track and redefining the purpose and function of skill levels. Basically, this is an anarchist's recipe to blow up the pyramid and do something better.

You might be able to do what Dan has done in his organization. As owner and CEO, he has total control, so that makes it easier. I'll take you down a slightly less traumatic approach that aims to preserve some essentials, like titles that reflect career progressions, while getting rid of the useless parts.

MANAGERS VERSUS EXPERTS

It was with great irony that I listened to our client, a large services company, tell me about their policy requiring their people to have a certain number of direct reports before attaining higher levels of advancement. People got their skill growth acknowledged through pay only if they became a manager! "So, how is that artificial constraint on career growth working out?" I asked them. The answer was that it wasn't. People were getting ready to leave because they couldn't be promoted without the availability of enough workers or managers "underneath" them.

In knowledge work, you want *all* of your workers to get better and to have that growth reflected in some form of recognition. The usual form that it takes is a "title change." Pyramids restrict that from happening by implementing a winner and loser distinction—if we only have one spot open on the hierarchy, and there are two (or more) really qualified people, we need to choose only one because that's how hierarchies work.

So, let's have our cake and eat it too, and separate the progression needs of those two or three specialists from the need to assign managerial roles. Yes, create two tracks.

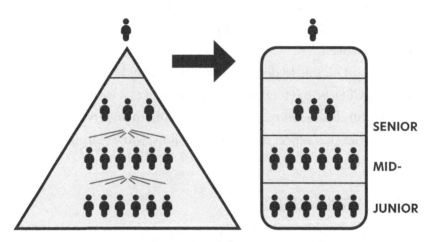

Figure 48: Progression Without Managerial Status

This solves another problem as well—it saves you from having to promote your best specialists into the noisy job of managing (or even a facsimile of it), a job that will reduce their productivity and the team's overall. As noted earlier, teams led by generalists perform better than teams led by the deep specialist. Choose someone with emotional intelligence who is good at facilitating others—that is, someone lacking a strong firefighter gene.

But there's more. As Dan's organization illustrates, promoting unmanaging in your organization saves you from needing as much managing anyway. Your workers are incredibly capable of performing a wide range of team and self-management activities.

The expert track does not need to have pyramid-style constraints. In fact, wouldn't it be great if all the workers found their way to the top? You can think of this as a column (rather than a pyramid) with layers.

TRADING IN YOUR PYRAMID FOR A LAYER CAKE

There are all kinds of ways to draw an organization's structure. The pyramid needs abandoning for sure, but the layered model that I just described needs one last tweak: let's flip it over so that junior people are at the top and "progression" is a matter of moving down the stack. I call it the layer cake model.

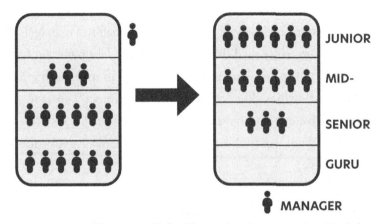

Figure 49: The Layer Cake Mentoring Organization Model

Each layer supports the layer above it; midlevels support the juniors, seniors support the mids, etc. And when I say the layer below supports the layer above, I mean the whole layer. Using this concept, we get rid of the ineffective single mentor model and instead go to a much more effective "group of mentors" model.

KEY SHIFTS FOR UNMANAGING THE ORGANIZATION STRUCTURE

1. **Separate the managerial from the skills function.** As discussed above, redefine your career progression strategy and structure. You can reduce the number of managers as well, as we noted in the story about Ben the CEO in section 3.

2. **Abandon military terminology.** You'll need names for each discipline and qualifying titles for the progression aspect of this. In both the manager track and the expert track, avoid the use of traditional "control" titles like director, manager, executive, etc. You can have

some fun with this in both tracks, and you can even involve your team in creating this. Some managerial function names sound less militaristic (think facilitator and coordinator), and others reflect a more servant-like posture (such as shepherd and sherpa), which more accurately reflects the team enabling managers do. If people are concerned that their title is not labor-market friendly (say, "chief technology gardener"), you can make a mapping to real-world titles (like "chief technical architect") so as to clarify the equivalent external career job designation. Or just do as Dan does and not worry about what they call themselves outside when they leave.

3. **Build the upside-down layer cake.** You'll need to define the layers for the expert tracks. Each layer should reflect a level of competency, as it normally does. Create a first draft or consider your current structure to assign people to their layers. Ultimately, you want the cohort for each layer to help define what people in the layer above need to accomplish or demonstrate in order to be eligible for progression (remember: progression is a downward movement). This is the layer-progression scorecard.

4. **Progression is an open book.** You'll need to make your own decision on this, but I believe you can be transparent about these changes. Once you have separated managing from expertise in terms of career growth and have a well-understood and validated progression scorecard, then you can move the whole process into the sunshine for all to see. The usual calculus of determining who to deny a spot in the hierarchy while promoting others becomes unnecessary—as is the secrecy behind it. Instead, people get promoted when they deserve it, not when a spot opens up. One of our clients even built scoring tools for individual work items and crowdsourced their use to evaluate completed work. This had a powerful effect in aligning people in that department on how

to think about doing the work and what success looked like on a work-item basis.

5. **Mentoring and assessing are team-based activities.** Each layer operates as a team and is responsible for the development and assessment of everyone in the layer above. This means that people get team mentored, which provides them with a richer learning experience. Likewise, decisions about whether someone belongs in the organization—in those cases where someone does not seem trainable—are made through group decision. You can still maintain control over that, but the scorecard can be a useful tool to give transparency to all involved.

6. **Let the less skilled measure the more skilled.** Steal that page from Ben's thumbs-up-thumbs-down playbook, where workers assessed managers rather than the other way around. Have each layer responsible for assessing how much the layer below (the more senior ones) has been helping them grow. This is valuable feedback.

One other potential benefit of this approach is that it probably, through transparency, will increase "trust" in the workplace, which some suggest correlates to a natural productivity boost.[74] Promotion decisions can be secretive discussions, which can provoke interruptive gossip.

CHAPTER 26

Where the Managers Go Next

It was something we could not figure out. Tania expressed extreme dissatisfaction with how we defined her job. I was at a loss, and my partner took his turn as well but with no success. Finally, we decided to meet with her together, the three of us.

We had hired Tania to run one of our large projects with a new client. They had ten or so people on the team, and they were designing a new website with several peripheral components. I had kicked the project off a few months before and things were going well, but with our business growing, I needed to get back to new clients and other challenges of scaling.

I had given her a comprehensive list of what she was supposed to do (and not do), and she had, from what I could tell, been doing a really good job of it. It is an easy job managing just one team on one project the way we teach and do.

After another ten minutes or so of us speaking with her, she blurted out, "I do understand what you want me to do, but I don't like it." Okay, I thought, we're getting somewhere!

And suddenly it was clear in her mind, and she finished the idea. "Hey, I really like telling people what to do! I want to do that in my job. It is what I like and what I am good at."

My partner and I sat back at the same time, smiled, and looked at each other. There was our answer. She wanted to be in charge of a self-managing team.

We laid her off the next day.

THE 5% PROBLEM

That was a good lesson for us, and a symptom we still see in our client's organizations. Not everyone likes to be an empowerer of people. Tania had a new job within a few days—the world, it turns out, has many jobs for people like her—so our two weeks of extra pay hopefully went to some good use. We call her situation the 5% problem.

If your organization has a traditional hierarchy and firefighter meritocracy, then you have a paradox:

- Most of your people are there *despite* your lack of a better management and organization model. They will become "unleashed" as you move toward better managing.
- A few of your people are there *because of* your management and organizational model. They will feel less comfortable with this change.

In the organizations we've worked with, this number is a single-digit percentage, usually not more than 5%. More often it is just a few people out of one hundred. These five percenters fall into two different groups as well:

- Like Tania, some prefer the exercise of vertical management power.
- Then there's the opposite type, those who effectively say, "Just tell me what to do. I don't want to have to choose, think, or innovate."

The first type, the vertical managers, tend to weed themselves out if the whole organization shifts to enlightened managing practices. Sometimes, though, leadership needs to do it for them.

The second type is usually someone who has either 1) been beaten down by the current system and lost their initiative or 2) someone who truly does not want to think that hard. The latter case is a hiring/firing problem—you have a knowledge work organization, and you probably don't have room for someone who does not want to be a knowledge worker.

I could make the "broken windows" argument that the seemingly unmotivated knowledge worker's very existence gives others an excuse to mimic their behavior, but I won't.[75] It is often hard to tell who they are until the Humble Gardeners really take control of the managerial system. You've already read the two-part vignette about the executive who assumed that half of their people were not good enough, until their managing changed. The "blossoming" of an individual can also be quite profound; we had a client tell us that one of their smartest people, who had been very withdrawn since hiring, had blossomed in the experience of being truly included and listened to in our trainings. Other people, only partly joking, said it was now hard to shut him up and get work done.

WHAT DO MANAGERS DO NOW?

The wizard, standing with his magic staff at his side, watched as the team moved off into the forest. They now traveled with the confidence that comes from knowing what needs to be done. That would serve them well in the days and months ahead. They had not asked the wizard to follow or visit them on the journey. The wizard looked down at the ground and asked, "What do I do now?"

One of the most common leadership questions that we get is just that simple. When managers are required to do less managing, they need less time to do it. For some, this feels uncomfortable.

You may not need as many managers. When teams get more self-sufficient and don't need to lean on managers, then the managerial load goes down. Likewise, when managers just lean back a bit and ask, "What now?" they often really mean, "Now how do I prove my value?" Here is a quick set of thoughts on how those in different managerial roles can respond to their new reality:

- **Department managers.** These are the firefighters, the deep specialists, your crème de la crème, right? Put them back to work! Those who have been in the gray zone of part-manager, part-worker can just shift back to doing more work, which they will usually love. Higher up in department structures, these managers can focus on improving the department's resources and prospects and promoting mentoring and general skills development.
- **Client managers.** When projects go bad, the CMs spend their time either as apologists to the client, which is hardly endearing, or as ogres who harass the team to speed up project work. With better delivery, the CM can shift to more proactive and strategic discussions with the client, seeking out new opportunities and building internal skill sets.

- **Requirements managers.** If you have these, they probably don't go away. Regardless of how ineffective their artifacts can be at certain stages of the process, they can still be useful. Meanwhile, the RMs themselves can focus more on the client's business needs as solution specialists and work to build their skills in that direction.
- **Project managers.** Okay, first of all, PMs are often overworked, so you could just let them have normal lives again. They can also serve as process facilitators (not owners) of the techniques described in this book. Still, you may have too many of them, and like our Tania, the more dominant ones will fiddle with your processes needlessly and often be discontent.

All that said, how these roles evolve will depend on many aspects of your business model. It will also depend on what else they can do. It may be that increasing worker productivity by just 20% allows you to just let the managers be. But keep your eye on them.

As challenging as the shift to a new way of managing and all the implications upon your organization will be, your long-term enemy in this process of change will be what we call "drift," the tendency of an organization to drift back to old or Tayloristic ways of working. The 5% can often be covert or even unintentional supporters of the forces of drift.

CHAPTER 27

The Challenge of Change

AgencyAgile hit another milestone. It was 2016, and now six years in, we had finally managed to get some good press. The phone was ringing.

Yet, as I noted in an Entrepreneur.com article, the shark was following us—every success brought more need to be successful.[76] Adding just one person to our tiny three-person team meant a huge increase in costs, and that needed to be matched by some added revenue. A good place to find that revenue is your existing clients. So, I reached out to one of my favorite agencies, The Starr Conspiracy (TSC), to check in. It had been a year or so since we helped them, and even if they needed just a little more, I could do a little business and see some old friends, including their awesome CEO, Bret Starr.

Kylie, who had been part of the leadership group we first trained, replied to my email and agreed to a phone call.

"How are things, Kylie? Great to hear your voice again." Funny how a voice can bring back so many memories, and Kylie's had done that for me.

"Jack! Yes, it has been a while. Interesting times here . . . a lot has changed," she replied, a bit too vaguely for me.

I sort of braced myself, not really knowing where this was going. I hoped she would say something like, "Yeah, pretty good . . . and we could probably use your help to fix things up some more." But this, sadly, seemed like it was going in a different direction.

"What's going on?" Yes, I know, lame, but it was the best I could do.

"You know, I think it surprised us all. We did like all of your trainings, but we didn't realize how they would impact us." She paused for a second. "We're running at about 50% utilization now, maybe a bit less actually."

OMG, I thought. My heart started racing. This is a complete disaster. Utilization is a measure of how busy people are, 100% meaning fully busy, usually with significant "billable utilization." When project failures compound on each other and create contagion, billable utilization takes a big hit. But 50% overall utilization? An agency with utilization that low usually means that clients are departing or, worse yet, that they are struggling to produce work.

My head was spinning as Kylie continued. "You know, we're not really sure what to do . . . do we have too many people now?"

Okay, I said to myself, it sounds like maybe a drop in revenue has caused this. If they had become less efficient, and were struggling to produce work, then they would feel as though they didn't have enough people. Whew. Some relief there, but I still couldn't parse the situation.

"Do you know what's going on with sales?" I figured, let's see if I can help with that.

"Sales are fine . . . we could use more for sure, but we're slightly up since you were here. But people are running out of things to do," she replied. And I was totally confused.

Then I figured it out. TSC used a retainer model—they charged clients a fixed amount every month, usually in a long-term contract, and then the teams work to deliver against that, usually a standard set of tasks, like email campaigns, social media posts, and other marketing content. But if sales were good, then that meant they were . . . I still couldn't make sense of this.

Time to go back to the basics, I thought, I must be missing something here. "Kylie, what do you mean when you say 'utilization'?"

"Oh, that's how busy our people are delivering against the retainers," she explained matter-of-factly. I gave a big sigh of relief. She and I had been having a conversation across different galaxies, maybe different universes.

"So, you're saying you are delivering work twice as fast as before; in other words, you're only needing half the effort to get things done? Like, your velocity is twice what it was?" My brain was still adjusting to this news.

"Yes! Maybe more!" she replied. "It's so strange. This has never happened . . . in fact, we used to struggle to get the whole month's work done. Now people are doing pet projects, working on our website . . . and things are kind of, um, calm."

Their transformation, as it turns out, had been much like the Project on Fire, which is maybe not so surprising, as I often shared that story at some point during our kickoff. But to this day, hearing their results remains one of the most vivid experiences for me. The time that had passed since the trainings and my utter lack of awareness of what they had been doing made their outcome seem like a miracle. And it was, and it wasn't. The Starr Conspiracy had accomplished something great, and it was far from easy.

The biggest challenge, according to them, was changing the managerial mindset, both in terms of how much managing gets in the way of people who want to get work done and how to get managers to stop doing what they've been doing and give things a chance to work.

THE TRUTH ABOUT CHANGE IN THE PROJECT-DRIVEN ORGANIZATION

There's a risk in recounting stories like that because the short version is always inadequate in its detail and likely overly positive. TSC backslid a few years after that conversation, having succumbed to the lure of creating a strong managerial class (using a technique from Entrepreneurial Operating System called Level 10)[77] and implementing a draconian workflow management system that literally sucked the fun out of the workplace. Productivity dropped, workers were unhappy, and they were taking a bath financially.

They invited me back to assess what was going on, which didn't take long to figure out. More challenging was figuring out why it happened at all. In the end, one very-well-intentioned executive decided they needed to be "modernized," and in that way, things needed "fixing." Ironically, that executive had been a huge fan of our original trainings but succumbed to the old managerial command and control mindset.

After I spent a day with them diagnosing all of this, then another day or two of reading them the unmanagement version of the Riot Act, they told me, "Enough, thanks, we got this." They dismantled most of those changes, and they rediscovered happy productivity and profits.

What struck me about this saga was that the managers, workers, and teams throughout who attended our first trainings experienced a golden age, fell into decline due to overmanaging, and then produced an unmanaging renaissance. The only thing that changed was their belief about managing and what managers should do.

Making great teams has little to do with workers or teams. They're the easy part. It is the managers and the leadership ethos that they operate under that needs to change and be sustained. It is cultural change, and it can be hard to do.

THE FOUR-STAGE CHANGE MODEL

Our AgencyAgile transformations follow a proven, research-based structure for enabling organizational change. Not surprisingly, it is essentially a Four Moments model—and in that way, the moments before and after the actual change (Go) matter most, affecting up to 80% of the failure/success rate:

- **Contemplation (Why):** You and others who need to change, improve by becoming aware of the sources and impact of your current behavioral choices. We get creative (and interactive) here in our trainings. In this book, I've used vignettes that help you see things differently and provided educational material about what works and does not. Share these resources. It is critical that everyone at every level of the organization gets deeply engaged with the Why and accepts the need for change.
- **Planning (What):** Once motivated, or at least informed, then the question of how we operate differently becomes the challenge. The bad news is that our behaviors—especially in the

workplace—typically form a self-reinforcing system. Hundreds of little scripts play constantly in our heads, so changing several of these at a time requires focus and also a very specific (and clear) set of new actions. While reading this book, you likely have been envisioning ways to implement what you've learned. To plan your organization's transformation, and since change is traumatic and also costly to productivity in the moment, your plan should consist of multiple steps, each one introducing a new way of working that replaces an old way of working. The order I've presented them in this book is not a bad place to start.

- **Implementing (Go):** Organizations are actually pretty good at change if they've prepared for it with the prior steps. Most change fails because it shows up one day on people's desks without a clear reason (Why) or coherent plan (What).

- **Sustaining (Grow):** Those in the organization will need a constant reminder of the new way, and its initiatives need diligent measurement. Even with expertly coached transformations like we do, the drift rate is significant over as little as six months from transformation. One challenge is that new hires, especially new managers who bring in their historical ways of managing (or a need to "show impact"), can work against your new culture.

In our experience, lasting organizational change is a job that never ends. But that's a good job for managers and leaders: to make sure our processes are the best they can be and stay that way. To enroll managers, we use a combination of approaches based on the model above, targeting the different organizational audiences in different ways during the first stage, then creating a unified cultural narrative around the planning and implementing stages.[78]

Whereas I am pretty sure that many managers reading this book will become much better managers as a result, I have no idea whether this book provides a sufficient basis for a leader to instigate a successful organizational change using these methods. Many of our clients remark that the external third-party role that we provide is highly useful in that regard and that it is not terribly replicable with internal resources.

SUMMARY

Section 5 went beyond the actions of single managers and explored the dynamics and challenges of making an organizational shift to unmanaging:

- **Inclusion is at the core of unmanaging.** This is demonstrated in the Four Moments and how unmanaging practices in general support a diversity-oriented values system.
- **NOCOs struggle with productivity and quality** due to fragmenting forces like multiple competing projects, multi-managed workers, and multi-allocated workers.
- **NOCO managers compete for the attention and focus of teams and workers** through a variety of means, including using highly costly meetings.
- **The meetings problem is a difficult one**, and any effective solution must raise the bar, making it more challenging to schedule a meeting, and also come with a firm leadership mandate establishing new behaviors.
- **The organizational pyramid is at the core of many problems** for project-driven organizations, and its very shape creates a set of behaviors and reward system that creates losers in order to name winners. You can relax this structure in many ways.
- **Some people won't like unmanaging.** Taylorism has its rewards for some personality styles.
- **Managers need to redefine their missions.** In general, the shift to unmanaging gets managers back to what they should have been doing otherwise. Managers are still needed and valuable.

- **Success is achievable, but the old ways will always fight their way back in.** An organizational shift is not a project but a change in values or renewal of behaviors that better align with values that have been underserved. In that way, you, as a leader, will need to apply the continuous diligence you apply to other topics (like sales and margin) to nurturing and sustaining your new organizational culture.

The Ingenious Manager

YOU'VE SEEN THE PLAYBOOK. You have the Why of the managerial mindset shift and also the What in the form of tools and techniques to implement new behaviors and help your workers and teams to prosper. But is it your job to do this? If not, whose job should it be?

Much of what we've covered could be labeled "project management." In fact, my many years of project and program management were instrumental in shaping the methods I have shared. But you don't need to be a project manager to implement these changes. Most project-driven organizations give many managers tremendous freedom to schedule meetings. This can be a problem, as I noted earlier, but it is an opportunity as well. While a pointless status meeting provides few returns on the time invested, meetings supporting the deployment of unmanaging techniques can be the beginnings of organization-wide transformations like the ones discussed in the previous section.

The people who prove instrumental to our AgencyAgile clients, people who are unmanagement torch carriers of a sort, come from any of the managerial roles. In some cases, they aren't even managers but workers with some influence and bravado.

The optimal initiator of the four key moments is, of course, an executive or someone with a leadership mandate. But influential client managers and department managers can be quite effective at setting up the needed meetings to make the Four Moments happen for teams.

The most important thing you can do is implement what you've learned. Embrace the Four Moments. Start using the practices. As you get the feel for them, you will see ways to apply them in almost all the work you do.

YOUR INTERNAL KEY MOMENTS

I was more than a bit surprised, as you know, that good managing might look a lot more like Siddhartha's mindful approach to life than the tyrannical, overbearing managers we see in media. Revisiting the research while writing this book confirmed that in my mind. When you're not executing one of the key moments, you'll need to be patiently waiting for situations in which you can once again flip the managerial narrative. They happen all the time.

> *"I can think, I can fast, I can wait"*
> —Young Buddha in *Siddhartha* by Herman Hesse

- **Fasting.** Like suppressing a hunger, you will need to suppress some of your older, patterned managerial reactions, everything from the base desire to just take action (somebody needs to do something!), exercise authority, be managerial, and act in other ways to assert your value as a manager. You may feel useless at times, but I hope your knowledge of the manager tax on productivity acts as a salve for your pride. Enjoy the fact that your inactivity can enable productivity. The work itself may not feel as satisfying as it could, but your work as an enabler matters.

- **Waiting.** Those impulses to be managerial are your enemy in another way as well. You'll need to slow down your decision-making so you can switch to question-making, which will help your thinking. You will do this by increasing your presence, your ability to observe in the moment.

- **Thinking.** Now that you understand how to see old managing and its myriad behaviors and problems, you'll need to start questioning the old ways of doing things. Seek out new key moments for your workers and teams, and craft new actions and methods for yourself. You will become a questioner and learner, and that will take you far both in terms of boosting productivity and with your fellow managers.

This last section is aimed at those last two topics, presence and questions, both of which are the key to making great ad hoc managerial decisions.

CHAPTER 28

The Virtue of Waiting

WE HUMANS MAKE HUNDREDS of choices every hour. We make so many decisions per day that the act of having to decide becomes fatiguing in itself. That's why decision familiarity is such a lovely and attractive path for us at times. For example, going to the same restaurant, ordering the same food with the same waiter at the same time of day allows us to surrender the need to make decisions, and this can feel relaxing and freeing, especially if the rest of your day was not.

And so it goes with managerial behavior. If you're always reacting, you will tend to go to that same restaurant, Taylor's Coffee Shop, and order the same old nonnutritious food. Familiar and easy, for sure, and nobody will criticize your choices.

Much like what we eat influences our health, the collection of managerial choices we make defines who we are as managers and our impact. Our unconscious, routine, and familiar choices affect our lives more than we realize, and those choices shape our experiences and beliefs. Taking time to observe these choices—to slow down—can be just what we need to make real change in ourselves and the work we do.

THE SPEED OF MANAGERIAL BLINDNESS

Work in project-driven organizations is chaotic, and it sometimes encourages managers to move quickly. Doing so makes good decision-making more difficult, and sometimes, that speed causes blindness. One interesting way to think about this is to ask yourself, "Do we really see things as they are, or do we mostly see only what we are looking for?" The answer? It depends on how fast we are going. This is the so-called top-down versus bottom-up processing conundrum, and it has to do with how our brains process information:

- **Bottom-up processing.** If our eyes fix on something, say an apple on a table (bottom), the brain uses the eyes (top) to identify colors and shapes and other related items nearby to determine what it sees. For each thing identified, the brain assigns a meaning.
- **Top-down processing.** Our brain (top) thinks there may be an apple somewhere nearby and uses our eyes to see if the actual apple (bottom) can be found anywhere in the visual scene. The eyes search for evidence of what the brain suspects is there because it already has a meaning in mind.

The answer is that most of what we do, because of the need for fast processing of decisions (at the speed of our immediate world), is top-down processing. In most situations, our eyes are looking *only* for the pieces we need in the visual field to confirm what the brain thinks is going on.

If you have ever been in a quiet, relaxing place, you've probably noticed your thinking style changes; you may have become more contemplative. This doesn't happen for everyone because some people like the constant buzz of neural processing or feel anxious about their current situation.

Contemplation is a luxury when, as a species, we are concerned about survival and safety. A manager who is suddenly aware of a project that might fail, not unfairly, might struggle to slow down.

When things are moving fast or we feel threatened, our brains tend to jump to conclusions to help us resolve the situation quickly (top-down processing). In this mode, we are prone to only see what we expect to see. While this works well in some situations, such as when we are rushing out the door and need to find our keys, it doesn't work well in complex situations—and that includes situations with people.

As illustrated in our earlier discussion of System 1 and the rider, our brains make assumptions about people that can get us in trouble. In a stressful situation, it's all too easy to see people as we expect them to be or wish they were.

When we see a challenging situation as we expect it to be, we miss its nuance and complexity. We lose the ability to question ourselves, in part due to our excessive speed, so we feel we already have the answer! These initial judgments can betray us and lead to poor decision-making because of their many assumptions. Mind you, they will be right from time to time, but that is better determined through slowing down and observing rather than taking uninformed action.

You may remember that fast processing of situations is done by System 1, which uses a connect-the-dots sort of analogical reasoning to connect information. System 1 has no problem making huge leaps to create meaning or a connection without much to base it on: "Hmm, he reminds me of Jonathan, but probably not as smart." And that's what it does for someone that you don't even know yet. It can steer you to both underassess and overassess people and situations, neither of which is particularly helpful.

Test it out sometime. When you're running errands sometime, just stop, watch people, and listen to your System 1 tell you all kinds of shit about them, most of which has no basis in fact. But it's delivered into your head as if it is a fact.

Great managing comes from slowing down and treating that System 1 commentary as the folly that it is. Bottom-up processing works, but you have to give it time; you have to make it happen on purpose. And it is a better way to assess and make decisions. It will help you ask better questions. Going slow and taking time to contemplate your decisions and actions is called *presence*, and it's a virtue of those who seek a better way to manage.

CHAPTER 29

Start with Stopping

*Leadership is first being, then doing. Everything
the leader does reflects what he or she is.*

—Warren Bennis

EXPERIENCING PRESENCE WILL ENABLE you to pivot from the rapid
and reactive processing of your mind, your reactive pathway. In exchange,
you will discover a reflective and contemplative process of exploration.

Presence will help you see things, as happened for me in the scoping
session vignette where Brad was taking people's cards off the wall. Rather
than listen to Brad's rationale for clarifying the wording on each card, I
watched what was really going on: he was undermining the purpose of the
exercise. Harnessing presence looks like all these things:

- **Learning to sense your *feelings*.** Yes, there's that word, but we'll
  break it down more specifically a bit later. There is more to how
  System 1 drives our actions, something deeper around the feelings

that it can trigger, what is known as a "reactive pathway." You'll need to learn how to deal with it when it happens.

- **Mastering the ability to slow down and observe.** The reactive pathway typically drives you to premature and uninformed action so as to relieve your discomfort. You'll need to wade through the discomfort to find what's really going on and make some choices.
- **Shifting to a "learning" mode.** You're going to be great at asking questions—it's fun and powerful.

You'll notice that none of this involves you taking action or making a decision. You're already good at doing those. Presence is what enables you to assess the current situation, formulate intelligent actions, and make excellent decisions more accurately.

Imagine what good decisions you could make if every decision was presented to you on a Friday evening, and you didn't need to respond until Monday morning. Best to not count on that, of course, but the point is that if you have time to pause—or if you make time to pause—then you'll stand a better chance of making better decisions.

SLOWING THINGS DOWN

Someone clever came up with the acronym STOP, which describes a process that you will follow to move yourself toward presence, and therefore, better assessment and decision-making:

- **S** = Stop, pause, wait
- **T** = Take a breath, anchor yourself, get present, slow your reactions
- **O** = Observe your feelings, allow them to pass, and release the emotions
- **P** = Proceed with questions, processing, decisions, and taking action

This model helps to break a pattern many of us have learned regarding challenging moments:

1. System 1 or other mechanisms alert you to a problem or threat.
2. You have a reaction, usually a physical autonomic response to the threat, like an increased heart rate, a sensation on the back of your neck, and other things that generally you would want to resolve or make go away.
3. Your discomfort with this will drive you to quickly choose a strategy for relieving, avoiding, or suppressing these physical responses.
4. And you will act out that strategy. Just make it go away.

This process is what is referred to as a reactive pathway. It is a pattern that all people do pretty much all the time. More on that in a bit. The problem, of course, is that the pathway is a chain reaction; if you can't stop it, it follows an inevitable course. Your tendency to rely on top-down processing and your biases will ensure that your response (#4) is not well considered. This results in personally biased assessments and choices like this:

Them: "I'm wondering whether we should put Sasha on this project?"

Inner me: Sasha, the guy who looks like a lame version of Jonathan? OMG, if he fails, then I will fail! Why would we use an "unknown quantity" like Sasha? My head hurts just thinking about it. I remember that awful project we had a few years ago where I almost got fired. I carried a bit of a stink on me for months. What was that manager's name? Sasha looks like him too!

Outer me: "For something like this, I think Jonathan is a better fit."

From the outer dialogue, nobody would guess what happened inside of me, and if it happened fast enough or I was also juggling another challenge or two, I wouldn't have either.

The first step to correcting this behavior is to STOP.

STEP 1: STOP

It's hard to stop, and we all need some help. This time, help comes from an unlikely place: your System 1. I have been hard on System 1, what with the negative effects of its sloppy reasoning. Yet to be fair, we owe our lives to System 1; so many of its interpretations are both correct enough and also valuable. System 2 will not notice the driver who ignored the stop sign, but it will happily tell you later that they were in the wrong. System 1 gets your foot to the brakes and steering left so that they just barely miss your brand-new car.

We can use System 1 to help implement the STOP model and reduce the reactive behavior that is often fueled by other parts of its relentless narrative. It all begins with programming System 1 to look for the right things. Since System 1 is so good at recognizing moments and quickly assigning them meaning, we just need to preassign the meaning it looks for. Here's a great way to remember to do something by programming your System 1:

Suppose I want to be sure to put the bocce ball set (that I store in my garage) in my car later today when I go to see my girlfriend, Kay. What I do is imagine a moment that System 1 will notice, give it a visual description (System 1 is always listening to you by the way), and give it instructions:

Me: "Hey, System 1!"

S1: "Hey, Jack, what up! I'm busy looking around— Hey, what's that? Oh, nothing. Anyway, make it quick. Doing important work here."

Me: "Okay, I am visualizing opening my car door before getting in to drive over to Kay's place later today."

S1: "Yes, you do that all the time. That's all? Hardly seems like anything to worry about."

Me: "You're right, but when that happens tonight, I will notice that I forgot the bocce ball set, stop, and put it in the back of the car."

S1: "You will?"

Me: "Yes, I am visualizing getting in and realizing later that I have forgotten it, which would be a disaster! I can see that moment clearly."

S1: "A disaster? Now I get it. I'm on it."

It works very well. Because your System 1, in this way, is a bit of a rockstar. Each situation will need a visualization, and you can attune it to the physical responses of becoming reactive. Make sure you give it a full instruction set, including a reminder to stop, take a breath, and observe your feelings before proceeding:

"When my manager Laura comes over with a problem and has that anxious energy to her, make sure I remember to STOP, pay attention to any feelings I have, and just take a breath. Remind me that I will be okay as well, and we will figure this out."

STEP 2: TAKE A BREATH (OR TWO)

Pausing, as described above, will give you the chance to observe your situation, but your reactive pathway is still driving you. You have slowed it down for a second. Now you need to start disabling it. This is what deep breathing does: it reconnects you with your body and less reactive parts of your brain and grounds you in the comforting calm of presence.

On one level, presence is just what it sounds like: feeling present in the room, in your space, and in this moment. There are plenty of good books on meditative presence and mindfulness techniques, so don't be shy about seeking out better teachers than me on this. Here are a few techniques that can be helpful as you pause and take a few deep breaths:

- **Permission.** Give yourself permission to do this, even if it means being different from those around you. It's as simple as thinking that to yourself. Jack Rosenberg, one of my therapists from long ago, wrote a book with a great list of permissions ("good parent messages") that may help you cultivate your sense of presence.[79] Each one embodies the words one might hear from a supportive parent:
  - You can trust your inner voice.
  - I have confidence in you; I am sure you will succeed.
  - You don't have to be afraid anymore.
- **Release your energy.** Paying attention to your physical presence, also called grounding, can provide a simple release of nervous and anxious energy, totally reframing your state of mind. Yes, it sounds New Agey, but there are decades of good science behind it. You can Google, "How to get grounded," and find a wealth of tools.
- **Clearing your head.** This is a simple mental exercise where you shift your attention to the top of your cranium and relax all of the muscles in your scalp. You'll feel it in your body right away. You can get much the same effect by holding your hand or hands on top of your head.
- **Feel your feet on the ground.** Shift your focus to your feet and your connection to the floor. Clench your toes, as if to grab the ground, and feel the strength of the floor.

- **Sit up (or stand up) straight.** Focus your attention on your spine, bringing yourself fully upright, whether standing or sitting. Notice how your whole body is connected.

All of these techniques have the benefit of focusing your mind on you, which your brain likes. You are familiar to it. When we aren't present, our minds are often detached, restless, or anxious. By breathing and giving yourself permission to be present, good decision-making comes more naturally.

STEP 3: OBSERVE YOUR FEELINGS

System 1 evolved to save us from *big* threats like predators, dangerous moments, and the risk of things highly unfamiliar. As a biological mechanism, it's fine-tuned for situations that are far more terrifying than the moment that you are in. Even in bad workplaces, nobody gets eaten by a saber-toothed tiger because they took sixty seconds to let their feelings settle.

Your System 1 reaction triggers feelings—usually ones that bring us discomfort like shame, guilt, apathy, grief, fear, anger, and pride. These feelings run deeper than emotions, being the invisible marks of life events that impacted us. By observing our feelings, even in the brief moment after taking a breath, we can diffuse the thoughts, biases, and emotions attached to them that might cloud our decision-making.

What follows is an amalgam of research and training using terminology from an excellent book by David R. Hawkins that I've used in my leadership coaching practice. In his book, Hawkins teaches a technique for eliminating feelings from our reactive pathways.[80] You will not be surprised when I tell you how deceptively simple it is: just wait.

And you don't need to wait long, though it may feel like forever to have to bear that feeling. Hawkins points out that in their simplest form, feelings are tied to memories. This can be thought of as being similar to the way System 1 connects the dots for us all the time.

You remember that awkward date when you were fourteen years old, and you have memories linked to feelings of shame, anger, sadness, whatever.

When you encounter a similar situation, System 1 (often poorly) recognizes the similarity and brings up the feelings mapped onto the original memory. This was a very useful technique when we were exposed to tigers and needed to recognize where tigers *might* be waiting to ambush us.

An easier way to see this in action is to observe animals, who also have strong reactive pathways (System 1, according to Kahneman, is the more "animalistic" of the two systems):

A friend of mine, Maddie, has a dog, Layla, a rescue, who doesn't like men with beards. In her past, there was a man with a beard who did something bad or scary to her, and her System 1 incorrectly connects the dots for her on a regular basis. Guys, shave before you meet Layla. She's a German shepherd that can run very fast—faster than you.

We unconsciously and quickly react to the discomfort of feelings, often because of the speed of the moment, psychological heat, and the presence of other feelings, and that shapes our actions.

One of the important side effects of our discomfort with feelings is our compulsion to do something with them. This is what drives the urge to react. Hawkins identifies the two main directions for this reactive energy: suppression and expression. Suppression has its own negatives, but in a managerial setting, and in terms of managerial actions, the latter, expression, is often a larger problem.

When we express our feelings, they are often projected onto other parties as emotions, including blame, distrust, and a whole litany of others. We have a very large catalog of emotions. Needless to say, emotions do us little good when making decisions either, and we are really bad at hiding our emotions. The sheer volume of our energy colors any actions that we take—especially when we are being reactive.

Our reactive pathway, which conjures up feelings that, in turn, dredge up emotions, guides us toward two default reactions toward others: nonresponse (which is often subverbally negative) or a very reactive judgmental response.

Fixing this? Here's the really cool part: Hawkins points out quite vividly—and I do hope you read his book—that the sensation of the feelings will pass from you in an amazingly short period of time, often just fifteen or thirty seconds.

While that sounds relatively fast, your reactive pathway probably sees it differently: fifteen to thirty seconds is an eternity because it is screaming, "YOU MUST REACT NOW, LIONS, I SAID LIONS!"

And that's why STOP can change everything.

Taking a moment to stop, take a breath, and observe yourself gives you the chance to do what's right in that situation: ask some questions and get System 2 back in the game.

STEP 4: PROCEED WITH QUESTIONS AND TAKE ACTION

Granted, the *proceed* in STOP sounds as if you should just do something, as if your actions are a dog scratching at a door, ready to go outside the moment it opens. Instead, proceed is really the beginning of the process of you being the awesome, contemplative manager.

And that leads to our final lesson for you in this book: how to ask the right questions so that you can find new answers and take new actions.

CHAPTER 30

Learner, Teacher, Manager

During grad school, I landed a prestigious internship at RAND Corporation, a think tank in Santa Monica, California. The internship worked out so well that they asked me to join the research staff, which was an amazing three-plus-year journey of learning. Yet one of the most profound things that I learned happened within the first few months and was not in any of the research papers that I read but, instead, was a lesson given in an unexpected way. It changed my ability as a thinker forever.

I was a bit of an oddball, as I was an MBA (almost), and there was only one other MBA among the 1,200-person research staff. As a result, they didn't really know where to put me, so I mostly reported to the CFO and an EVP for special projects. That got me introductions, through association, with all of the senior leadership, all of whom were researchers, mostly double or triple PhDs. A choice few were given instructions to make sure I learned what it was like to be at RAND, how it worked, and so on. I was more like a pet monkey, I think. They liked to play with me.

One day, they invited me to a meeting with a visiting scholar. This guy comes into the conference room that's already filled with a dozen or so of our six-sigma researchers, and they all dive in, talking about Afghanistan. I felt grateful that one of my dad's best professor friends was from Afghanistan, so I understood maybe 30% of what they were saying.

After forty minutes of dense policy and political discussion, the meeting winds down, and the guest is ushered out. The conversation shifts to the departed guest. The sharpest guy in the room, Dick, smiles, looks at me, the MBA monkey, and says, "What do you think, Jack? Should we hire him?"

I knew this was a test and that they weren't really asking for me to approve the hire. Shit, what can I say? I looked at the table, and the best I could come up with was, "I think he had a lot of answers. He seemed quite knowledgeable." Dick laughed, slapped the table, and said, "Exactly! That's why we're not going to hire him." I didn't get it and just looked blankly at him. Everyone else in the room sort of chuckled.

They waited to see what the monkey would say to that.

It made no sense to me, so I just shrugged, giving up: "Okay, I'll bite."

He replied, "Answers are the end of all learning." He went on, now that he saw I was getting it. "He was way too much into having answers. Every time we gave him a question, he answered. If I bring up a question to you, what you should be thinking about is, 'Is that question even the right question? Or what is it that led him to ask that question? Are those things true?' And we saw none of that thinking in our guest, so he does not belong here. We're running an organization where we get paid to think of what's not being thought about."

What a huge takeaway. I had to remember where I was, working among the top 1% of policy thinkers in the world. RAND is special—it is a premier knowledge work organization, with a decades-long record of producing highly innovative work. Billions of dollars in policy research money flow through their departments.

The biggest trap is thinking that we know things. We run the risk of limiting our learning by assuming that we know. When one stops wondering who someone is or what they're capable of, that's when they lose the ability to see that person's potential. Creating and uncovering questions is one of the most important aspects of enabling your teams: question-driven discussion *creates* new knowledge. Reciting information does not.

This shift requires patience and bravery. But doubting yourself, especially what you think you see and know, is what the smartest people do. It makes them learners.

PRESENCE ENABLES THE SHIFT FROM JUDGER TO LEARNER

In her very fine book, Marilee Adams describes one of the most important moves that any manager can make, and you'll recognize its necessity in much of what we've already discussed.[81] In her model, there are two postures, the Judger and the Learner. What she highlights so well is the difference in the kinds of questions these managers ask. The Judger typically asks questions like:

- What did you do wrong?
- Who is to blame?

- Why can't they perform?
- How can I prove I'm right?
- How can I protect my turf?
- Why aren't we winning?
- What could we lose?
- Why bother?

Another great researcher/author on this topic is Edgar Schein. In his book *Humble Inquiry*, Schein digs deeply into the origins of why questions often are not asked.[82] He would refer to the above Judger questions as being confrontative.

They have a presumptive posture, such as "Why isn't it done yet?", which presumes that it should be. Some confrontative questions are almost not questions but rather really a prompting question that seizes control, decreasing the sense of ownership (even morale) on the part of the recipient:

- "Why did we not get Josh to fix it?"
- "Why did we think that Alisa could handle it?"
- "Why did you say yesterday that you were almost done?"

In the end, both Adams's and Schein's examples demonstrate reactive pathway-based questions, questions that are not really questions, but seek to use expression as a way of resolving the negative feelings within the questioning manager.

The Learner, in contrast, shifts away from the Judger's blaming, fault-finding posture toward a much more reflective, humble style of inquiry:

- What am I responsible for here?
- What am I assuming?
- What is the most helpful thing I can do?

- What are my goals?
- How can I help?
- What do our stakeholders want?
- What steps can we take?
- What's possible?

This open-ended question style tends to open up conversation, and because of that, you as a Learner will help others learn too.

SHIFTING TO TEACHER MODE

You can help people better assess the situation, especially when you do have some useful information, by using diagnostic questions, a form of Learner questions that help the questioner and questionee learn from the situation, often by connecting cause and effect. The questioner sometimes knows the answer, but the design of the question is to get the questionee to think more deeply about the situation and allow the questionee to retain a sense of control and mastery in the situation:

- "What was the hardest part about this so far?"
- "What changed from what we first knew?"
- "What needs fixing here?"
- "What are we missing?"
- "What things or actions might have caused that?"

This can be extended further by using process questions, which help everyone involved to think more broadly about the situation. These make great group questions and tend to broaden the conversation, adding a layer of process learning as well. Again, often the questioner may know at least some of the answers, but there is value in mentoring everyone into the Learner mindset, by asking rather than stating:

- "What are our options from here?"
- "How could we do it better next time?"
- "What else do we need to cover in this discussion?"

These latter two question styles, as Schein notes, make for much better decisions, which matches with one of our most persistent themes throughout this book: engaging with others, rather than dominating, makes pretty much everything, even a real bad situation, better. It's just as Andreas the saddle maker taught us.

THE MAGICAL MANAGER

The magic of asking the right questions and moving from Judger-style questions to Learner-style questions is a matter of mastering your own speed:

- **Stop.**
- **Take a breath or three.** Get present, and then start checking out what your feelings are.
- **Observe.** Notice your feelings and let them settle back down. Notice the others and stop to hear what has been said. This is the moment that you need to start asking questions, internally at first and then externally. The Learner questions are especially useful at this point, as is Schein's most-favored question style: questions for which you do not have the answer. Here's one: "What's another way of looking at this situation?"
- **Proceed.** Do this through diagnostic and open-ended questions to build your understanding of the situations, and then shift to process questions to help get everyone else aligned on what the situation really is and what could be done at this point. You can even put your managerial decision into a process question in order to gain "enrollment" by others. "If we were to do X to try to fix this, how might that work, and what else would we need to do?"

Smart people move slowly. Most people answer too quickly. In managers, this comes from many sources, including reinforcement from the pecking order and firefighter syndromes; people pay attention and give recognition to the fast ones.

What you will find is that by waiting and letting conversations unfold, you can illuminate situations with some really good questions, often subtly pointing out the things people said without much reflection and emphasizing great points that people glossed over.

Being smart, as Dick at RAND pointed out, can be easier than trying to be smart. It is far easier to find the missing questions that reveal the fallacies of someone's blurted-out idea than to have a truly defendable (much less great) answer. Usually, the rest of the people in the room are still stuck in a reactive, trying-to-answer mode, so your questions will be a gift that helps steer them toward better answers.

People will start to look at you for the questions, not the answers. You will have a reputation as a magician who can see better paths through situations that trigger everyone else's reactive pathways. They will be inspired by and admire you for your calm.

You'll be on your way then, with the patience and knowledge to choose only the actions that will be useful and to use your mind and your questions to guide everyone else to success.

SUMMARY

The techniques in this section are really quite grad-school level, in that they are far more challenging than the somewhat simple mechanics of various techniques discussed earlier in the book. That is intentional. I can tell you from my personal experience and from observing our coaches and their personal growth that this largely personal work will not only profoundly change your stature as a manager but also as a person.

The reactive pathway is not something that appears only at work. It pervades our lives and has a massive influence on how we respond to others.

It shapes our relationships and colors our overall experience of life.

I wish for you all the rewards of this journey, as well as its challenges, which will help you learn. Those people who are most challenging to you, in the words of my amazing life coach of thirty years, will be your best teachers. Embrace them for the opportunity they provide. When encountering people whose decisions I find challenging to accept or who treat others in ways that are difficult for me to watch, I have to admit I find great relief by merely repeating in my head, "Thank you, my teacher."

The Unmanager's Manifesto

- **We are fans of our humanity.** We are all more gifted, capable, and motivated than we can ever see.
- **We work better together.** The best outcomes happen when we work together with trust and transparency. We assume and expect that everyone has positive intentions.
- **Taking turns makes more winners.** Our great gifts of individual motivation and related dominant behavior styles can threaten group success and the growth of others. We take turns and go no faster than the slowest.
- **The speed of the team is the speed of the organization.** It is our job as leaders, first and foremost, to enable productivity and growth by optimizing the four key moments: Why, What, Go, and Grow.
- **Relinquishing control unleashes our human potential.** Control is a toxic organizational behavior when practiced upon others. Leading with authority and empowering mentorship brings out the best in teams and individuals.

- **The collective outperforms the silo.** Our collective wisdom works better to resolve and manage our challenges than managing vertical or chaotic structures.
- **Direct communication beats intermediaries and documentation.** Richness in communication is key to getting things right. Alignment between the team and our customers is our top priority.
- **We are present, on time, and connected.** We speak in realities, stay connected, and value alignment of purpose, understanding, and action. We help each other when needed. We share so others can learn.
- **Questions are the best way to learn and lead.** All good learning comes from questions—we answer when asked but not before. We lead with questions that inspire leadership and growth in others. An answer discovered is far more valuable than an answer told.
- **We work together better in person.** Communication is best done as a group, in rich and collaborative formats, colorful and interactive.
- **Conversation and communication often outperform systems.** Our innate fascination with tools often steers us away from effective ways of working. We prefer to turn off tech and keep systems simple, to create better communication.

Endnotes

1   The working title of that book was *How to Run a F**king Agency, by the Guy Whom You Said Could Not Run an Agency.* Clearly, I was not unhinged at all.

2   Mintzberg, Henry; Managers, not MBAs: a hard look at the soft practice of managing and management development, 2004, Berrett-Koehler Publishers in English - 1st ed.

3   The name of our company is a bit of a misnomer as we don't "do" agile really; nor do we only work with agencies. It sounded catchy, and the domain was available. I tell myself that while there are better names, there are also worse ones.

4   The Why Moment also embodies many of the great differences between Japanese and Western management styles and is called *Ba*, which (roughly) means "a shared place." Ikujiro Nonaka, "A Dynamic Theory of Organizational Knowledge Creation," *Organization Science* 5, no. 1 (February 1994).

5   The name *agency* really means an organization in service of many clients, which is a situation many departments and teams in non-agencies find themselves in these days as organizational silos are broken down by the rapid demands of business.

6   My writings on Agile are mostly on Medium.com (https://medium.com/@jackskeels) but you can also find a more full selection on this book's online resources page: https://unmanagedbook.com/resources

7   Coase, Ronald Harry. *The Nature of the Firm* (London: Macmillan Education UK, 1995).

8   Geometric growth here refers to a multiplicative relationship of some form; in this case, manager-to-manager coordination for four managers is more than twice as costly as it was for just two managers, something closer to four times more costly, multiplication rather than addition.

9   AgencyAgile gathered this data in a 2019 client forum by asking clients how much productivity they gained by adopting better techniques.

10 https://www.nobelprize.org/prizes/economic-sciences/1991/coase/facts/

11 I use the term *Software Agile* to denote the specific methods and applications of this concept to software development. The word *agile* (note the lower case *a*) is used more broadly in business to characterize change initiatives aimed at agility, innovation, etc., and as such is a bit of a platitude, rather than a practice.

12 Software Agile was designed to solve the problems of long-term, dedicated teams working on one large project.

13 See https://agilemanifesto.org/ © 2001, the cited authors.

14 From Rico, David F., Hasan H. Sayani, and Saya Sone. *The business value of agile software methods: maximizing ROI with just-in-time processes and documentation.* (Fort Lauderdale: J. Ross Publishing, 2009).

15 https://books.google.com/ngrams/graph?content=manager&year_start=1800&year_end=2019&corpus=en-2019&smoothing=3

16 https://fashion-history.lovetoknow.com/fashion-history-eras/history-needles-sewing

17 From Oliver Burkeman, *Four Thousand Weeks: Time Management for Mortals* (New York: Farrar, Straus and Giroux, 2021) 18–19, citing from Lewis Mumford, *Technics and Civilization* (Chicago: University of Chicago Press, 2010).

18 S. E. Scullen, M. K. Mount, and M. Goff, "Understanding the Latent Structure of Job Performance Ratings," *Journal of Applied Psychology* 85, no. 6 (2000): 956–970.

19 Adapted from my original article published in *MediaPost Agency Daily,* Dec 17, 2017, How Good (Or Not) Are Your Agency Managers?

20   Mintzberg, Henry. "Structure in 5's: A Synthesis of the Research on Organization Design." *Management Science* 26, no. 3 (1980): 322–341.

21   Maslow, Abraham H. *Maslow on Management.* John Wiley & Sons, 1998.

22   It is important, when quoting scientists and others from the early twentieth century to remain mindful that although some of their findings remain relevant and useful today, others have become dated and, in many cases, wholly inappropriate. Maslow, for example, held a strong position on eugenics, which influenced the development of his principles regarding how relative (often experiential) superiority affect group dynamics.

23   Tost, Leigh Plunkett, Francesca Gino, and Richard P. Larrick. "When power makes others speechless: The negative impact of leader power on team performance." *Academy of Management journal* 56, no. 5 (2013): 1465–1486.

24   From RAND's original report on the Delphi Technique for improving group decision-making. Helmer, Olaf. "Analysis of the future: The Delphi method." (1967). https://apps.dtic.mil/sti/pdfs/AD0649640.pdf

25   Likert was an under-appreciated genius, in my opinion, on the scale of Ronald Coase. A good starting point is this book: Likert, Rensis. *New Patterns of Management* (New York: McGraw-Hill Book Company, Inc., 1961).

26   Buckingham, Marcus, and Ashley Goodall, "Reinventing Performance Management," *Harvard Business Review* 93, no. 4 (2015): 40–50.

27   If you are an Agile practitioner, you now probably realize that the so-called fifteen-minute stand-up rule—that the stand-up should be limited to a fifteen-minutes duration—is complete BS. The stand-up should always take as long as is needed because it is the best way to have those conversations.

28   Chaddad, Fabio. "Both Market and Hierarchy: Understanding the Hybrid Nature of Cooperatives" (International Workshop, Rural Cooperation in the 21st Century: Lessons from the Past, Pathways to the Future, Israel, 2009).

29   Paul S. Martin, *Twilight of the Mammoths: Ice Age Extinctions and the Rewilding of America* (Berkeley: University of California Press, 2005).

30   Saavedra, R., Earley, P. C., & Van Dyne, L. (1993). Complex interdependence in task-performing groups. *Journal of Applied Psychology,* 78(1), 61–72. https://doi.org/10.1037/0021-9010.78.1.61

31   As a side note, the variability of the machines contributed to the poor quality: the complexity of fitting a car together meant that any slight deviation in a given part might impact whether other parts would fit later on.

32 To this day, I'm sure that I could have gotten through that Multivariate Calculus class in undergrad if I had only taken it like four more times; the people who did well in it sounded like they were from another planet when they talked about the assignments.

33 Sandra Seagal and David Horne, *An Introduction to Human Dynamics* (Human Dynamics International, 1992).

34 We've modified Seagal's model slightly and also renamed each style and dropped dated, loaded terminology to be more effective when we're teaching the this topic. We call it mVAK (or modified VAK), as her terminology was not really workplace friendly as it included defining people as "mental" or "emotional," both of which can carry some serious pejorative baggage.

35 More than one executive with decades experience at RAND told me this, so I take it as fact, despite not being able to find any published research on the topic.

36 This shows up in workplace survey data like the 2015 Campaign.us survey that showed decreased engagement in more-junior workers. https://web. archive.org/web/20150925004928/https://www.campaignlive.com/article/ survey-70-employees-low-morale-ad-companies-job-hunting/1364561

37 A good place to start: Gagné, Marylène, and Edward L. Deci. "Self-determination theory and work motivation." *Journal of Organizational behavior* 26, no. 4 (2005): 331–362.

38 Wikipedia lists over 170 cognitive biases, but a more authoritative source might be: Jonathan Barron, *Thinking and Deciding* (New York: Cambridge University Press, 2023).

39 You can beat this number through method, which is what we teach, but also by reducing project complexity. If your projects are very routine and familiar, using the same tools for the same problems and with an established and tested (repeatable) process, your rework rate should be much lower. But then that would also indicate your work is somewhere between the corners on our work-styles triangle, more routine or formulaic, containing significant product- or process-driven attributes.

40 Credit for these goes to the Standish Group, an amazing research organization that studies project success rates and factors that drive them, and their biannual *Chaos Report*. www.standishgroup.com

41 You can earn certificates and accreditations in project management, but unlike medical or accounting professions, project managers are not governed by any regulations and rarely receive best practices guidance.

42   In many ways, project management drew its techniques from Taylorism, including the prodigious use of time standards and the manager as the controller.

43   A video of this narrative can be found on our resources page, with the title *The Ignorance Gap*. https://unmanagedbook.com/resources

44   An AgencyAgile study, published by *Digiday*, showed that project failure rates increase with the newness of technology and technique. https://agencyagile.com/agency-research-digidays-the-hidden-cost-of-agency-freelancers-study-summary/

45   The Standish Group has noted that almost 60% of the causes of projects being challenged or failed were directly connected to problems of scope and alignment between all of the parties involved: The Chaos Report, 2014; The Standish Group; p. 9.

46   The research field of LEC (Law, Economics, and Contracting) includes fascinating work on the "enforceable bounds of contracts," which, in essence, suggests that contracts are rarely as detailed as they might be because of a diminishing return on that detail versus the benefits of simply agreeing on a contract. This is even more true in the world of one-off projects.

47   On the client side, the project may have finally been approved after years of budget requests and political jockeying. The managers who "own" the project may have been better off if the project had not been funded.

48   In case you're curious why we have such great stories, it is because we only do our work with live projects. It is the only type of training that actually works and is sustainable after the trainer leaves.

49   This is another of the lessons that was incorporated into Software Agile: it can be better to have the team just define and build a piece of scope and validate it afterward than spend weeks or months writing a "complete scope" that nobody understands and is often incorrect.

50   One of many on this topic: March, James G., and Zur Shapira. "Managerial perspectives on risk and risk taking." *Management science* 33, no. 11 (1987): 1404–1418.

51   This roughly corresponds to a term used in management research called VUCA, which stands for volatility, uncertainty, complexity, and ambiguity.

52   Moløkken-Østvold, Kjetil, and Magne Jørgensen. "Group processes in software effort estimation." *Empirical Software Engineering* 9, no. 4 (2004): 315–334.

53   Moløkken, Kjetil, and Magne Jørgensen. "Expert estimation of web-development projects: are software professionals in technical roles more optimistic than those in non-technical roles?" *Empirical Software Engineering* 10 (2005): 7–30.

54   https://unmanagedbook.com/resources

55   To the degree that this is true, it may also contribute to some of the myopia around requirements documents. If an RM produces a document and then asks for another in-the-know person to review it, they will probably get positive feedback, despite it being highly useless for someone who has no understanding of the project.

56   These are from comments that we have collected, postevent, in a retrospective with the vendor/agency and (usually) client.

57   We've also seen clients get less demanding of the team once a face has been put to it.

58   Brooks, Frederick P. "The Mythical Man-Month." *Datamation* 20, no. 12 (1974): 44–52.

59   In well-run Software Agile projects, it is largely the *only* meeting in the day that has any potential managerial involvement. The rest of the day? Go.

60   Daniel Kahneman, *Thinking, Fast and Slow* (New York: Farrar, Straus and Giroux, 2011).

61   The "systems" reflect two different processes but do not correspond to any specific physical organization of, or location within, the brain.

62   Levitin, Daniel J. The organized mind: Thinking straight in the age of information overload. Penguin, 2014.

63   Mark, Gloria, Victor M. Gonzalez, and Justin Harris. "No task left behind? Examining the nature of fragmented work." In *Proceedings of the SIGCHI conference on Human factors in computing systems*, pp. 321–330. 2005.

64   Murray, Susan L., and Zafar Khan. "Impact of interruptions on white collar workers." *Engineering Management Journal* 26, no. 4 (2014): 23–28.

65   This list was inspired by a book I highly recommend, John Mackey and Rajendra Sisodia, *Conscious Capitalism: Liberating the Heroic Spirit of Business* (Boston: Harvard Business Review Press, 2014).

66 In a traditional workplace, everyone has just one manager—that's why drawing a pyramid is actually accurate. It is called the manager's span of control and is often stated as a ratio: "most managers have six employees, which results in a 1:6 span of control."

67 In case you're wondering, I do think there are excellent DEI consultants out there, but their excellence comes from their approach: they embed in the organization so they can *manage behaviors*, achieving similar effects to what I describe here. The futility of the shame-based approach was recently noted by researchers Mahzarin Banaji and Frank Dobbin, in their *Wall Street Journal* article, "Why DEI Training Doesn't Work—and How to Fix It"; September 12, 2023; https://www.wsj.com/business/c-suite/dei-training-hr-business-acd23e8b

68 Romano, Nicholas C., and Jay F. Nunamaker. "Meeting analysis: Findings from research and practice." In *Proceedings of the 34ᵗʰ annual Hawaii international conference on system sciences*, pp. 13-pp. IEEE, 2001.

69 I made a few fun podcasts with my writing partner Steve Prentice on this topic, one of which was *I Hate Your Stupid Meeting*, which you can find on www.TheArtof.Management

70 My article, *Inhuman Trafficking*, (MediaPost, May 2015) where the word *trafficking* refers to the process (often automated) of scheduling workers in a very fragmented way, as if context switching and multi-allocation had no dehumanizing effect. https://agencyagile.com/inhuman-trafficking/

71 *Digital Taylorism*, by the staff of *The Economist*. Sept 2015. https://www.economist.com/business/2015/09/10/digital-taylorism

72 The correct question would be, "How much did we (managers) underestimate Josh's work this week?"

73 For a more thorough dissection of this topic, I recommend the two books, *Abolishing Performance Appraisals* (Coens, Tom, and Mary Jenkins. *Abolishing performance appraisals: Why they backfire and what to do instead*. Berrett-Koehler Publishers, 2000) and *Pyramids are Tombs* by Joe Phelps, a former client (and mentor) of mine (Phelps, Joe. *Pyramids Are Tombs: Yesterday's Corporate Structure, Like the 20th Century, Is History*. IMC Pub., 2002).

74 https://slack.com/blog/news/future-of-work-research-summer-2023

75   This refers to the sociological phenomenon where one broken window in a
     neighborhood, left unrepaired, will lead to more broken windows because
     it signals that nobody cares. From: Wilson, James Q., and George L. Kelling.
     "Broken windows." *Atlantic monthly* 249, no. 3 (1982): 29–38.

76   https://www.entrepreneur.com/leadership/
     you-can-never-elude-the-shark-but-you-can-learn-to-swim/278146

77   To be honest, when I first read this book, I wished I had written it. It has its
     challenges in the clients we've worked with. Gino Wickman, *Traction: Get a
     Grip on Your Business* (Dallas: BenBella Books, Inc., 2012).

78   I made this sort of approach the subject of a keynote that I did for an indus-
     try group several years ago. Look for *Values Are Not Enough: The Keys to
     Unlocking Enduring Agency Transformation,* which you can find on our on
     our online resources page. https://unmanagedbook.com/resources

79   Jack Rosenberg et al., *Body, Self, and Soul: Sustaining Integration* (Atlanta:
     Humanics Limited, 1989). Also, you can find the two lists (Good Father and
     Good Mother) reproduced on websites like this: https://stillinthestream.
     com/2022/01/22/good-parent-messages/

80   David R. Hawkins, *Letting Go: The Pathway of Surrender* (Carlsbad: Hay
     House Inc., 2014) 20–28.

81   Marliee Adams, *Change Your Questions, Change Your Life* (Oakland: Berrett-
     Koehler Publishers, 2009).

82   Schein, Edgar H., and Peter A. Schein. *Humble inquiry: The gentle art of
     asking instead of telling.* Berrett-Koehler Publishers, 2021.

Acknowledgments

THIS JOURNEY STARTED with my parents, Jack and Joyce, two talented economists who hoped their kid would be smart. I am grateful for the journey it gave me, as I am for my dad's love and his belief in me through my many pinball bounces. He loved teaching as well as research, and I see more and more of him in me every day.

In *Illusions*, Richard Bach wrote that our true family often is not the one we were born into. So I am thankful to those in my true family, including Mike Goldenberg, my teacher, coach, sage, sherpa, mirror, thought partner, and many other things. Many of the ideas in this book were nurtured in our weekly conversations that spanned decades. Another family member is Greg Morrell, my business partner of over a decade, the brother I never had. I thank him for his patient support of this project. And speaking of patience, my thanks to Kay, my partner, who has been a constant source of encouragement and support, and is the record holder for how many times anyone outside me and the editors has read this book.

Thanks to my career's many pinball bumpers: Chuck Hanby at Del Monte, who fired me from being a plumber and told me to go back to college because it was where I belonged; two close friends who passed too early, Wally Baker and Bryan Martin, whose early deaths propelled me forward; Paul Keshian, an MBA classmate who in the summer of 1998 told me I was "stupid" for not applying for the RAND internship, knowing full well I don't like being called stupid; my boss at Sapient, who said I was not a good manager, which I didn't like either; Ivan Todorov, the CEO of Blitz Agency, who gave me a job and the ultimately the chance to learn from the Project on Fire.

Thanks for the trust and partnership of our AgencyAgile clients, the thousands of leaders and managers of agencies and other project-driven organizations who put their faith in a promise of a better way of doing things, and most of all to those who made these crazy ideas work better than I could have imagined. Of note: Ming Chan, CEO of The 1st Movement, who gave us our first AgencyAgile gig; Dan LaCivita of Firstborn; Jon Christensen and Nick Gower at FutureFriendly (now part of EY); Tim O'Neil of Reactive (now part of Accenture); Justin Kabbani at Hardhat Digital; Steph Bailey at Inlight; Ned Johnson at WPP/GTB; Monte Masters of BottleRocket and Jacqui Hartnett of Starmark International, for their endless advocacy of our work; the leadership team (Beau, CJ, and Andy) at LaneTerralever; Chris Locke and Deanna Derocha of HelloWorld; Kim "Kimfer" Flanery-Rye of Yesler; Joe Phelps of Phelps Agency, an early mentor from grad school who wrote quite the book, *Pyramids Are Tombs*; Melissa Rowe of RAND; Jose Villa of Sensis; and last but not least, Bret Starr of the Starr Conspiracy, for a conversation at the end of a very long liquid lunch, when he said, "Dude, you gotta write a book."

Leaders in the industry that kept me inspired, including: Marla Kaplowitz, Chick Foxgrover, and Mollie Rosen from the American Association of Advertising Agencies; Tom Beck and so many members of the Society of Digital Agencies; Leah Power of the Institute of Canadian Agencies; thenetworkone; Magnet; Mirren; Taan Worldwide; The Canadian Agency Network; AMIN Worldwide; and many others.

Thank you to the amazing AgencyAgile team, especially Steve Wages for his business insights; Dave Foster, a brilliant mind filled with questions;

and the many other amazing teachers and coaches who have been with us through the years, including Lauren, Steve Knapp, Kate, Allen, and Allegra. And a special thanks to Maya Krauss for her continuous support and facilitation of the village that made this happen. Without her, this whole project would be in shambles.

And thanks, at last, to the village that makes books happen: Jesse Winter and Duo Storytelling, for their structural insights and editing; Steve Prentice, my podcast partner and an early supporter of my writing effort; and Victoria Wolf for her wonderful design work, and Sharon Woodhouse for her seasoned guidance in getting us into print.

Index

About the Author

JACK SKEELS is a former RAND senior analyst, and currently CEO of AgencyAgile, an Agile transformation and coaching firm that helps agencies, consultancies, and other complex service organizations go better, faster and happier. His career includes leading Sapient's 105-person Los Angeles office, and founding and executive roles in multiple startups. He is a coach to executives, a thought-leader and evangelist to industry, and wakes every day driven to create a revolution in leadership and management practices, optimal organization design, and delivery excellence.

Jack is recognized as an outstanding speaker, writer, and educator. He speaks at over 15 industry and association events per year, including Ad Age, Digiday, SoDA (annual meeting and The SoDA Academy), 4A's conferences, Advertising Week, Magnet Global, Miss Collective, TAAN, Bureau of Digital, and others. With over 35 published articles, his work frequently appears in leading publications such as: Ad Age, Entrepreneur.com, Ad Week, MediaPost, and Campaign.us.

Jack is a two-time Inc-500 Award winner and entrepreneur, with several successful startups to his credit. In addition to a bachelor's in Industrial Engineering and an MBA with honors in Entrepreneurship and Finance from the Marshall School of Business, he has held several graduate-level teaching roles, including associate professor at the RAND-Pardee School of Public Policy.

Made in the USA
Las Vegas, NV
24 January 2024

84822740R00203